Gilles Van Grasdorff is a journalist specializing in Tibetan affairs and he maintains close links with the Tibetan communities in exile. He has written many books on the subject; *Tibet: My Story* which was co-written with Jetsun Pema – the Dalai Lama's sister – was published by Element Books in 1998.

HOSTAGE
OF BEIJING

THE ABDUCTION OF THE
PANCHEN LAMA

Gilles Van Grasdorff

ELEMENT
Shaftesbury, Dorset • Boston, Massachusetts • Melbourne, Victoria

© Element Books Limited 1999
Text © Presses de la Renaissance 1999

First published as *Panchen-Lama: Otage de Pékin* in 1998

First published in the UK in 1999 by
Element Books Limited
Shaftesbury, Dorset SP7 8BP

Published in the USA in 1999 by
Element Books, Inc.
160 North Washington Street
Boston, MA 02114

Published in Australia in 1999 by
Element Books and distributed
by Penguin Australia Limited
487 Maroondah Highway, Ringwood,
Victoria 3134

Translated by Géraldine Le Roy
Cover illustration: Telegraph Colour Library
Cover design by Mark Slader
Design by Behram Kapadia
Typeset by Bournemouth Colour Press, Parkstone
Printed and bound in Great Britain by
Creative Print and Design (Wales), Ebbw Vale

British Library Cataloguing in Publication
data available

Library of Congress Cataloging in Publication
data available

ISBN 1 86204 561 5

Contents

Acknowledgements   IX
Foreword   XI
Introduction   XV

PART I
The Ninth Panchen Lama (1900–1937)   I
 1 The 'Continuity of Consciousness'   3
 2 British Intervention   10
 3 The Chinese Exert Control   23
 4 First Attempts at Modernization   37
 5 Death of the Thirteenth Dalai Lama   53
 6 Rise of the Regent, Reting Rinpoche   59
 7 Search for the Fourteenth Dalai Lama   69

PART II
The Tenth Panchen Lama (1938–1989)   83
 8 A Corrupt Regime   85
 9 Selection of the Tenth Panchen Lama   97
10 Arrival of the People's Liberation Army   109
11 The Panchen Lama's Formative Years   122
12 The Tibetan People Rebel   133
13 Democratic Reforms'   143
14 The Seventy-Thousand Characters (1)   155
15 The Seventy-Thousand Characters (2)   168
16 Imprisonment and Rehabilitation   179

PART III
The Eleventh Panchen Lama (1989–1999)   189
17 Puppet of Beijing   191
18 The Child Elected by Tibet   203

Conclusion   211
1999   215

Notes   216

Appendix   223
  The Fourteen Dalai Lamas   225
  The Lineage of the Panchen Lamas   226
  Boundaries of Tibet, India and China   232
  Colonies of Tibetan refugees in India and Nepal   233
  The Main Prison and Labour Camps   234
  Major Dates in the History of Tibet   236

Glossary   243
Bibliography   247
Index   251

On one star, one planet, my planet, the Earth, there was a little prince to be comforted. I took him in my arms and rocked him.

ANTOINE DE SAINT-EXUPÉRY, *The Little Prince*

(translation by Katherine Woods)

To His Holiness the Dalai Lama

To all the Tibetan prisoners who are victims of Chinese repression, and to the youngest of them all, the Eleventh Panchen Lama, Gendün Chökyi Nyima.

I dedicate these thoughts to my mother, in memory of the secrets we shared with so much tenderness.

Acknowledgements

Knowledge about Tibet, its history, its culture and its religion is fairly recent, with each piece of research adding to the construction of the whole story. Through trial and error, Tibetology makes known a land and a people threatened with extinction. I extend my gratitude and friendship to everyone who made this book possible, in particularly Laurent Deshayes, author of the important *Histoire du Tibet*, for taking the trouble to read my manuscript and for contributing his extensive historical knowledge.

The book could not have been written without the particularly warm welcome of the Tibetan government in exile and of all the Tibetan community in India. I am particularly grateful to the former representative of His Holiness the Dalai Lama in France, Dawa Thondup, who recommended that I embark on this tragic adventure and warned me of the numerous pitfalls I would encounter. My thanks also go to the present representative of His Holiness in Paris, Ms Kunzang D Yuthok.

In Dharamsala, I am particularly grateful to: the secretary of the Department of Information and International Relations, Mr Tempa Tsering, who has also been a long-standing friend and support; all the Tibetan government in exile and Ms Jetsun Pema, for her daily fight; Venerable Samdhong Rinpoche, chairman of the National Assembly of Tibetan People; my friend Palden Gyatso; Dr Tenzin Chödrak; and the Nechung oracle, Venerable Thubten Ngobub. How can I thank Venerable Tsayul Tenzin Palbar, present *kalön* of the Department of Security, who guided me through the very complex story of the Ninth and Tenth Panchen Lamas? My humblest gratitude to You, Venerable, as well as to all the Tibetans I cannot mention so as not to put the lives of their families in Tibet at risk.

I also gratefully thank the translation team: M Topden Tsering who translated from Tibetan into English, in Dharamsala; and Géraldine Le Roy, who translated from French into English, for her talent, constant help and faith in this work.

I also wish to thank: M Louis de Broissia and M Claude Huriet for their constant support; Léon Zeches and André Heiderscheid; Pierre Dutilleul, Alain Noël and their families; Ian Fenton for his support; my friend Jean Lassale who gave me advice and support in most difficult times, when I was on the brink of giving up; my friend Ngawang Dakpa and his large family; Sandra Franck; Roland Barraux, who got everything started; Anne-Marie and Maître Gilbert Collard; and Marie.

The following credits are given with thanks for the use of images in the plate section: 12) © Stone Routes/Tibet Image Bank; 13) © Tim Nunn; 14) © Tibet Images/Ian Cumming; 15) © Eitan Simonor; 16) © Tibet Information Network/TIN; 17) © Tibet Information Network/Tibet Image Bank; 18) © TIN/Tibet Images; 19) © Alliance for Research in Tibet (A.R.T.). The remaining images are © Dir Dharamsala, or from the collection of the author.

Author's note on the text

Tibetan written and spoken forms diverge considerably. I have therefore simplified the transcription of Tibetan names and tried to apply a method as close as possible to spoken Tibetan. Although I have standardized the phonetic renderings of Tibetan names, the names and terms cited in quotations may vary considerably.

With Chinese names, I have usually adopted the official transcription – Pinyin, devised by the Chinese after the occupation of Tibet – except for well-known names such as Mao Tse-tung. Tibetan place names have been phonetically transcribed; I have not used Chinese transcriptions. I refer to Shigatse, for instance, instead of Xigaze, and Kumbum instead of Taer.

Words explained in the Glossary are followed by an asterisk the first time they are used.

Foreword

The silence of a child echoes around the world.

The publication of *Hostage of Beijing* serves as a timely and well-documented reminder – for readers who are new to recent happenings in Tibet and those who might have forgotten – of the iniquitous actions taken against a young child.

Beyond its historical interest in setting out the development of the two most famous lineages of spiritual masters of Tibet – the Dalai Lamas and the Panchen Lamas – the book denounces the unbearable situation of a child who is presently held captive for political reasons, the aim of which appears to be the obliteration of the Tibetan nation and its culture. And yet such a situation reveals many paradoxes.

The first is that an atheist State – communist China – proclaims to be the only authority competent to choose and appoint 'living Buddhas'. Of course this does not mean that Beijing's masters have suddenly been converted to spiritual values. On the contrary, they aim to eradicate – or at least control – Buddhism in Tibet, a religion they irremediably associate with 'separatism'. To that purpose, according to a terminology which seems to stem from the Cultural Revolution, Beijing declares a desire 'to crush the snake's head', that is to say, the head of the supreme spiritual and temporal leader of Tibet, the Dalai Lama.

The following is a summary of the facts recorded in this book, which judiciously examines point by point the official Chinese version and contrasts it with the truth of the Tibetan people.

In 1989, the second hierarch of Tibetan Buddhism, the Tenth Panchen Lama, died. The search for his successor – the child in whom he would be reincarnated, according to Buddhist beliefs – was immediately launched, with the 'blessing' of Beijing. The search raises significant issues concerning the future of Tibet, because it is the Eleventh Panchen Lama who will in turn appoint and train the successor of the present Dalai Lama.

On 14 May 1995, in accordance with his duties and with

centuries-old rituals, the Dalai Lama recognized Gendün Chökyi Nyima, a six-year-old boy from a poor nomadic family, as the Eleventh Panchen Lama. The Chinese, unwilling to accept the intervention of a man to whom they had denied all spiritual authority, abducted the boy and his family and appointed in his place another child, of the same age and from the same village, after a rigged drawing of lots from a golden urn. Since then, the young Gendün has not been seen or heard.

Simultaneously, a harsh campaign of religious persecution (although the word 're-education' is more commonly used) was once more waged against Tibet and its monasteries. Pictures of the Dalai Lama were banned. Monks were told to accept the child appointed by Beijing as the Panchen Lama and to reject definitively the spiritual authority of the Dalai Lama. Arrests, the closure of monasteries, many deaths, and exile followed. Unfortunately we have become all too familiar with such actions.

The second paradox is the silence of the Western nations. In full view of the world, China – the most populated country on Earth, a permanent member of the United Nations Security Council and a signatory to the Universal Declaration of the Rights of Man and the International Convention for the Rights of Children – abducted a six-year-old child and no official voice was raised in protest. We refuse to believe that trade requirements or fear of China should take precedence over the more essential duties of concern, courage and respect for other human beings. Does this mean that the issue is too complex, too alien to our sensitivity? Any culture and true spirituality is worthy of our respect and concern, all the more so when it is threatened with genocide.

At issue here is a child whose only crime was to be born, a child who has already spent more than two years of his brief life confined by the Chinese, who has been deprived of his childhood and who, because of so-called reasons of State, has become 'the youngest political prisoner in the world'. The mere phrase should be enough to arouse general indignation, especially when this child, whose silence grips us, has something so essential to say.

First, he reminds us that in him we can see the situation of all oppressed children everywhere. How can we pretend that international law will be respected or hope that our fundamental moral values will make things any better for the millions of children around the world who are exploited, beaten, raped and murdered, if we cannot take care of one single child who is in the news worldwide as a victim of State terrorism? As well as an individual human tragedy, this is an exemplary case, a matter of credibility which calls into play our responsibilities as 'witnesses'.

The second message Gendün Chökyi Nyima might deliver were he not condemned to silence, emanates from the soul of Tibetan culture itself, a culture that has been bled dry and almost annihilated, and whose ultimate survival is intimately related to his fate. What could Gendün say? That the essential values of respect, tolerance, compassion and joy that have been nurtured for centuries in Tibet are now available to all humanity? That, all phenomena being interdependent – according to Buddhist philosophy – each one of us is entrusted with a spark of universal responsibility and moral duty towards an endangered culture that was developed in a closed and fragile world? That our responsibility extends also to the environment, which is in as much danger there as in our world?

Of course we do not want to substantiate the idea that ancient Tibet was some kind of lost paradise, as some people would like to believe, or that the values it represents belong exclusively to Tibet. But there, maybe more than anywhere else, they are woven into the social fabric and are part of everyday life, forming a strong moral code. Our main concern today is that these values remain alive, and that they may also serve as a mirror wherein we might find reflected our own human conscience.

The third message enshrined in Gendün's silence concerns the major issues of the future – the rights of man, the environment, peaceful coexistence between nations, conservation of heritage, preservation of the diversity of cultures – all of which will be particularly challenging in Tibet. Our attitude and the determination with which we face our future will also influence the fate of this nation – and of this child. This is why, to our mind, it would be a failure on the part of all humankind to enter the twenty-first century without Tibet and without Gendün.

In 1996, in response to the tragedy of Tibet, 343 French deputies and senators – that is to say, over a third of the nation's representatives – signed an 'Appeal of French members of

Parliament for Tibet'. In 1996, they took the decision to 'sponsor' the young Gendün Chökyi Nyima, hostage of Beijing; for politicians in a democracy, it is a duty – and a matter of conscience and honour – to do their utmost to uphold Freedom, Justice and Truth, especially when they are endangered or ridiculed.

Gilles van Grasdorff and his team, through this book, are part of the attempt to break the silence surrounding this child, a silence which embraces the fate of an entire nation and of all humanity.

Louis de Brossia, Deputy for the Côte d'Or, Chairman of the Parliamentary Group for Tibet in the National Assembly.

Claude Huriet, Senator for Meurthe-et-Moselle, Chairman of the Association of Friends of Tibet in the Senate.

Introduction

On 14 May 1995, His Holiness the Fourteenth Dalai Lama, Tenzin Gyatso, officially recognized Gendün Chökyi Nyima as the reincarnation of the Tenth Panchen Lama, who died in Shigatse on 28 January 1989. The boy chosen was born in Lhari, in the district of Nagchu, on 25 April 1989. Shortly after the announcement, the child and his family disappeared.

Why did the Dalai Lama choose 14 May 1995? Those close to him say, simply because that day was considered an auspicious one. The announcement, prior to any from Beijing, put an end to many rumours and uncertainties, for China had declared several times that it alone had the authority to choose the reincarnated child. The Tibetans rejoiced when they heard the news on the radio, but, sadly, their joy was short lived.

On the same day, on the road to Lhasa, Chadrel Rinpoche, head of the Democratic Management Committee of Tashilhunpo* monastery, managed to get through to the monks there by phone. He just had time to give them a message before the line was abruptly cut.

On the following day, 15 May, a 'work group' arrived in Tashilhunpo, composed of 50 cadres from the Board for Public Security, the Religious Affairs Bureau and the Chinese People's Political Consultative Conference (CPPCC). They arranged daily meetings with the monks and declared that Chadrel Rinpoche had changed his mind (something the monks never believed) and no longer recognized the child appointed by the Dalai Lama. From then on, support for Gendün Chökyi Nyima was viewed as treason, and punished as such. On 17 May, Chadrel Rinpoche was arrested in Chengdu, in Sichuan. A few days later, he was replaced at the head of the management committee by Sengchen Lobsang Gyaltsen, a layman wholly in the pay of the Chinese communists. He had also been among those who had sent the Tenth Panchen Lama to jail in 1964.

On 24 May 1995, the CPPCC condemned the Dalai Lama's announcement and declared it 'invalid and illegal'. Shortly after, the child recognized by His Holiness was abducted, together with his parents, and secretly taken away. Since then, the Chinese have not revealed his place of detention and even today it is not known for sure where he is.

Towards the end of 1995, a farce of politico-spiritual dimensions took place within the temple of Jokhang* in Lhasa. Its main protagonists were two Chinese officials – Luo Gan, representative of the State Council, who was close to Premier Li Peng, and Ye Xiaowen of the Religious Affairs Bureau – and the governor of the Autonomous Region of Tibet (ART),[1] who had joined with numerous officials, dignitaries and monks for the ceremony of the Golden Urn. Following an imperial tradition dating back to the Manchus, the Eleventh Panchen Lama was to be chosen by the drawing of lots. But on this occasion it was obvious that one of the ivory tablets in the urn was longer than the others, and this was the one picked out. (For a full account of the ceremony *see* Chapter 17.)

The child thus elected by China was of the same age as the one chosen by the Dalai Lama, and from the same village. In fact, even while the fake lottery was taking place, little Gyantsen Norbu was waiting behind a red curtain, already dressed in ceremonial attire. It was reported that the child was a relative of a certain Raidi, a Tibetan member of the Communist Party's regional committee since 1977.

At the beginning of 1999, Gendün Chökyi Nyima, his parents and his brother were still missing. After being pressed by experts from the United Nations Rights of Children Committee, the Chinese ambassador declared that his government had 'taken over guardianship of the child at his parents' request'. The experts demanded to meet him, but in vain. Chadrel Rinpoche and his secretary, Jampa Chung, were given long prison sentences. In Tashilhunpo, the atmosphere remained tense, with communist officials constantly hanging around the monastery.

Rooted as it is in the Buddhist theory of reincarnation, the history of the Dalai Lamas and Panchen Lamas is unique. From the time of the Fifth Dalai Lama, Ngawang Lobsang Gyatso (1617–82), an important part of the history of Tibet has revolved around these two spiritual authorities, the former living in the Potala in Lhasa, and the latter ruling the monastery of Tashilhunpo, near Shigatse in the province of Tsang, approximately 190 miles from the Tibetan capital.

I have not attempted to recount the history of all the Dalai Lamas and Panchen Lamas. One book would not suffice since in Tibet one tragic event follows another: the invasion of the country by Chinese communist forces in 1949; the uprising of the Tibetan people and the departure into exile of the Dalai Lama in 1959; and the silencing of the Tenth Panchen Lama. The appearance of a local administration controlled by Beijing, and now the removal of the Eleventh Panchen Lama and his replacement by another child, have once more made the ambiguity of relationships between Tibet and China obvious to the international community, an ambiguity often exacerbated by rivalry between the Dalai Lamas and the Panchen Lamas. It is essential therefore to explain these two roles in both historical and spiritual terms.

The path chosen by Tibetans for their daily practice of Buddhism dates back to the first centuries of our era. It is in fact possible to consider the Emperor Trisong Detsen (755–97)[2] not only as an outstanding conqueror who gave the Chinese empire cause for fear on several occasions, but also as the person who first introduced Buddhism into the country when he invited famous Indian scholars and pundits to Tibet to translate texts and commentaries on the sutras★ and tantras.★

In the seventh century, from the north of India came Padmasambhava[3] – whom the Tibetans also call Guru Rinpoche.★ Under the emperor's patronage, he initiated, with his disciples, the construction of the first Buddhist monastery in Tibet, Samye, in the high valley of the Brahmaputra, between Lhasa, then just a village, and Tsethang in the valley of Yarlung, the birthplace of the Tibetan empire. The emperor, in fact, saw this new way of thinking as a political tool, something that could perhaps unite the common people with the Tibetan nobility, which was still supported by priests of the Bön★ religion which had originated long before Buddhism in the region of Changchung, in the west of Tibet.

Although Buddhism was declared a State religion in Tibet as

early as 779, it nonetheless remained restricted to a minority of people. In the ninth century it underwent a period of decline and there were many persecutions, particularly under the reign of Emperor Langdarma who saw himself as a champion of ancient beliefs. Many Buddhists were also persecuted in China between 842 and 846. But with the assassination of the Tibetan ruler, by a monk called Pelgyi Dorje, the dynasty died out in Central Tibet. The imperial domain, which had already lost a large part of its territories, then split into various rival principalities. The lineage which had ruled over Tibet for many centuries survived only on the borders of the plateau, in the south-west and east of the country.

However, thanks to Buddhism, Tibet pursued its cultural development throughout the eleventh century. With the support of the kings who ruled small estates in the south-west, Indian masters were invited to Tibet to propagate the religion. The most famous was indisputably Atisha,[4] who revived teachings that had become moribund and re-emphasized the importance of monastic discipline. This second dissemination of Buddhism was strengthened by Tibetans who, in the face of considerable hardship, went to India to meet famous spiritual masters. In this way, Buddhism became established as one of the building blocks of Tibetan culture, merging with it and sometimes even adopting aspects of local beliefs. These adjustments led to a religion which was halfway between shamanism and Buddhism – as reflected in the importance given to the oracles' trances. There were also more superficial adaptations: for instance, because of the harsher climate, the clothes worn by Tibetan religious people were different from those worn by Indian Buddhists.

Nevertheless, these developments did not affect the transmission of traditional Buddhism. Just as the vastness of India encouraged the development of numerous Buddhist universities, Tibet also boasted several Buddhist lineages or main Buddhist schools, four of which still exist today: Nyingmapa, Kagyupa, Sakyapa and Gelugpa. In the course of time, to their advantage, these schools restored ancient feudal rights and created monastic seigneuries. Religiously speaking, they all derived their legitimacy from the three great branches of Buddhism: Hinayana, Mahayana and Vajrayana, which they all respected. The Nyingmapa school, established in the imperial era in the eighth century, groups together the teachings introduced into

Tibet by Padmasambhava. The Kagyupa school – school of oral transmission – appeared in the eleventh century. It split into a dozen groups, among which the Karma-Kagyupa group played an important political role up until the seventeenth century. The Sakyapa lineage – named after the monastery in western Tibet where it originated – was founded by Khön Könchog Gyelpo in the eleventh century. With the support of the Mongols, it ruled over Tibet in the thirteenth century. The Gelugpa school – 'the Virtuous' – resulted from the reforms initiated by Tsongkhapa[5] in the fifteenth century. Internal struggles and their links with the Mongols enabled the Gelugpa to reach the highest political power by the middle of the seventeenth century. It is to this lineage that the Dalai Lama and the Panchen Lama belong.

The ethical rules of Hinayana form the foundation of Tibetan Buddhism, which is also based on the generous aspirations of Mahayana and on Vajrayana techniques for more esoteric practices. The differences between the lineages lie in their approaches to spiritual practice. The Nyingmapa approach is qualified as the 'direct path'; the Kagyupa give precedence to the close relationship between master and disciple; the Sakyapa are famous for the perfection of their rituals and metaphysical studies; and the Gelugpa emphasize monastic life and profound philosophical study.

Certain religious people, be they monks or laymen, are recognized as *bodhisattvas*.* In this context, the Panchen Lama could be assumed to hold a higher rank than the Dalai Lama, for Tibetans consider the Panchen Lama an incarnation of Amithaba[6] (*Eupame* in Tibetan), the Buddha of Infinite Light. They also recognize Eupame as the spiritual father of Chenrezig,[7] the *bodhisattva* of Perfect Compassion, from whom the Dalai Lama is believed to emanate.

Chenrezig is seen as the protector of Tibet, its mountains and its people. A legend explains that he appeared as a monkey to create the human species in those desolate areas and, according to some versions, founded the first hermitages there. One day, as the monkey was meditating, he heard cries of distress. He quickly left his cave and discovered a female demon, with whom he fell deeply in love. Their union produced six children, who in turn procreated. Their offspring became the Tibetan people.

The accession to power of the Dalai Lamas has been a long process. After several centuries during which Tibet was ruled by Sakyapa and minor Kagyupa lineages in turn, the Gelugpa took precedence. To understand their political ascent, it is necessary to go back to the sixteenth century, to the time of Gyalwa Sönam Gyatso (1543–88), whose life and work were decisive for the Tibetan people, initiating a trend that lasted until present times.

It is reported that in the course of a raid led by Tümed Mongols against a nomadic Tangut tribe settled in Amdo, in the north-west of the Tibetan plateau, two Gelugpa monks were found among the Tanguts' prisoners. As a result of their resolute determination, the two monks managed to attract the attention of Altan Khan, the ageing prince who ruled over the Tümed Mongols at that time. They talked to him at length about their spiritual master, Gyalwa Sönam Gyatso, and persuaded the prince to change his way of life.

Convinced of the virtues of Buddhism, Altan Khan asked Gyalwa Sönam Gyatso to meet him. The encounter took place in 1578 and was followed by the conversion of the Mongol nations. The prince, wanting to raise the lama* above the common run of people, conferred on him the title of *dalai*, a Mongol word meaning 'ocean' (of wisdom), whose Tibetan equivalent is *gyatso*. From then on Gyalwa Sönam Gyatso's successors took the title of Dalai Lama.[8]* The title was also given retrospectively to his two previous incarnations, so Gyalwa Sönam Gyatso thus became the Third Dalai Lama in this spiritual lineage. But there is something else of significance here: by establishing relations with the Mongols, Gyalwa Sönam Gyatso took a stand in the secular quarrels of his time. As a result of his actions, the fledgling Gelugpa lineage acquired very useful protectors who would ensure its authority and future in Tibet – even though this would require over 50 years of struggle.

In 1642, for the first time in Tibet, a Dalai Lama, the spiritual leader of the country, also held temporal power. With the help of Mongol armies, Ngawang Lobsang Gyatso, the Fifth Dalai Lama, set in place the constitution which the Tibetan government was to keep until the 1950s. He established Lhasa as the capital and installed his government in the Potala.* He organized temporal hierarchies within the country and initiated relationships with China, which he visited in 1653 at the invitation of the first Manchu emperor, Shunzhi, who considered the Dalai Lama one of his spiritual masters. As a result, 250 years of cordial relationships and mutual allegiance ensued, based on respect for spiritual authority on the one side and for secular power on the other. Tibet's internal reforms were decisive: feudal lords were gathered under a single authority, a central government was structured and trade developed, thus enabling foreign colonies – Mongol, Chinese or Nepalese – to settle on Tibetan land, and the arts and sciences to flourish.

Within the Gelugpa lineage the Dalai Lamas are often associated with the Panchen Lamas. The title Panchen comes from the first syllables of the Sanskrit word *pandita*, meaning scholar', and from the Tibetan adjective *chenpo*, meaning 'great'. Contrary to the claim of the authorities in Beijing that they were responsible for the title, the institution of the Panchen Lamas was created by the Fifth Dalai Lama.

The story of how this came about is actually very simple. In Shigatse, in the province of Tsang, west of Lhasa, the first Dalai Lama (Gendün Drub, 1391–1475) founded a monastery called Tashilhunpo, and, consequently, was its first abbot. Two centuries later, in 1600, Tashilhunpo was ruled by an abbot (Lobsang Chökyi Gyaltsen, 1570–1662) who was to play an essential part in the rise of the Fifth Dalai Lama, Ngawang Lobsang Gyatso. The two men held each other in great esteem, and the 'Great Fifth' – the name Tibetans gave to Ngawang Lobsang Gyatso – looked on the abbot as his tutor. It is acknowledged that Lobsang Chökyi Gyaltsen was a lama of great erudition. When, at the age of 31, he had been raised to the rank of abbot of Tashilhunpo, he had designed 23 magnificent pictures made of embroidered satin, numerous tapestries, paintings, brass and clay statues, and generously donated various pieces of furniture and religious artefacts to the most destitute monasteries, especially in the Kokonor area, in Amdo. One of his first acts had been to ordain the Fourth Dalai Lama, Yönten Gyatso, and to teach him the *Kalachakra*.[9] Later on, under the rule of the 'Great Fifth', he completed the writing of five volumes of sacred aphorisms and helped the spiritual and temporal leader of Tibet to organize the monastic hierarchy responsible for the management of religious estates. It was reported, with great awe, that he ordained some 50,000 novices and presided over the ordination ceremonies of around 100,000 monks.

It is said that texts which had remained secret at the time of the first dissemination of Buddhism would have revealed to the Fifth Dalai Lama that his tutor and master, Lobsang Chökyi Gyaltsen, was an incarnation of Amithaba, the Buddha of Infinite Light. When Ngawang Lobsang Gyatso conferred on the abbot of Tashilhunpo the title of Panchen Lama, his three previous incarnations were retrospectively given the same title. That is how Lobsang Chökyi Gyaltsen became the Fourth Panchen Lama and one of the highest Gelugpa authorities in the country. Usually, this role was not considered to have any temporal authority.

Why did I decide to write this book? Freedom has been all but totally suppressed in Tibet for decades, and Buddhism, treated harshly by Chinese invaders since the 1950s, struggles to survive. And yet nowadays it is still impossible to separate the practice of Buddhism from the Tibetan national identity, despite almost 50 years of Chinese occupation.

In spite of everything, it is very difficult to understand the so-called new 'freedoms' granted by a communist power that does virtually nothing to promote the development of Tibetan culture, which it sees as the legacy of a feudal past full of superstitions. Why, since the early 1980s, have the Chinese invaders allowed the renovation of some monasteries but destroyed some 6,000 others? For Tibetan people, monasteries were, and still are, centres of intellectual and cultural life, and symbols of national interest, whereas for the Chinese they are merely 'national museums' and 'monuments revealing the work of the people'.[10] The monastery of Kumbum, for example (in the Tibetan region of Amdo, which now forms the Chinese province of Qinghai), which was built in the sixteenth century in the birthplace of Tsongkhapa, the founder of the Gelugpa lineage, has now been reduced to a popular tourist attraction. The surroundings are inhabited by Chinese settlers (you would think you were in China rather than Tibet) and the dusty road leading to the sanctuary is flanked by Chinese stalls and shops. This applies to nearly all the renovated monasteries: tickets are sold at the entrance to each temple, there are group visits, and every day crowds of noisy Chinese tourists can be seen taking pictures, insulting the monks, and profaning the holy places by turning prayer wheels with their feet and sitting on the throne of His Holiness, in full view of the monks. The Chinese police and soldiers, confident of their impunity, and sometimes completely drunk, enjoy harassing and beating the monks. Guides are always on hand to tell the tourists that religion is just an obscure faith and that there is no deity. The communist authorities consider that Tibetan people are lacking in discernment, and declare that religion will be annihilated by civilization.

All this gives cause for concern over the fate of ten-year-old Gendün Chökyi Nyima, the eleventh reincarnation of the Panchen Lama and the youngest political prisoner in the world.

I wanted to write this book to denounce further interference by Chinese communists in a purely Tibetan issue. By appointing another child in place of the Eleventh Panchen Lama, Beijing are gambling with time. If, unfortunately for the Tibetan people, the Fourteenth Dalai Lama were to disappear, it would be the duty of the Panchen Lama to recognize his reincarnation. Were the true Panchen Lama to be replaced by a puppet in the pay of the Chinese Communist Party, the continuation of the lineage of the Dalai Lama would again be in question. The new Dalai Lama chosen by him, undoubtedly pro-communist, would then acknowledge that Tibet belongs to 'motherland' China. At that point, in full view of the indifferent nations and political powers of the world, the final assimilation of an entire nation and the eradication of a 1,000-year-old culture would be assured. Fifty million Chinese people have disappeared in *laogai** (camps) since the communists came to power in China. Over 1 million Tibetans – one in six – have been victims of the genocide carried out in their country since 1949. The real issue concerning Tibet is whether its people will survive as anything more than a collective memory. Are we going to stand by and let such a unique nation, civilization and way of life disappear?

I have written this contemporary history of the Panchen Lamas in order to denounce Beijing's shameful behaviour towards a child, Gendün Chökyi Nyima, whom nobody has seen since he was kidnapped in 1995, after being officially recognized as the Eleventh Panchen Lama by Tibetans in exile. His fate concerns all of us, for his disappearance is an absolute injustice and a matter for our universal conscience. Quite simply, this book aims to save the lives of a ten-year-old child and his family, imprisoned in Tibet or China.

I hope I have helped readers to understand what is at stake, so that they will realize the seriousness of these events, which, although related to the age-old history of Tibet, concern the country's present survival. China must agree to stop all transfers of population, cease its policy of assimilation, and put a stop to the destruction of Tibet's cultural and religious heritage, and to all harsh actions taken against a people, which, until the communist invasion, had lived in freedom.

PART I

The Ninth Panchen Lama
(1900–1937)

I

The 'Continuity of Consciousness'

*I was granted the precious and
uncommon opportunity to be reborn as a
human being.*

THUBTEN GYATSO, THIRTEENTH DALAI LAMA

Shortly before his death in 1933, the Thirteenth Dalai Lama wrote:

> ... if you are not able to defend yourself now then the
> institution of the Dalai Lama, other venerable incarnations and
> those who protect the teachings will be wiped out completely.
> Monasteries will be looted, property confiscated and all living
> beings will be destroyed ... official property will be confiscated.
> The people will be slaves of the conquerors and they will roam
> the land in bondage. All souls will be immersed in suffering
> and fear. And the night shall be long and dark.[1]

This reads like a prophetic vision. But, equally likely, it was this
outstandingly wise man's assessment of the future of Tibet after his
rule, which he wished to make known to his people.

Tibet first came into contact with the Western world around the
turn of the nineteenth century. This new development in its history
took place through the Russian Empire and especially through
British India. The attitudes and events of the time clearly explain the

isolationist tradition of Tibet – Lhasa, the capital, for instance, was called the 'Forbidden City'. The distinctive geography of Tibet reinforced this attitude, and was in turn considered by the government to be an effective barrier against invaders. Also, at that time, between 1815 and 1875, four Dalai Lamas met an early death. It is possible that the palace of the Potala[2] will one day reveal its terrible secrets, but for the time being we have only the explanation given by W W Rockhill, who considered that the young Dalai Lamas led a confined and somewhat unnatural life, and were subjected to all sorts of constraints. In addition, exacting feats of intellectual development were required so that from childhood on they could adapt to the role they had to play. It was therefore obvious that only children with a sturdy constitution could go through such ordeals and come of age in good health. In the nineteenth century, the Dalai Lamas who did not survive into adulthood may have had little physical or mental resilience, and may thus have died of natural causes. Another possibility is that these premature deaths occurred as a result of the struggles for power between various political groups.

At that time, the government of British India tried to resume the relations initiated with Tibet in the eighteenth century, when an emissary of the East India Company had stayed with the Sixth Panchen Lama. But first, disagreements about the borders between the two countries had to be resolved. The British were hesitant, wondering whether it was better to negotiate directly with the Tibetans or to use the Chinese as intermediaries. It should be pointed out here that in spite of the fact that the two countries had signed treaties as independent and free States,[3] the Chinese empire had already been describing Tibet as a political dependency for a long time.

As a result, British diplomats held to a simplistic vision of the situation. They considered, in effect, that Tibet came under Chinese authority – a prejudice again reflected in their attitude towards Chiang Kai-shek after World War II. Nevertheless, the British signed agreements with Beijing that were supposed to solve all matters concerning communications and trade in both Tibet and Burma. On 17 March 1890, a first text delineated the boundary between Tibet and Sikkim and established norms of communication

4

for relations between the Tibetans and the British authorities in India. On 5 December 1893, a new Anglo-Chinese agreement granted Britain several commercial rights in the south of Tibet, between the borders of Sikkim and Bhutan. As the Tibetans had not been allowed to take part in negotiations, they considered these agreements worthless and refused to take them into account. From then on, the number of incidents increased.

The Thirteenth Dalai Lama, Thubten Gyatso (1876–1933), had just turned 12 when in 1888 he presided over the enthronement ceremonies of the six-year-old Ninth Panchen Lama, Chökyi Nyima, son of a herdswoman and an unknown father, who was born in the year of the Eighth Panchen Lama's death.

Often suffused with the supernatural, Tibetan history records that in 1888: 'Crops were plentiful, cows and sheep gave birth to magnificent offspring, and flowers and fruit were more beautiful than ever.'[4] In accordance with tradition, the search for the reincarnation of the Eighth Panchen Lama was controlled by the highest administrative authority of Tashilhunpo. The Kashag★ and the Council of Khenpo★ also took part. Oracles went into trances and monks prayed without cease, their incantations also guiding the search.

Under the guidance of the superior of Tashilhunpo, a delegation went to Lhamo Latso, a mystical lake of many powers. In 1509 the Second Dalai Lama, Gyalwa Gendün Gyatso (1475–1542/3), had ordered that the monastery of Chökhorgyal be built there, about 90 miles from Lhasa. Speaking for other adepts of tantrism, he described the lake as follows:

Those who wish to be enlightened in this life can find here the ideal place to meditate. The lake will reveal everything. Its magical waters reflect the emptiness of appearances and events underlying our conventional view of their nature. It guides the mind of the yoga to the sublime union of two levels of truth: the ultimate, and the visible reflection.

Regarding reincarnation, some Buddhist scholars prefer the term 'rebirth'. They assume, in effect, that the word 'reincarnation' implies that it is the 'soul' that becomes incarnate, which is not in line with their beliefs. They believe, too, that there are four types of rebirth. The Fourteenth Dalai Lama, Tenzin Gyatso, explains:

> The most common rebirth concerns a being who is unable to influence his incarnation, for whom the quality of rebirth is entirely dependent on his past deeds. At the other extreme is a Buddha who has been completely freed, who takes on a physical body solely for the purpose of contributing to the development of sentient beings. The third possibility applies to a being who, because of past spiritual achievements, is able to choose, or at least influence, the place and nature of his future rebirth. The fourth possibility is called a 'blessed manifestation'. This person is endowed with blessings which go beyond the normal abilities required to accomplish useful tasks such as teaching religion. Such a person must have had a particularly strong aspiration to help other people in his past lives to have been given such power. Although some forms of rebirth seem less likely than others, I cannot say for sure which one I belong to.[5]

To facilitate the search for their incarnation, high-ranking religious people often leave a will indicating the place of their next birth, with the names of their parents as well as material clues describing the landscape, features of the house, and so on. A lama's rebirth is recognized by a simple declaration from his peers, but the reincarnation of the leader of a school or the superior of a particularly important monastery involves a more complex procedure, including a visionary dream and the consultation of oracles. The final choice occurs when the 'candidate' is able to distinguish, among many similar objects, those which belonged to the previous incarnation. This is how Thubten Gyatso (the Thirteenth Dalai Lama) and Chökyi Nyima (the Ninth Panchen Lama) were chosen.

The following explanations by the Fourteenth Dalai Lama may help us to understand better the Buddhist interpretation of the concept of rebirth, which is essentially based on the idea of the continuity of consciousness:

If we consider the physical world, for instance, it is possible to trace back the origin of all the constituents of our present universe – even at a microscopic level – to an initial point where all elements of matter are spread out in 'space particles'. These particles result from the disintegration of a previous universe. Therefore a continuous cycle occurs: the universe develops, disintegrates and comes back to life.

Our mind works in a similar way. It is absolutely obvious that we possess what we call 'mind' or 'consciousness': our experience testifies to that. It is also obvious that what we call 'mind' or 'consciousness' is liable to change when faced with different conditions and circumstances. That it varies from one moment to the next is proof of its nature, and of its predisposition to change.

It is also obvious that at its most base level, the 'mind', or 'consciousness', is closely linked with physiological body states; in effect, it depends on them. However, there must also be a substratum, an energy, a source which enables the mind, in its interaction with material particles, to create living beings with consciousness. On the material level, this substratum is also undoubtedly a continuation of the past. Therefore, if we trace the origin of our actual mind and our present consciousness, we discover that, as with the origin of the material universe, we go back into the infinite past of the mind continuum, for which there is no origin. Consequently there must be rebirths to make it possible for the mind to continue.

Buddhism believes in universal causality: everything is subject to change as well as to the law of cause and effect. It leaves no room therefore for a divine Creator, nor for the 'spontaneous generation' of beings. On the contrary, everything appears as a consequence of cause and effect. This is why the present state of the 'mind', or 'consciousness', is the result of previous moments.

Causes and effects fall into two main types: there are substantial 'causes' – which are at the root of what happens – and various 'agents', which contribute to the creation of causality. As for mind and body, although one may affect the other, it cannot become the other's substance, nor can one be the substantial cause of the other. This is the basis on which Buddhism acknowledges the idea of rebirth.[6]

At the end of the nineteenth century the situation had looked promising, with two young reincarnations filling the Tibetans' hearts with happiness. Since 1886, because the Dalai Lama was not yet old enough to rule (traditionally, he cannot assume secular power until he is 18), the country had been administered by a regent, Demo Trinle Rabgye, who had succeeded regent Kundeling Chökyi Gyaltsen. At the time, the Kashag, the main organ of government, was composed of four members: one monk and three laymen. Two departments depended directly on this institution: the secretariat, or monastic council (Yigtsang), and the Finance Office (Tsigang). The former was ruled by four monks who, under the supervision of the Dalai Lama – or, at the time, the regent – were in charge of religious matters. In the latter, four laymen took care of the secular management of the State. The equivalent of a parliament could be summoned according to three different procedures. At ordinary meetings, about 20 people attended: the eight members of Yigtsang and Tsigang, plus representatives of the three great Gelugpa monasteries close to Lhasa – Drepung, Ganden and Sera – and laymen. When specific issues were debated, the group was increased to 30 people. For the most important issues, extraordinary sessions were convened, under the authority of the Dalai Lama or the regent; and for a plenary session, 400 members were necessary.

In spite of all the hopes Tibetans placed in both reincarnations, these years of regency were not happy ones. Indeed, the preceding ones had not been either: Lungtok Gyatso, the Ninth Dalai Lama, had died at the age of nine; his successor, Tsultrim Gyatso, had lived only until the age of 21; Khedrup Gyatso, the Eleventh Dalai Lama, had died at 18, and Trinle Gyatso, the Twelfth Dalai Lama, at the age of 19. In accordance with Tibetan tradition, people readily believed that the spiritual and temporal ruler of Tibet made a precious contribution to the development of his country 'by departing for the Realm of Happiness'. Was this to be the lot of the Thirteenth Dalai Lama and the Ninth Panchen Lama?

Selected from the country's major monastic institutions, among the most important regents in Tibetan history were Tengyeling,

Demo Kundeling, Tshomöling and Reting. The title of regent (*desi*, in Tibetan) was conferred for the first time by the Fifth Dalai Lama (Ngawang Lobsang Gyatso, 1617–82) on his administrator Sönam Chöphel, who died in 1656 or 1658, and later on Sangye Gyatso[7] – certainly the most famous regent – in recognition of their administrative capabilities and erudition. After the death of the Seventh Dalai Lama (Kelsang Gyasto, 1708–57), the tradition changed and famous reincarnated lamas were appointed as regents.[8] Yet, since 1757, when a reincarnated lama was chosen as regent for the first time, the institution has continued to deteriorate. The allegiance of monasteries like Drepung, Ganden or Sera to men who were suddenly granted enormous power in part explains the terrible ills which befell the country. The regents have been the main agents for the most chaotic and enigmatic chapters of Tibetan history.

2

British Intervention

Think of death: think of freedom.
MONTAIGNE

Most Tibetan people consider the Dalai Lama an absolute and undisputed authority. This was probably true of Thubten Gyatso and Tenzin Gyatso, the Thirteenth and Fourteenth Dalai Lamas, but has not always been so. Before that, in the two centuries following the Great Fifth, the Dalai Lamas' rule over Tibet was so weak that they only left behind spiritual traces of their reigns. For most of the time, power was in the hands of administrators, regents or ministers. In the early eighteenth century, when Tibet entered into close relations with the Manchu empire, the power of the regency became so great that one of the first administrative reforms of the occupying forces was to suppress the regent and create a cabinet of ministers.

The Sixth Dalai Lama was deposed by the Mongol leader Lhabsang Khan and sent into exile in Amdo, with the consent of the Imperial Manchu Court of Beijing; in 1728 the Seventh Dalai Lama was sent into exile in China by the emperor. The Eighth Dalai Lama survived adolescence, but was urged to leave control of the country's political affairs to a lay minister. A religious regency was instituted after his death in 1757. And there is good reason to believe that the Ninth, Tenth, Eleventh and Twelfth Dalai Lamas were 'encouraged' to leave their human form![1]

The Thirteenth Dalai Lama, Thubten Gyatso,[2] took over the temporal leadership of Tibet in 1895, the year of the Wood Sheep in the Tibetan calendar, when he was just 19. It is thought that not long after his enthronement, Demo Rinpoche, who had acted as regent during the Dalai Lama's minority, probably tried to murder him.

Demo Rinpoche would no doubt have been an excellent administrator had he not been surrounded by relatives and friends who were greedy for power. The years of his regency passed in a climate of corruption. Executions followed upon confiscation of properties, and there were rumours of strange poisonings and suspicious disappearances.

One particular rumour suggested that Demo Rinpoche and his relatives intended to get rid of the Thirteenth Dalai Lama. Thubten Gyatso had just taken his full monastic vows (gelong) and it is unknown whether he was aware that the years of regency preceding his accession to power had not been happy ones for the Tibetan people. Those who were close to the young Dalai Lama readily acknowledged his great intelligence. His cleverness, indeed, was equalled only by his religious purity. However, the fact remains that Norbu Tsering, a brother of Demo Rinpoche, asked for help from a lama called Nyagtrü, from Nyarong in eastern Tibet, who in turn called upon the deity Shinje Tsheda using black magic rituals. The lama, who was reported to have reached a high level of spiritual development, thanks to the help of Shinje Tsheda, agreed to prepare a particularly powerful yantra – a diagrammatic symbol of a divinity or group of divinities, usually composed of geometric designs and mantras.* In this particular yantra, various mantras were inscribed around the figure of a man with outstretched arms and legs, but the name of Thubten Gyatso and the year of his birth, chiwa, were written within the body of the figure. The lama inserted the yantra in the sole of a very beautiful pair of boots which Demo Rinpoche gave to Sogya, a tutor of the Dalai Lama from the western province of Kham.[3] In this way, Norbu Tsering hoped to put an end to the life of the Thirteenth Dalai Lama.

At the time the Nechung oracle* went into several trances. During one of them he declared that the life of the Thirteenth Dalai Lama hung only by a thread and that a pair of boots given to Lama

Sogya should be found as soon as possible. The Dalai Lama immediately summoned the lama, who explained at length how he had been given the present. He also specified that the boots seemed very strange and suspicious, for his nose started to bleed each time he put them on. An order was immediately given to bring in Sogya's boots. They were placed before the Dalai Lama and completely taken apart. When the *yantra* concealed in the inner sole was discovered, Thubten Gyatso instantly ordered the arrest of Demo Rinpoche, Norbu Tsering and Nyagtrü.[4] Demo Rinpoche died shortly afterwards under house arrest in Lhasa. The rumours increased; one said that he had drowned himself in a huge copper tank filled with water. It was also reported that Norbu Tsering and Nyagtrü had been executed in jail. The Kashag confiscated all the properties of the former regent and declared that in future no reincarnation of the Demo lineage would ever again be recognized.[5]

Only someone with the Thirteenth Dalai Lama's strength of character could have remained cool-headed in the face of what was happening within Tibet. When some monasteries denounced the nepotism of the monastic authorities, as well as the obvious lack of education of members of the monastic Council and the Assembly, the ruler's answer was almost immediate: the right of inheritance would play no key role in the appointment of *kalön**, and candidates would have to provide evidence of their skills for all other positions. He also issued a warning to the monasteries, enjoining them to respect the word of the Buddha and to act with honesty.

Regarding external affairs, the Thirteenth Dalai Lama had to face the emergence of new threats to the already precarious Sino-Tibetan balance. In August 1894, Russia and Britain took advantage of the onset of war between China and Japan[6] and moved their pawns forward on the giant chessboard of Asia. Tibet was a key element in their game plan.

With the weakening of the Qing empire, the Manchus had lost interest in Tibetan affairs and their influence had become minimal. For example, in the course of the century, wars against the Dogras of Ladakh in 1841, and Nepal in 1854 and 1857, and the uprising of the eastern province of Nyarong in 1860–5, had all been settled without Manchu intervention. The overthrow of the regent Reting Ngawang Yeshe Tsultrim Gyaltsen in 1862 had had no direct effect on relations between the Manchu empire and Tibet, or, at the very most, it had motivated the new emperor Tongzhi to send a letter to the Tibetan prime minister. Tibetan authorities had even selected the Thirteenth Dalai Lama without resorting to the lottery system instituted in 1793 by the Manchu Emperor Qianlong,[7] another indication of just how marginal the influence of the Manchu commissioners, the *ambans*,★ had become on the government of Lhasa.

However, at that time, Sino-Tibetan relations turned out to be far more complex than could have been expected at first sight. They were further complicated by the Tibetan concept of a *chöyön*★ relationship between the leaders of Tibet and China. This term referred to a symbiotic link between a religious figure and a lay protector; and so to the Tibetans, the Dalai Lama and the Manchu emperor represented a spiritual master and his lay protector, rather than a subject and his lord. Both countries thus assumed that coexistence, albeit one fraught with compromises and ambiguities, was to their advantage. Their interests, in any case, converged on one point: they both distrusted strangers, whoever they might be.

Unfortunately, Tibet was no longer a buffer state shown as a white area on maps. The influences of the Russian and the British empires had a neutralizing effect: the first Anglo-Afghan war (1838–42) was hardly over when the Russians successively occupied Tachkent in 1865, Samarkand in 1868, Bukhara in 1869, Khiva in 1873 and Khokand in 1876. Then after the second Anglo-Afghan war (1878–80), the Russians took Turkmenistan in 1881, Merv in 1884, and Pamir in 1895. They would again pursue their political strategy of deployment in Asia after the 1917 Revolution and the communists' accession to power.

At the turn of the century, the relationship between the Dalai Lama and the Panchen Lama was one of mutual respect, but signs of rivalries between their respectives parties were common. The Panchen Lama's territory covered a wide area around Shigatse and the monastery of Tashilhunpo; many other districts had also been united with it. Under the permanent pressure of their respective parties, the two spiritual authorities of Tibet seldom met.

As traditionally required of each Dalai Lama, Thubten Gyatso went on a pilgrimage to the monastery of Chökhorgyal, in 1900. He extended his trip to Samye, where he contracted smallpox, but he recovered and continued on to the Tibetan capital. The Ninth Panchen Lama heard about the Dalai Lama's illness and, in 1902, decided to visit him. It was said that the two men spent so many hours talking that the master of Tashilhunpo almost forgot to leave. It was also reported that late into the night, Thubten Gyatso took a lantern and guided his guest to the main gate of Lhasa, where he bade him goodbye. Unfortunately, the conflicting events of the time and the political ambitions of those in the service of these two men were to put their friendship to the test and plunge Tibet into sadness and anxiety.

The British were obsessed with the fear of being beaten by the Russians in the diplomatic game with Tibet. Rumours of a possible delivery of Russian weapons to the government of Lhasa increased their apprehension. Dispatches from St Petersburg arrived in London, mentioning the strange friendship between Thubten Gyatso and a Russian national, a Buriat monk called Dorjieff, who had acted on several occasions as an intermediary between Tsar Nicholas II and the Dalai Lama. The Tibetan government was not in total agreement with London's somewhat simplistic view which held, in particular, that Tibet came under the authority of China. Beijing and London had even signed various agreements relating to commercial and transport issues in Burma, Sikkim and Tibet without consulting the government of Lhasa. For instance, on 17 March 1890, an agreement delineated the border between Sikkim and Tibet. The Tibetan government was understandably unhappy about this and, not surprisingly, Thubten Gyatso had the boundary stones set up by the British destroyed. Another agreement, on 5 December 1893, allowed a permanent trade mart to be established in Yatung in Tibet, at the entrance to the Chumbi valley, a narrow gateway to Sikkim and Bhutan.

The efforts of Lord Curzon, Viceroy of India, to open up relations with Tibet led to the 1903–4 British invasion. But by forcing Tibet out of its voluntary political isolation, the Anglo-Indian aggression thrust the Land of Snows into the forefront of the international scene to face the might of China, Russia and Britain.

The Tibetan army desperately tried to halt the British troops led by Francis Younghusband.[8] The British military escort, led by the British Agent J Macdonald, originally amounted to only 200 men, but with support forces this was increased to some 3,000. The clash between the two armies led to the death of several hundreds of Tibetans.

Lhasa was filled with consternation. Convinced there were traitors within his party, the Dalai Lama dismissed three members of the cabinet. He also knew that he could expect nothing from You Tai, the new *amban* who had arrived in 1902, so he decided to flee rather than submit. He appointed as regent the head of the Gelugpa lineage, the *ganden thriba*★ Lobsang Gyaltsen, to take charge of state affairs in his absence. The Dalai Lama's departure was embarrassing for both the British and the Chinese, so much so that the *amban* sent a message to Beijing requesting the deposition of His Holiness. The Chinese complied with this request as if they had some right or power over the Dalai Lama.

Thubten Gyatso went to distant Mongolia, where he hoped to obtain the help of the Russians. After a four-month journey, the Thirteenth Dalai Lama arrived in Urga, the capital of Outer Mongolia, where he was welcomed, with all the honours due to his rank, by the Buddhist temporal and spiritual leader of the Mongols, the *Jetsun dampa*.

It was reported that over 20,000 people came out from the town to welcome the Dalai Lama and bow down before the highest incarnation in Buddhism, and that an artillery salute announced the arrival of the God–King of Tibet. Elsewhere, crowds of pilgrims set off from Siberia, China and Turkestan.

The British were alarmed on hearing that Thubten Gyatso was in touch with the Russian consul in the Mongolian capital, and that he had been given presents on behalf of the tsar by Ambassador Pokotiloff who was en route to his post in Beijing. The entry of the Anglo-Indian army into Lhasa forced the regent to act and he signed a convention with the British in Lhasa on 7 September 1904, the year of the Wood Dragon in the Tibetan calendar. Under this agreement, Tibet recognized the suzerainty of Britain over Sikkim and agreed to open trade relations with India. The opening of a trade mart in Yatung was confirmed and others were created in Gyantse and Gartok, where British troops were allowed to be stationed. Moreover, Tibet was to sever diplomatic relations with all other foreign countries.

The British presence in Tibet was, in fact, a Pyrrhic victory for the empire, for London once again found itself in an embarrassing situation with China and Russia. The government, backed by the Viceroy, Lord Curzon, then disowned the operations led by Francis Younghusband, thus negating any benefit which might have come from this policy, which they considered too adventurous. In addition, over the next few years, Lord Morley, the Secretary of State for India in London, instigated a diplomatic retreat. More important, the British initiated negotiations with the Manchu empire to obtain its acceptance of the Lhasa Convention, in its amended form. The resulting agreement reaffirmed Manchu hegemony over Tibet and almost excluded the British from Tibetan political affairs, if not from commercial matters. This attitude immediately prompted a new Chinese policy of annexation towards Tibet.

For the first time in its history, China expended concerted efforts to gain direct control over Tibet and the semi-autonomous Tibetan principalities of Sichuan. The Manchus considered that it was time to address the fact that the Tibetan government, headed by the Thirteenth Dalai Lama, no longer obeyed the *amban* – and therefore the emperor. They also thought that since 1904 there had been a real danger that Tibet would become a British protectorate, like Bhutan and Sikkim.

At the end of 1904 and during the first months of 1905, China published an edict in Batang in eastern Kham (which had been joined to the Chinese province of Sichuan since the early eighteenth century), reducing the number of monks in monasteries and forbidding all recruitment for the next 20 years. Already estates had been confiscated and Chinese colonists settled in the area. They were given full support by French Catholic missionaries who had been living there for some fifty years. This prompted an immediate reaction from the Tibetan religious and lay population and led to an uprising in the town and later in the whole region. The *amban*, Feng Tsuen, one of the instigators of the Sinicization of the area, was put to death along with his escort. Four French priests were assassinated in the following weeks.

Retaliations followed immediately, and were extremely violent.

The officials of the province of Sichuan sent troops to Batang as well as to all Tibetan principalities of the province. The monastery was razed to the ground and the monks murdered. Then Beijing appointed Chao Erh-feng to complete 'consolidation'.[9] Great lamaseries were besieged for several months. They were fiercely defended by hundreds or thousands of monks who only succumbed due to lack of food and water. Their shaven heads were cut off and hung by the ears in trees.[10] Chao was nicknamed 'the butcher of lamas'.

By 1908, eastern Kham was completely dominated, but it was no longer merely a military operation. In fact, Manchu China had decided to bring the whole region permanently under its direct rule. Chao Erh-feng implemented regulations which would one day be applied to all Tibetan people: the inhabitants of eastern Kham were now subjects of the Chinese emperor and under the jurisdiction of a Chinese magistrate; all taxes – some of them very unfair – were to be paid to the Chinese, and those traditionally paid to Tibetan chiefs and monasteries abolished; all inhabitants were subject to Chinese law. He even tried to change traditional dress and funeral customs. Schools were opened and young Tibetans forced to learn Chinese.

In Lhasa, the *ambans*, including You Tai, took advantage of the Dalai Lama's absence and the British retreat to proclaim that, immediately after the signature of the Lhasa Convention, China had compelled London to submit to its authority. The *ambans* were also busying themselves with high-ranking officials, trying to Sinicize the élite, appointing officials in their pay, making plans to form a powerful army and trying to secularize the Tibetan government by creating lay councils. They were also planning to build roads and telegraph lines and even considered exploiting the country's large natural resources. As an immediate consequence, a Chinese school opened in Lhasa in 1907, and a military college in 1908.

As soon as the officials of Tashilhunpo heard of the departure of the Dalai Lama to Mongolia, they put pressure on Chökyi Nyima, the Ninth Panchen Lama, to travel to India. Officially, the reason given was that he wanted to visit major Buddhist sites in the country; unofficially, the officials wanted him to meet the Prince of Wales (the future George V) in Calcutta. The news immediately aroused anger in Lhasa. The government denounced the move, at a time when the Dalai Lama was away in the high plateaux of Mongolia, as extremely awkward and expressed the view that at least some solidarity was expected from the rulers of Tashilhunpo.

The news of the Panchen Lama's departure for British India was not entirely unexpected. Younghusband had met one of his representatives in Khamba Dzong as early as 1903, in what was possibly a first attempt on the part of Chökyi Nyima to reinforce his power in the face of the Dalai Lama's efforts to assert his own authority. At that time, Lord Curzon had contemplated appointing a British agent in Lhasa; however, a compromise was found and it was agreed that the agent would settle in Gyantse and go to the Tibetan capital whenever needed. In spite of the viceroy's directives, Younghusband had refused to include the nomination of an agent in the Lhasa Convention, signed with the regent in 1904. A separate agreement was drafted, on which were affixed all the seals of Lhasa, except that of the regent, *ganden thriba* Lobsang Gyaltsen.

Frederick O'Connor was in due course appointed trade agent in Gyantse. He had already met the Panchen Lama while taking part in an expedition to western Tibet under Captain Rawling's command, and it was O'Connor who suggested his trip to India. In the short term, he pushed London to support the Panchen Lama, to take advance of his opportunity to break away from the Dalai Lama's control and fill the political vacuum left by the Tibetan ruler's absence – one which China would not hesitate to use to its advantage.

Lord Curzon's invitation to visit India reached Gyantse in September 1905, but the Panchen Lama remained unconvinced and reluctant. O'Connor promised that his government would protect him against the anger of the Dalai Lama and the authorities in Lhasa. However, no sooner had Chökyi Nyima left Shigatse, than a semi-official message from Beijing reached the British trading post stating that the Chinese government would refuse to recognize any agreement the Panchen Lama might sign with the British government in India.

Meanwhile other events were taking place. Sudden changes occurred in the British administration in Calcutta: in December 1905, Lord Curzon left his post and was replaced by Lord Minto. Shortly thereafter, in London, Lord Balfour's Conservative government gave way to the Liberals led by Campbell-Bannerman. Younghusband left Lhasa, leaving behind a situation that was more embarrassing than beneficial. No wonder that the new head of the British government immediately decided to appoint the authoritarian Morley to rule Indian affairs from London. The consequences of these changes were soon to be felt.

Meanwhile, in Calcutta, the Panchen Lama, who knew nothing of these disruptions, was expecting the support of the British administration. He was greatly disappointed when he realized that Lord Minto considered the possibility that he might be attacked by Beijing or Lhasa of no consequence. This reaction implied that the Panchen Lama would be refused the military assistance he had come to seek in Calcutta. Lord Minto also remained vague when Chökyi Nyima requested that the empire's representative in Gyantse should keep in close touch with his monastery so that he could immediately inform the Calcutta authorities of any emergency. Disappointed, Chökyi Nyima completed his tour of Buddhist sites in India and headed back to Tashilhunpo.

The return of the Panchen Lama to Shigatse empty-handed marked the end of Frederick O'Connor's intervention in Tibetan affairs. He had tried to save what he could from the political debris left by Lord Curzon. In fact, the British representative had even incurred Lord Minto's gratitude. It was Morley who had put an end to O'Connor's plan. Morley let it be known that relations with the Panchen Lama should be reduced to their simplest terms and that there was absolutely no question of intervening in Tibet's internal affairs or in relations between the Panchen Lama and the government of Lhasa or the emperor of China.

The Dalai Lama was kept informed by his agents of everything that was happening in his country. It was said that he became violently angry with the Panchen Lama, but possibly the facts reported to him had been exaggerated. In any event, Thubten Gyatso believed for a long time that the Panchen Lama had obtained the agreement of the Prince of Wales and the British government before he declared himself supreme ruler of Tibet.[11]

Meanwhile, relegated to painful exile, the Thirteenth Dalai Lama turned to Russia. He sent Dorjieff, his monk attendant, to St Petersburg to meet Tsar Nicholas II and ask him 'for protection from the dangers which threaten my life, if I return to Lhasa as is my intention and duty'.[12] But Russia had just been defeated in the 1904 conflict with Japan, and the 1905 Revolution had weakened whatever was left of imperial power. Tsar Nicholas II delayed settling the Tibetan issue. Eventually he came to think that there was no reason to intervene in the affairs of Lhasa and to this effect sent a very courteous letter to the Dalai Lama on 7 April 1906:

> A large number of my subjects who profess the Buddhist faith had the happiness of being able to pay homage to their great High Lama during his visit to northern Mongolia, which borders on the Russian Empire. As I rejoice that my subjects have had the opportunity of deriving benefit from your salutary spiritual influence, I beg you to accept the expression of my sincere thanks and my regards.[13]

Thubten Gyatso's troubles increased even more with the deterioration of his relations with the principal incarnate lama of Mongolia. The Thirteenth Dalai Lama's biography says: 'Although the *Jetsun dampa* had great respect for the Dalai Lama, because he saw that the Mongolian people revered the Dalai Lama more than himself, he gradually came to resent and dislike the Dalai Lama and wanted him to leave Mongolia.'[14] No doubt this deterioration in his attitude was aggravated by the fact that the Mongol was a dedicated epicure and the Tibetan a disciplined monk: divorce was inevitable.

An anecdote summarizes their somewhat complicated relationship: the increasingly hostile feelings between the two leaders were in part due to a difference of opinion about the height of their respective thrones. Thubten Gyatso wanted his to be higher than that used by the *Jetsun dampa* in his previous incarnation! The current *Jetsun dampa* insisted that their thrones be the same height.

In the meantime, in Tibet in the summer of 1905, the Kashag and the abbots of Drepung, Ganden and Sera implored the *amban* You Tai to ask the emperor of China to restore the Dalai Lama's titles. Simultaneously, they sent a message to Thubten Gyatso, urging him to come back to Lhasa as soon as possible. The Dalai Lama eventually agreed to leave Mongolia in April 1906, the year of the Iron Horse in the Tibetan calendar. When he reached Amdo in October 1906, he was met by Chinese officials who instructed him to stay at the monastery of Kumbum until further notice. There is no doubt that this decision had been taken by Zhang Yin Tang, who was anxious to settle the Tibetan issue. The moment he assumed his post, he had asked the government of Beijing to give him time to strengthen his position in Tibet and implement reforms which would put the country under the complete domination of China.

As Thubten Gyatso was fearful of meeting the *ambans* in Lhasa, he spent a long year in Amdo. He then decided to adopt a completely different strategy. Rebuffed by Tsar Nicholas II, he sought an accommodation with the Manchu empire which had deposed him in 1904; but at the same time he also tried to improve his relations with the British who were still ruling India.

It seems that Thubten Gyatso himself ordered the regent Lobsang Gyaltsen to ask the emperor to invite him to Beijing so that he could explain the reality of the situation in Tibet. Highly satisfied with the British diplomatic retreat, China hurriedly paid off the war debts that the Lhasa government was committed to pay under the terms of the 1904 Lhasa Convention.[15] By following this course of action, Manchu China clearly showed its international partners that it had suzerainty over Tibet; according to Beijing, the 1906 Sino-British Convention in respect of Tibet could only be interpreted as recognition of Tibet's status in international law.

The Thirteenth Dalai Lama reinstated the three *shapes** he had sent to jail in 1903, accused of being pro-British. He promoted them to the position of *lönchen,** which transformed them into co-prime ministers with authority over the Kashag. Thubten Gyatso did not expect much from St Petersburg, because Russia had just signed (on 31 August 1907) an agreement with London concerning Persia, Afghanistan and Tibet, ratifying the vassalage of Tibetan territory. None of the countries involved had been invited to the meeting; even worse, none had been informed. The convention signed between Britain and Russia validated the Sino-British Convention of 1906 by recognizing the suzerainty of China over Tibet. Thubten Gyatso made sure that a verbal message was delivered to the British representative in Beijing as follows: 'The Dalai Lama now desires friendly relations with India, and thoroughly understands the position of affairs: whereas in 1903 the circumstances which led to the rupture were concealed from him by his subordinates.'[16]

After spending a year in the monastery of Kumbum in Amdo, the Thirteenth Dalai Lama was invited to China. Accompanied by a party of 250 people, Thubten Gyatso first reached the well-known Buddhist sanctuary of Wutai Shan. After a stop in Baoding, the official convoy arrived in Beijing on 28 September 1908, the year of the Earth Monkey in the Tibetan calendar. This was the first visit of a Dalai Lama to Beijing since the time of the Great Fifth.

3

The Chinese Exert Control

*Even the most beautiful spring flower wilts
and fades away.*

RIGDZIN TSANGYANG GYATSO, SIXTH DALAI LAMA

Built for the Great Fifth, the monastery and palace known as the
'Yellow Temple' was renovated to accommodate the Thirteenth
Dalai Lama during his stay in Beijing – at a reported cost of 2
million *taels*. The welcome ceremony with the emperor and empress
had been carefully planned for 6 October 1908, the year of the Earth
Monkey in the Tibetan calendar. But Thubten Gyatso had come to
Beijing as an independent ruler, not as a vassal, and when he was
told that he would have to bow down before the ruler of Manchu
China and sit on a 'low seat' he flatly refused, and the first meeting
was immediately cancelled. Numerous consultations followed until a
final compromise was reached.

The second audience was planned for 14 October. The Dalai
Lama was to meet first Empress Cixi, then Emperor Guangxu, and
it had been agreed that he would merely bend the knee before their
majesties. On the day of the meeting, as tradition required, the Dalai
Lama sent his presents, from a list that had been carefully drawn
up: for the empress, two gold statuettes, one of Shakyamuni
Buddha[1] and one of the Vajrapani bodhisattva,[2] and a copy of the
Kangyur;[3] for the emperor, two statuettes of Shakyamuni Buddha;
and for each of them a rosary of 108 coral pearls, gold, furs and a
yellow horse. On 30 October, a big banquet was held in honour of

the Tibetan ruler. On 3 November, the birthday of the empress, an exchange of titles took place, during which the ageing Cixi affirmed her authority over Tibet. She treated the Dalai Lama as a simple vassal and published an imperial edict which once again revealed the empire's ambitions for annexation:

> In the past, the Dalai Lama was given the title 'Perfect Buddha of the West'. The title will now be 'Very Submissive and Most Perfect Incarnate Buddha of the West'. He will be given a grant of 10,000 *taels*. With this title, the Dalai Lama will return to Tibet very soon. On his journey, officials will escort and protect him. He must exhort his supporters to abide by the laws and to practise virtue. Anything he may have to tell Us should first be reported to the *amban* in Tibet, as required by regulations; he will then await Our decision.

While in Beijing, the Dalai Lama sent emissaries to the British, French, American and Russian embassies, but the political importance of this initiative was minimized by the fact that the Chinese did the same, with a note stipulating that the Dalai Lama was available to meet guests at the 'Yellow Temple' any day of the week, except Sunday, between 2 and 5pm. Access to the Dalai Lama was further restricted by the fact that the Chinese allowed only brief meetings. A letter of that time sent by the American minister in Beijing, W W Rockhill, explained that he had probably been a witness to the end of the Thirteenth Dalai Lama's temporal power.

However, Thubten Gyatso took advantage of his stay to try to obtain the assistance of France in the building of a telegraph line in Tibet. But his efforts came to nothing.[4]

The death of Emperor Guangxu at 3pm on 14 November 1908, followed on the next day by the empress's death at 2am, precipitated the Dalai Lama's departure. But first he attended the enthronement ceremony of the last Manchu emperor, the two-year-old Xuantong, better known as Puyi. The newly appointed regent, Prince Ch'un, asked the Dalai Lama to preside over the funeral ceremonies. On 19 December, Thubten Gyatso celebrated a final public worship in Beijing and left two days later. He had pleaded in vain for independence, and the future seemed very dark.

The Panchen Lama found it hard to come to terms with the failure of his Indian trip. As soon as he arrived back in Tashilhunpo, he hastened to assure the two *ambans* in Lhasa – the Chinese Lien-yu and the Manchu Zhang Yin Tang – of his unconditional faithfulness to the emperor. The Manchu's reaction did not satisfy him completely, and he became aware too of a noticeable strengthening of Chinese power in Tibet. He feared possible retaliations. He also felt anxious about possible government interference, because Lhasa suspected him of wanting to destabilize the country.

When Chökyi Nyima heard that the Dalai Lama was on his way to Beijing, he sent an emissary to Lhasa to tell the *ambans* that he, too, wished to visit the Chinese capital. The Panchen Lama's request did not succeed for the Chinese refused to welcome the two leaders at the same time. While the Dalai Lama was still on his way back to Tibet, to the monastery of Kumbum, the two *ambans* urged the Panchen Lama to resume relations with the Kashag, mainly because Lien-yu and Zhang Yin Tang considered that this might lead to the possibility of settling the Panchen Lama in the Potala, the Dalai Lama's palace. Faced with this new refusal and the growing scepticism of the Tibetan authorities, Chökyi Nyima then asked to be received by the Dalai Lama on his return to Lhasa.

Thubten Gyatso arrived in Kumbum on 26 February 1909, in the year of the Earth Bird, and set off to reach Lhasa by early summer. The two *ambans*, as well as all the great religious and lay dignitaries of the country, insisted on going to meet him. They joined him in Nagchu, the first frontier post between China and Tibet. The Dalai Lama reached the capital on 25 December 1909; there had been five years of forced and trying journeys since his departure for Mongolia in 1904.

Outside of the town, he was greeted by an important group of dignitaries and monks, who stood in a line on one side of the road, and Chinese officials and soldiers, who stood on the other. The Dalai Lama exchanged friendly greetings with the Tibetans, but he passed the Chinese with raised head and a faraway look in his eyes, as if he did not see them. The Chinese did not say anything, but their hearts swelled with dark rage.[5]

As the Dalai Lama quickly got back to work, carrying on regardless of the authority of the empire's delegates, Beijing hastened to send troops to Lhasa in order to control the Tibetan ruler – an interference that could only be condemned by foreign powers. To gain time, the Chinese Foreign Office informed New Delhi that it was necessary to police the trade routes between British trading posts in Tibet and India. An agreement between Britain, China and Tibet, signed in Calcutta in 1908, had in fact left China in charge of commercial routes in Tibet. The British diplomats were no fools, however, and henceforth expected military intervention in Lhasa.

Beijing immediately got in touch with Chao Erh-feng, who was waging war with his troops in Kham. He had at his command several thousand men who would stop at nothing. Wherever the Manchu warlord went, he spread terror and caused much bloodshed. While still fighting in northern Kham, he sent one of his best generals, Chung Yin, to Lhasa to subdue the Tibetans.

The news of the deployment of forces deeply upset the Dalai Lama, who, on his way back to Lhasa, sent a message to Britain and all the ministers of Europe in China expressing his distress and despair:

> Though the Chinese and Tibetans are of one family, yet the Chinese officer Chao and the *amban* Lien are plotting together against us, and have not sent true copies of our protests to the Chinese Emperor, but have altered them to suit their own evil purposes. They are sending troops into Tibet and wish to abolish our religion. Please telegraph to the Chinese emperor and request him to stop the troops now on their way. We are very anxious and beg the Powers to intervene and cause the withdrawal of the Chinese troops.[6]

He had also dispatched a message to the government in Beijing:

> We, the oppressed Tibetans, send you this message. Though in outward appearance all is well, yet within big worms are eating little worms. We have acted frankly, but yet they steal our hearts. Troops have been sent into Tibet, thus causing great alarm. We have already sent a messenger to Calcutta to telegraph everything in detail. Please recall the Chinese officer

and troops who recently arrived in Kham. If you do not do so, there will be trouble.[7]

The Dalai Lama turned once again to France, whose ambassador in Beijing had received the emissaries of Lhasa. But neither gold nor gifts were able to move Paris. The authorities let the Tibetan tragedy happen without interfering. Meanwhile, the *amban* Lien-yu attempted to convince the Dalai Lama that all his fears were groundless. It was his duty to put forward the official explanation for the Chinese army's presence on Tibetan soil, which was that troops had been sent as part of a simple operation to control trade marts. As soon as Thubten Gyatso realized that the truth was somewhat different and that soldiers had entered Lhasa, the monasteries of Drepung, Ganden and Sera rose up, but this only hastened the progress of the Chinese soldiers.

The Tibetans celebrated *Losar,** the Tibetan New Year, with blood and tears. In temples and monasteries, the population prayed even more than usual, and monks constantly performed rituals and made offerings (*pujas**) to the *Dharmapalas*, the protective deities of Buddhism, so that the new year would be more fortunate. Everywhere a strange fervour prevailed.

On 12 February 1910, in the year of the Iron Dog, the Dalai Lama, after first appointing as regent *ganden thriba* Tenpe Gyaltsen, the head of the Gelugpa lineage, took advantage of a particularly dark night to leave the Potala under the protection of 100 guards and attendants. He immediately headed for Gyantse, intent on going to British India for a second period of exile.

Informed of the Dalai Lama's flight, General Chung Yin, commander of the Chinese troops, sent 200 heavily armed troops after the Tibetan ruler, whom they were instructed to bring back, dead or alive. Bloody encounters occurred between Chinese troops and the Tibetan rearguard, but eventually Thubten Gyatso reached Yatung on 20 February. On the following day, he managed to cross the border 'on a very bad horse', dressed in 'shabby old red clothes'. On 25 February he headed for Kalimpong in the north of India, expensively attired in a 'Chinese dress of red velvet' and a 'watered-silk waistcoat'; brimming with emotion, dozens of Tibetans living in the area formed a guard of honour.

'The Tibetans', wrote Sir Charles Bell, 'were abandoned to Chinese aggression, essentially caused by the British military expedition to Lhasa and its subsequent withdrawal.' Not surprisingly, an edict was published in response to the Dalai Lama's escape, depriving him once again of his temporal role. But this time, the Chinese went much further: assuming they had some kind of authority in this issue, they also deprived him of his status as an incarnation. The edict was posted in the streets of Lhasa:

The Dalai Lama of Tibet has received abundant favours from the hands of Our Imperial predecessors. He should have devoutly cultivated the precepts of religion in accordance with established precedent in order to propagate the doctrines of the Yellow Church.[8] But, ever since he assumed control of the administration, he has shown himself proud, extravagant, lewd, slothful, vicious and perverse without parallel, violent and disorderly, disobedient to the Imperial Commands, and oppressive towards the Tibetans.

In July 1904, he fled during the troubles and was denounced by the imperial *amban* to Us as lacking in reliability. A Decree was then issued depriving him temporarily of his titles. He proceeded to Urga, whence he returned again to Xining. We, mindful of his distant flight, and hoping that he would repent and reform his evil ways, ordered the local officials to pay him due attention. The year before last he came to Beijing, was received in audience, granted new titles, and presented with gifts.

On his way back to Tibet he loitered and caused trouble; yet every indulgence was shown to him in order to manifest Our compassion. In Our generosity we forgave the past. Sichuan troops have now been sent into Tibet for the special purpose of preserving order and protecting the Trade Marts. There was no reason for the Tibetans to be suspicious of their intentions. But the Dalai Lama spread rumours, became rebellious, defamed the *ambans*, refused supplies, and would not listen to reason.

When the *amban* telegraphed that the Dalai Lama had fled during the night of February 12 on the arrival of the Sichuan troops, We commanded that steps be taken to bring him back. At present, however, his whereabouts are unknown. He has been guilty of treachery and has placed himself beyond the pale of Our imperial favour. He is not fit to be a reincarnation of Buddha. Let him, therefore be deprived of his titles and his position as Dalai Lama as punishment. Henceforth, no matter where he may go, no matter where he may reside, whether in Tibet or elsewhere, let him be treated as an ordinary individual. Let the imperial *amban* at once cause a search to be made for male children bearing miraculous signs and let him inscribe their names on tablets and place them in a Golden Urn, so that one may be drawn out as the true reincarnation of previous Dalai Lamas. Let the matter be reported to Us, so that Our imperial favour may be bestowed upon the selected child, who will thus continue the propagation of the doctrine and the glorification of the Church.

We reward Virtue that Vice may suffer. You, lamas and laymen of Tibet, are Our children. Let all obey the laws and preserve the peace. Let none disregard Our desire to support the Yellow Church and maintain the tranquillity of Our frontier territories.[9]

In the first months of Thubten Gyatso's exile, the *amban* tried to persuade the Panchen Lama, among others, to take the place of the Dalai Lama. Urged by his entourage, the Panchen Lama even went to Lhasa. He first visited the Jokhang, where he spent some time praying. Then he moved into the Norbu Lingka*, the Dalai Lama's summer palace. This was a terrible blow for the Tibetans, who were shattered by such casual behaviour. Their anger increased even more when they saw the Panchen Lama fraternize with the *amban* Lien-yu, whom everybody hated. The two men often attended performances of Tibetan opera together and were seen side by side at numerous parties. Puzzled, the Tibetans interpreted this new and disconcerting situation as an underhand attempt on the part of the Chinese to gain control over the master of Tashilhunpo. Faced with the hypocrisy and lies of the Manchu delegation, the Panchen Lama proved far too weak. But how could the population express their dissatisfaction, let alone their disgust? During the Butter Festival, one of the highlights of the New Year celebrations, while Lien-yu and Panchen Rinpoche (the name given by Tibetans to the Panchen Lama) were carried in palanquins around the streets of Lhasa, with all the pageantry due to the Dalai Lama, people gathered around them and threw mud and socks. In the streets of the Tibetan capital a song could be heard:

> There was a monk on Jokhang's roof
> Who might have been a thief,
> But dawn arrived
> He ran away
> And nothing was achieved.

The 'monk' referred to the Panchen Lama, and 'dawn' to the beginning of Tibetan resistance. The latter was embodied in the person of the religious Jampa Tendar and by Trimön, the Secretary of State for Finance, whom the Dalai Lama had commissioned to organize, in secret, the struggle against the invaders.

Faced with the difficulty of putting the Panchen Lama in the place of the Dalai Lama while the latter was still alive, Lien-yu offered to cancel the edict deposing the Tibetan ruler, provided he would agree to return to Lhasa. The conditions required by the Chinese delegation in the capital reflected a new policy towards Tibet: the Dalai Lama would be allowed to return to the Potala unharmed, but not to resume his political prerogatives.

But they had not realized that Thubten Gyatso was taking advantage of his period in exile to meet various Westerners – in particular, Charles Bell, the British political officer in charge of relations between India, Bhutan, Sikkim and Tibet. He was learning from him all the tricks of modern politics, which he intended to develop as soon as he returned to his country. From Darjeeling, where he was staying, the Dalai Lama analyzed the circumstances which had led to two occupations of Tibet in six years. His idea of the world had broadened, meanwhile, and he had a new vision for the future of Tibet. Thubten Gyatso's answer to the *amban* was a good demonstration of his attitude. His intention was to initiate a new era in relations between China and Tibet by introducing for the first time what was to become a fundamental strategy: the use of Britain and India as mediators for support against China.

His position was all the more strengthened when he received a message from the Panchen Lama informing him how the Chinese felt towards him. On receiving the Dalai Lama's answer, Panchen Rinpoche left Lhasa to go back to his own monastery in Shigatse. Charles Bell, who was very knowledgeable about the Tibetan world, judiciously commented:

> The spirit of the Tibetan Constitution is against his [the Panchen Lama] acting as Regent, though it would be unsafe to assert that such an appointment could never be made. In any case a Regent has not the power of a Dalai Lama; he is largely under the control of the National Assembly in Lhasa. Thus, were a Panchen Lama to act as Regent, there would almost certainly be friction between him and the Lhasan authorities, who would side with their National Assembly.[10]

But events in China were to dictate what happened next. The Manchu Chinese empire, which had already been in disarray for some time, now disintegrated completely in the face of the political upheavals caused by the nationalists in China. The Republican Revolution broke out in 1911. On 12 February of the following year, the child emperor Puyi abdicated. On 15 February, General Yuan Shikai was elected provisional president of China. But the country had been through fire and put to the sword. Almost everywhere, soldiers rose up. From North to South and East to West, provinces reclaimed their independence from the decadent empire and entire Manchu garrisons were murdered. Sichuan was among the rebellious provinces. Chao Erh-feng, the strong man of the empire, was executed in Chengdu.

When the Chinese soldiers in Tibet heard of the uprising and the creation of a republic in their country, they attacked and plundered the residence of the *ambans* and captured them. All Chinese soldiers stationed in Tibet were ordered to go to Lhasa. In the meantime, an army was raised and left Sichuan to subdue the Tibetans who had rebelled. From India, the Dalai Lama and his government co-ordinated the military campaigns that led to the defeat of the occupying forces.

Thubten Gyatso's return to Tibet became all the more necessary, and he had already asked his ministers to go back to Lhasa. In Shigatse, the Panchen Lama carefully observed the development of the situation and offered to act as an intermediary between the Dalai Lama and the Chinese. On the other hand, he also reminded the British of their promise to provide arms and ammunition and he asked His Majesty's representative to give him two hundred guns, two machine guns and ammunition with which to defend Shigatse.

When the Panchen Lama received no reply, he became concerned for the future of his party and feared persecutions. He again addressed the British trade agent in Gyantse and begged him to ask the authorities of his country to arrange a meeting with the Tibetan ruler in Ralung or Kangma. Almost simultaneously, a similar request reached the British agent in Yatung from the Thirteenth Dalai Lama. But, fortified by previous experience, His Majesty's government had no intention of interfering in any agreement the two lamas might make. In spite of having officially taken refuge behind the Anglo-Russian Convention signed in 1907, which stipulated mutual non-interference in the affairs of Tibet, the British made sure behind the scenes that the meeting between Thubten Gyatso and Chökyi Nyima in Ralung would produce the results they expected.

In April 1912, the Tibetans compelled Chinese officials and soldiers – some 3,000 men, according to some sources – to lay down their arms. They were eventually allowed to leave the country via India. In the fifth month of 1912, the year of the Water Mouse, the Dalai Lama left Darjeeling for Tibet. After a short stay in Chumbi, he triumphantly entered Lhasa in January 1913 (the year of the Water Ox).

Although the Chinese nationalist government had no intention to make changes in the policy towards Tibet, the Dalai Lama saw the last Chinese soldiers leave Lhasa. Even before the Dalai Lama had reached the capital, General Yuan Shikai sent him a telegram apologizing for the exactions of the armed forces on Tibetans and restoring his title.

But the Dalai Lama did not fall for this Chinese manoeuvre. He answered that he did not need anyone to restore a title he had never lost, and, more important, that he now 'intended to exercise both temporal and ecclesiastical rule in Tibet'.[11] Since the 'priest–patron' (*chöyön*) relationship between the Dalai Lamas and the Manchu emperors had come to an end with the disappearance of the ruling dynasty, all links with China were now completely severed. For the first time for almost 200 years, there was no Chinese official representative or soldier on Tibetan territory.

Twenty-two days after his return to Lhasa, the Dalai Lama proclaimed independence and reaffirmed his rule over the whole of Tibet:

I, the Dalai Lama, most omniscient possessor of the Buddhist faith, whose title was conferred by the Lord Buddha's command from the glorious land of India, speak to you as follows:

I am speaking to all classes of Tibetan people. Lord Buddha, from the glorious country of India, prophesied that the reincarnations of Avalokitesvara,* through successive rulers from the early religious kings to the present day, would look after the welfare of Tibet.

During the time of Gengis Khan and Altan Khan of the Mongols, the Ming dynasty of the Chinese, and the Ch'ing dynasty of the Manchus, Tibet and China co-operated on the basis of [a] benefactor and priest relationship. A few years ago, the Chinese authorities in Sichuan and Yunnan endeavoured to colonize our territory. They brought large numbers of troops into central Tibet on the pretext of policing the Trade Marts. I, therefore left Lhasa with my ministers for the Indo-Tibetan border, hoping to clarify to the Manchu Emperor by wire that the existing relationship between Tibet and China had been that of patron and priest and had not been based on the subordination of one to the other. There was no other choice for me but to cross the border, because Chinese troops were following with the intention of taking me alive or dead.

On my arrival in India, I dispatched several telegrams to the Emperor, but his reply to my demands was delayed by corrupt officials at Beijing. Meanwhile the Manchu Empire collapsed. The Tibetans were encouraged to expel the Chinese from central Tibet. I, too returned safely to my rightful and sacred country, and I am now in the course of driving out the remnants of Chinese troops from Do Kham in eastern Tibet. Now, the Chinese intention of colonizing Tibet under the patron–priest relationship has faded like a rainbow in the sky. Having once again achieved for ourselves a period of happiness and peace, I have now allowed the following duties to be carried out without negligence:

1 Peace and happiness in this world can only be maintained by preserving the faith of Buddhism. It is, therefore, essential to preserve all Buddhist institutions in Tibet, like the Jokhang and Ramoche temples in Lhasa, Samye and Taduk in the South of Tibet, and the three great monasteries ...

2 The various Buddhist sects in Tibet should be kept in a distinct and pure form. Buddhism should be taught, learned and meditated upon properly. Except for special persons, the administrators of monasteries are forbidden to trade, loan money, deal in any kind of livestock, and/or subjugate another's subjects.

3 The Tibetan government's civil and military officials, when collecting taxes or dealing with their subject citizens, should carry on their duties with fair and honest judgement so as to benefit the government without hurting the interests of the subject citizens. Some of the central government officials posted at Ngari Korsum in western Tibet, and Do Kham in eastern Tibet, are coercing their subject citizens to purchase commercial goods at high prices and have imposed transportation rights exceeding the limit permitted by the government. Houses, properties and lands belonging to subject citizens have been confiscated on the pretext of minor breaches of the law. Furthermore, the amputation of citizens' limbs has been carried out as a form of punishment. Henceforth, such severe punishments are forbidden.

4 Tibet is a country with rich natural resources; but it is not scientifically advanced like other lands. We are a small, religious and independent nation. To keep up with the rest of the world, we must defend our country. In view of past

invasions by foreigners, our people may have to face certain difficulties, which they must disregard. To safeguard and maintain the independence of our country, one and all should voluntarily work hard and with the help of special messengers, inform the government of any suspicious facts, however small. It is useless to provoke serious crisis between two nations about minor facts.

5   Tibet, although thinly populated, is an extensive country. Some local officials and landholders are jealously obstructing other people from developing vacant lands, even though they are not doing so themselves. People with such intention are enemies of the State and our progress. From now on, no one is allowed to obstruct anyone else from cultivating whatever vacant lands are available. Land taxes will not be collected until three years have passed; after that the land cultivator will have to pay taxes to the government and to the landlord every year, proportionate to the rent. The land will belong to the cultivator. Your duties to the government and to the people will have been achieved when you have executed all that I have said here. This letter must be posted and proclaimed in every district of Tibet, and a copy kept in the records and the offices in every district.

Yuan Shikai attempted to sabotage the newly recovered authority of the Dalai Lama by trying to bribe the ministers of the government at Lhasa and to take advantage of the Panchen Lama's weakness. The brain behind these manoeuvres was a man called Lu Singchi, a furrier living in Calcutta, whom Beijing decided to send to Lhasa to take up the vacant post of *amban*. But the British had prohibited travel to Tibet via India and Lu Singchi was unable to leave. But, being a man of agile mind and, more important, considerable means, the Chinese trader made use of Tibetan agents who travelled the length and breadth of the country, to spread false information put out by Beijing. In this way Lu Singchi also remained in touch with the situation in Lhasa.

Internal threats continued to weigh heavily on Tibetan political life. During Thubten Gyatso's periods of exile in Mongolia, China and India, numerous officials and monks of Gelugpa monasteries had taken up the cudgels on behalf of China or the British empire with the sole aim of undermining the Dalai Lama's authority and bringing about his deposition in favour of the Panchen Lama. But numerous monks of the monastery of Drepung had refused to fight against Chinese forces. The monks of Tengyeling, however, had opened their door to the enemy, thus compelling the Tibetans to besiege the monastery for a long time. Collaboration also existed in the aristocracy. This is why the minister Tsarong, who had largely compromised himself with the enemy, had been executed with his son in 1912 by supporters of the Dalai Lama. Such events inflicted deep wounds, ones that would be difficult to heal. In the streets of Lhasa, the Tibetans sang:

> The bird we call a magpie flew in
> Half his feathers black and half white
> After the great cuckoo bird arrives,
> The time for talking could be right.[12]

4

First Attempts at Modernization

Three regrets lie heavy on my heart.
RIGDZIN TENZIN GYATSO, SIXTH DALAI LAMA

The Dalai Lama was deeply disappointed by the tripartite convention between Britain, China and Tibet, signed in Simla on 3 July 1914. Not only had China refused to sign the documents, as had been expected, but in his view the concessions to Britain had been too generous. All the mountainous region in the south-east had been ceded to form the North-East Frontier Agency (NEFA), what is today the Indian state of Arunachal Pradesh. With the signing of the convention by Britain and Tibet, and a commercial agreement between the two countries, the realm of the Dalai Lama joined the ranks of independent nations, but there was a high price to pay. Convinced that the strength of the country lay in its modernization, the Tibetan ruler decided to launch a vast campaign of reforms. One of his first priorities was to create an efficient military organization. This was to be a hard task in a country deeply influenced by Buddhism, where military professions were denigrated at all levels of the social hierarchy. In the nobility as well as among the common people, resistance to militarization was extremely strong.

At the time, all sorts of rumours circulated in Lhasa, including some about poisonings, and growing numbers of people gathered in the streets to sing songs. Yet misunderstandings between the Thirteenth Dalai Lama and the Ninth Panchen Lama became less frequent, and they even visited several sites of pilgrimage together. However, the past remained deeply engraved in the memory of the people.

When Thubten Gyatso decided to set up a modern army in order to defend Tibet's borders, he appointed Jensey Namgang as its commander-in-chief. He was born in 1885 to a peasant family in Phembo, north of Lhasa, where his father owned a small farm and also made arrows, but it was in Lhasa, while a servant to the director of the school for religious officials in the Potala, that he attracted the attention of His Holiness and became his favourite.

It was Jensey Namgang who directed the manoeuvres of the Tibetan rearguard when the Chinese attempted to capture the Dalai Lama in 1910. At the ferry in Jagsam, with a handful of men, he stopped the advance of 200 Manchu troops for two days, thus enabling the Tibetan ruler to reach British India unharmed. He followed the Dalai Lama into Mongolia and China during his first exile, and he spoke fluent English, Mongolian and Hindi and had an excellent grasp of Russian. The man did not possess the calm and dignified courteousness so cherished by the Tibetan nobility, but this did not prevent him from assimilating avant-garde ideas and developing a progressive vision – which was what Tibet most needed.

As early as 1911, the Dalai Lama set up a Department of War in India and secretly sent Jensey Namgang into Tibet to organize resistance and drive out Chinese soldiers. Amidst the turmoil of fighting in Lhasa, and in spite of the overt support of the Tengyeling monastery for the Chinese garrison, the new department ordered the arrest and execution of certain pro-Chinese ministers, among them the father and son of the Tsarong family, a noble family with a glorious past. Jensey Namgang knew them, but was unable to do anything to save them. However, the Dalai Lama allowed Jensey Namgang to marry the two daughters of the Tsarong family and made him the heir of the Tsarong family and its fortune.[1] From then on, His Holiness's favourite took the name of Tsarong Dabzang Dradul.

When calm returned to Lhasa, Thubten Gyatso often went alone up onto the roof of the Potala, where he enjoyed flying kites, far away from all distractions. Only Tsarong was allowed to dress casually and go up there to visit the Dalai Lama. They would spend long hours talking together and exchanging memories.

In the meantime, Tsarong set to work. Even though he did not always have the Dalai Lama's consent to raise an army equal to his ambitions, he was able to rely on 4,000 men, as well as several thousand militiamen from Kham, commanded by another early supporter, Jampa Tendar. Tsarong started to send his best recruits to India or Sikkim to be trained; large supplies of weapons and ammunition were bought from Britain and the new army was soon able to parade in British uniforms and, on their manoeuvres, to follow commands delivered in English. A brand new arsenal completed the picture. This fresh importance attached to the defence of the country and to the army almost immediately aroused the hostility of the major monasteries. They saw Tsarong and his friends as men who were capable of creating a power which, in the short term, would put their own at risk. But the new policy enjoyed the full support of the Dalai Lama, who was well aware of the need to be able to defend with arms an independence whose recognition had been so difficult to achieve.

Charles Bell[2] had often discussed the issue with him and, strangely, the Gurkha representative in Lhasa had even explained to him that the Tibetan army needed to number 30,000 men to be efficient in the field. He had also advised him to send officers to India for special training.

But the implementation of the government decision required a lot of money. There were two solutions: either the taxes on goods imported from India could be increased (which would require the agreement of Calcutta), or new taxes could be levied. The latter was obviously the less popular option. The already tense atmosphere in Lhasa was heightened by all sorts of rumours, in particular one concerning the forced enrolment of monks into the army. The Dalai Lama immediately issued a decree making it clear that monks would not be allowed to join the army, but it did little to calm the situation. A leader of the monastery of Sera even told Charles Bell: 'This proposal to increase the army is strictly disliked by the monks, who feel that it is against the Buddhist religion.'[3]

The enrolment of just one man from each family, the purchase of weapons and the creation of training centres around Lhasa would increase the cost of such an enterprise considerably, and obviously displease both the aristocracy and the high dignitaries of the major monasteries, who feared an increase in the government's power, but Tsarong was determined to overcome all opposition. Soldiers were already being trained in the camps of His Majesty's army, with the most promising being sent to Shillong and Quetta for further military training.

The country's modernization was not restricted to the military. To achieve the opening up of Tibet to the modern world, young noblemen were sent to Russia and Britain to learn modern techniques to exploit natural resources, produce electricity, and so on. Tsarong imported machines to print banknotes, which gradually replaced copper coins, and stamps were also issued. In spite of the monasteries' total opposition, an English school opened in Gyantse.

The Dalai Lama and his government were also faced with the problem of constant uprisings in eastern Tibet. Nearly all the old generals were deployed to defend the country's territorial integrity; they also had to remind local lay and religious landlords that they now had to take their orders from Lhasa. Jampa Tendar, the religious minister of the Kashag who had been delegated to Kham, was particularly successful in making powerful landlords bow to authority. At the end of 1917, a brutal and bloody Chinese assault almost took the Tibetans by surprise in Riwoche, in northern Kham. This was the first opportunity for the soldiers to put their new fighting techniques into practice. Not only were the Chinese forces repelled, but the Tibetans also managed to recover territories that had been lost to the fearsome Chao Erh-feng. The victory led to a truce in Rongbatse in August 1918. In answer to China's request that disagreements between both countries be settled once and for all, the Dalai Lama made it quite clear to Beijing that he would stick to the Simla agreements and eagerly wished China to ratify the convention.

The army had won acclaim for its actions in the field and yet it still faced opposition from the conservative aristocracy and high-ranking religious dignitaries who feared its growing power. Some young officers, mostly trained in British India, went a bit too far in showing off their progressive ideas, and rumours of disagreements between civilians and soldiers spread throughout the Tibetan capital. In November 1920, the traditionalists' fears increased with the arrival in Lhasa of a British mission headed by Charles Bell. Tsarong took advantage of the visit to make known his military views. During a stormy session of the National Assembly, in which the abolition of an additional tax levied by the military authorities was being discussed, the four *tsipön*⋆ of the Finance Office, led by Lungshar,[4] opposed the presence of representatives of the army. Affronted, a handful of young generals in full dress, led by Tsarong, noisily interrupted the session and started to quarrel with the *tsipön*.

In 1922, as the Tibetans were celebrating the festival of *Mönlam Chenmo*⋆ for the year of the Water Dog, over 50,000 monks converged on the capital. A new rumour – that Tsarong wanted to set up a military government – spread around the Forbidden City. The arrest of an important abbot from Drepung, who was considered too conservative, aggravated the situation. Encouraged by Lungshar, the monks immediately headed for the Potala and the Norbu Lingka, the Dalai Lama's summer palace, to demonstrate their opposition to militarization, to Tsarong and to modernization. Panicking, Tsarong ordered that 100 rounds of ammunition be given to his personal guard. He too carried a gun.

The excitement reached its climax when the Dalai Lama, who had been kept informed of the events happening on the streets of Lhasa, intervened. He had never doubted Tsarong's faithfulness, but he reprimanded the generals who had stormed the National Assembly, as well as Lungshar who had done nothing to calm the situation; two of his officers – *dapöns* Shazur and Tsogo – were dismissed, and a cabinet member – *kalön* Kunsangtse – was sacked for making conservative remarks. The Dalai Lama also deposed the abbots who had been responsible for the unrest among the monks and instructed them to exert more control over them, otherwise he would take ruthless action. Thubten Gyatso thus tried, but in vain, to reconcile these two groups with diametrically opposed views.

Tsarong, however, never recovered his past popularity, even when calm returned. Tibetans related the incident in a song:

> Cabinet ministers sit in sessions
> But do they have any real plans?

They should cut out the roots
And not just trim the branch![5]

The situation was so unfavourable to Tsarong that the Dalai Lama decided to send him away to Yatung to inspect the National Mint.

Once the Bell mission had left, in October 1921, Thubten Gyatso pursued his plans for modernization. He had already obtained the Assembly's agreement to increase the strength of the army. It was then decided to recruit 500 soldiers each year so as to eventually reach a total strength of 17,000 men. A telegraph line was set up in Gyantse and connected to the Anglo-Indian network. Again, on his suggestion as well as that of Charles Bell, the Dalai Lama gave his agreement to the building of a British school in Lhasa. Tibetan society was evolving: in his time, Tsarong had expressed the wish that Tibet become a member of the International Postal Union; he also wanted to have a typewriter made in India with a Tibetan keyboard, and envisaged cars on the roads and motorboats on the country's numerous lakes. But Tsarong was not the only one to want to shake off the yoke of tradition: Commander Surkhang liked to organize polo matches and had a tennis court built in the capital, and men now had their hair cut in the English fashion.

While in Yatung, Tsarong and his wife, Rinchen Dolma Taring, decided to go on a pilgrimage to India and Nepal. They reached Darjeeling in the winter of 1924 and visited Calcutta, Bombay, Bodh Gaya, Benares, Kushinagara and Kathmandu. The couple and their retinue were received everywhere with much respect and dignity. In Nepal, the Maharajah Shamsher sent his son and grandson to call on Tsarong. In Gyantse, Frank Ludlow, the director of the English school, asked his pupils to form a welcoming guard of honour.

However, the period of modernization did not last long. In 1925, the anglophobia of the monasteries and the conservatives forced the Dalai Lama to back down. As the result of a combination of circumstances skilfully manipulated by his detractors, Tsarong lost his appointment as commander-in-chief of the Tibetan army and the officers who had remained faithful to him were discharged for trivial reasons. For example, three generals – Dingja, Doring and Sambo – were reduced in rank for having had their hair cut during their training in Shillong and Quetta, outside Tibet. A nephew of Thubten Gyatso, Dzasa Trumba, was appointed at the head of the army. Tsarong never came back to sit beside the Dalai Lama, and gradually he drifted away from political life. From then on, the army, which had been so dear to him, fell into a state of neglect. Tibet withdrew into itself.

Behind all these events lurked a man whose ambition was equalled only by his conceit – an evil being of excessive selfishness, an extremely clever man but one whose sole aim was to seize power, sooner or later, and to crush all those who tried to oppose him, giving the highest rewards to those who agreed to submit – under threat of banishment! Dorje Tsegyal Lungshar had undoubtedly become the Dalai Lama's favourite and the person he listened to the most. Lungshar's voice dominated debates in the *tshongdu* (the National Assembly) and nobody dared oppose him. He spent his time scheming and plotting and he always seemed to know which way the wind was blowing. He may not, however, have been familiar with the words written by the Great Fifth, Ngawang Lobsang Gyatso, who used a scene from an Indian epic as a reminder that there are many false gurus and that people can easily be deceived by them:

One day Ravana appeared as a beautiful animal to fool everybody. He led numerous living beings to the barren lands of confused lives and abducted the beautiful Sita, who was a symbol for joy and prosperity.[6]

Up until then, nothing had stopped him. One of Lungshar's principles had been never to challenge the monasteries' high-ranking dignitaries or to do anything that might annoy them. Aware of the power of the monasteries, however, he knew how to use the monks to achieve his own ends. It did not take him long, therefore, to take advantage of the weakness of Thubten Gyatso's nephew and use it against Tsarong. It is even reported that Trumba had wept before his uncle when Lungshar had denigrated Tsarong and accused him of intending to plot against the State. The Dalai Lama may have remembered how, in the early eighteenth century, Miwang Pholanay, one of the Tibetan army's senior officers, had overshadowed the Seventh Dalai Lama; but he also knew the faults of his nephew, who was an opium addict.

Aware of the Dalai Lama's concern and his wish to correct the government's financial problems, Lungshar was among those who championed the idea of extending and increasing taxes: to raise the taxes on salt and furs, and to impose a fixed tax of 5 per cent on all goods traded at the Tibeto-Indian border. (Negotiations were not completed until 1929.) The monasteries and the nobility were also concerned, and as early as 1920 a special investigation office was set up. At the time, Lungshar also carried out investigations into revenue frauds in a number of monasteries, including Tashilhunpo. His report was extremely serious, and the subsequent measures taken by the government were to initiate one of the saddest chapters in the country's history.

When he returned to Tibet after his second period of exile, the Dalai Lama had made direct contact with the Panchen Lama to ask him to contribute to the costs of the 1912 conflict with China. Based on what had happened previously in 1791, at the time of the war against Nepal, he had asked for a quarter of the total costs of this second war (which had led to the *de facto* independence of Tibet) and an additional quarter for the expense of the wars between Tibet and Britain of 1888 and 1904, in total some 27,000 *ke*[7] of grain. Initially, Chökyi Nyima had opposed the government's instructions, but then he agreed to co-operate and pay part of the sum asked for by the Dalai Lama. Unfortunately the affair did not stop there. In 1917, Thubten Gyatso instituted a new regulation called the 'Order of the year of the Fire Snake', which required the donation of a seventh of the taxes in kind levied by Tashilhunpo in the district of Gyantse and the imposition of transportation duties for the peasants of the Shigatse area, who had previously been exempt from such paid services because they were subject to the Panchen Lama's authority. In 1922, the revenue investigation office imposed an additional annual tax on Tashilhunpo of 30,000 *ke* of grain and 10,000 silver coins. One year later, the government instituted the 'Order of the year of the Water Pig', which extended the 1917 order to the whole of Tsang, thus including a large part of the estates belonging to the Panchen Lama's monastery.

The Panchen Lama interceded directly with the Dalai Lama, but without success. Chökyi Nyima got in touch with the British trade agent in Gyantse and begged him to act as mediator. He bluntly refused to intervene in a strictly internal matter.

The controversy continued for several years until, disappointed by the behaviour of both Lungshar and certain officials who had not forgiven his highly ambivalent attitude during both the Dalai Lama's exiles, the Panchen Lama decided to flee. He made his first attempt in 1923, on a visit to hot springs in the district of Lhatse, but because he felt he was being closely watched he was unable to take advantage of this opportunity to go into exile.

Amidst much confusion, on the night of 15 November 1923, once his last instructions had been given to the monastery's senior dignitaries, the Panchen Lama left Tashilhunpo. His personal chamberlain, Lobsang Gyaltsen, his two favourites and a number of officials were included in the convoy – of around 100 people and 200 mules – which headed for Mongolia across the plains of Changthang and the vast Northern steppe, on roads heavily blocked with snow and in Siberian cold. Nobody got wind of the Panchen Lama's sudden departure, not even the Tibetan government's representatives in Shigatse.

When Lhasa heard of Chökyi Nyima's escape, Lungshar immediately ordered 300 men, armed to the teeth, to set off in pursuit of the Panchen Lama and bring him back, dead or alive.

A street song said:

> Lungshar the hunter
> None so heartless can be found.
> His deer is the Panchen Lama
> Tsogo is his hound.

With the help of caravanners who were crossing the high northern plains with their camels, the Panchen Lama escaped his pursuers. Before his departure, in order to prevent civil war, he had been careful to address a letter to the Dalai Lama expressing his wish to visit monasteries. Because Tashilhunpo was left without an administrator, Thubten Gyatso appointed his nephew Trumba to the post.

In Tashilhunpo, as well as in the district of Shigatse, monks ran away to join their spiritual master. Many of them – including the Panchen Lama's father – were arrested and thrown in jail. The government authorities in Shigatse passed a law stating that runaways would be flogged.

The Panchen Lama arrived in northern China in 1925, the year of the Wood Ox in the Tibetan calendar. When the news reached Lhasa, it became obvious that China would take advantage of the Panchen Lama's presence, even though fights between warlords over the last ten years had reduced their own country to a state of anarchy. The Chinese had one simple aim: to destabilize Tibet by playing on the rivalry between the Potala and Tashilhunpo. History was repeating itself. In the end this policy of interference in the affairs of the high plateau was facilitated by the territorial ambitions of the governors of Sichuan and Qinghai – Liu Wen-hui and Ma Pu-fang – who both wished to annex the areas of Tibet neighbouring their semi-independent states.

As for Chökyi Nyima, he also tried to use the lords of the former empire against Thubten Gyatso. First, he sent delegates to an important conference for the reorganization of China, which had been set up by the pro-Japanese warlords of the north. He then sought, successfully, to create stable relations with Chiang Kai-shek's Kuomintang, with French diplomats acting as intermediaries. As a result, a Panchen Lama Office was opened in Nanjing to represent officially the exiles from Tashilhunpo. In the meantime, the Panchen Lama tried to resume relations with the Dalai Lama, but the first exchange of letters brought no hope of an amicable settlement of their dispute.

While the Panchen Lama was struggling to find support to have his lawful rights recognized, Tibet was still prey to intrigues. A newcomer to the political entourage of Thubten Gyatso was Thubten Kumbela, who in 1925 was appointed by the Dalai Lama to head a new department – *Drapchi Lotru Laygung* – which merged together the National Mint, the Arsenal and a small hydroelectric plant in Drapchi, in the suburbs of Lhasa. Thanks to Kumbela electricity was brought to the capital. He was a monk endowed with great intelligence, and he quickly rose up through the ranks of power. As he had the ear of the Dalai Lama, it was obvious that

Kumbela would soon cross the path of Lungshar, who hated him, so he was aware that his high position depended in great measure on Thubten Gyatso's favours. In the narrow corridors of power in Lhasa, Lungshar knew that there was no room for two favourites with such insatiable ambition. Since the removal of Tsarong, the monk and the *tsipön* from the Finance Office were the only two left close to Thubten Gyatso. And here Kumbela had the advantage over his rival: his religious status. He also created something of a sensation in Lhasa by driving around in one of the Dalai Lama's two cars, an Austin A-40 (the other was a Dodge). Tibetans used to jostle in the streets to see him go by, and put out their tongues to greet him.[8]

Time passed. On 7 September 1926, one of the Panchen Lama's officials, Tsa Serkhang, met His Royal Highness King George V of England, while on a visit to Beijing. The latter expressed his wish that 'the unfortunate domestic differences which had led to the Panchen Lama's departure from Tibet would soon be adjusted and that His Holiness would be able to return to his homeland in the near future'.[9] At that time the British government already seemed to be acting as mediator, but it was convinced that, as long as Lungshar remained influential in Lhasa, it would be impossible to bring up the issue of the Panchen Lama's return to his monastery with the authorities in Lhasa. In February 1927, Chökyi Nyima spent a long time unburdening his heart to W F Williamson, whom he had met when the latter was the British trade agent in Gyantse. In expressing his regret at having left Tibet, he said: 'It was a serious mistake on my part.' The Panchen Lama even talked about his return by sea, via India. On other occasions, Chökyi Nyima's message was more explicit: he acknowledged to Colonel Bailey, then Political Officer in Sikkim, and to the maharajahs of Bhutan and Sikkim, that the Chinese climate did not suit him very well and begged them for help 'in all private or official matters'. And in a long letter to O'Connor, dated 4 December 1927, the Panchen Lama recalled their friendship and the British pledge to give him all the assistance he might need. He wrote: 'I want you to advise me on how I could return to Tibet very soon.'

All these letters served as preliminaries to the Panchen Lama's return to Tashilhunpo. Chökyi Nyima's first official request reached Colonel Bailey in April 1928, at the beginning of the year of the Earth Dragon in the Tibetan calendar. But Bailey knew that the Dalai Lama would eventually dictate his own conditions. This was why he suggested to his government that the Panchen Lama be granted political asylum in India, in Darjeeling or Kalimpong, two places which he knew the Tibetan ruler could not object to, for he had himself stayed in those towns. Bailey's suggestion was rejected, for the British authorities thought it less dangerous for the time being to leave the Panchen Lama in China.

Months passed in this way, with one negotiation following another, but the situation was not resolved. Some of Chökyi Nyima's plans verged on the farcical. For instance, he considered raising a Mongolian army, with the assistance of the Russians, to attack Lhasa and expel the Dalai Lama.[10] Supporters of Chökyi Nyima then declared their intention to put the matter in the hands of the Chinese authorities, because their endeavours with the British had come to nothing; they wanted, they said, to create a new party in Tibet and to overthrow the Dalai Lama. With Chiang Kai-shek's victory and the reunification of China in 1927, there was hope that the new government, which considered Tibet merely a Chinese province, would help the Panchen Lama to return to Tashilhunpo. It is not clear whether Chökyi Nyima knew about all these goings-on at the time or whether he was manipulated. In any case, a report in *The Times* mentioned the arrival of representatives of the Panchen Lama in Nanjing to beg the Kuomintang government to rule Tibet and unite it with the Republic, because they were afraid that their country 'might become a second India'.

In Lhasa, the situation was particularly tense. The Panchen Lama's nephew had just escaped from the place where he had been detained with several members of his family. He was recaptured in Shigatse and sent back to the capital, where he and all his relatives were then put in chains.

In June 1930, J L R Weir, the new British Political Officer in Sikkim, received a letter from the Panchen Lama which confirmed his fears that the master of Tashilhunpo might call on Chinese troops to help him return to Tibet. The letter read:

Except for one or two individuals, all Tibetans have great faith in me and they are expecting my return. I also desire to go back to Tibet at once, but you are aware of the danger I would have to face there if I were to return without outside assistance, and I cannot take this risk. The Chinese would help me by sending their troops if I were to seek their assistance ... If many Chinese troops arrive in Tibet, it will be a great hardship on the subjects, the religion will suffer and self government will disappear. In consideration of the above dangers I have postponed my return ...

The Tibetan government of Lhasa taking no notice of past or future, consider my (absence) a trifling matter and continue to ignore me ...

For the protection of our lives, it is essential for me to take an army if I go to Tibet, otherwise the evil people of Tibet may not do the right thing. In the circumstance, I would request that you will kindly arrange to help us in lending arms and ammunition for our mutual benefit. In case you find it inconvenient to supply munition, I would request a considerable sum of money which if granted I shall repay on my arrival in Tibet.[11]

At the time, the main British worry was how, and to what extent, their own interests in Tibet would be affected if the Panchen Lama drew closer to China. British policy was based on the idea of Tibet as a buffer zone, free of all Chinese or Russian influence and control. Yet His Majesty's representatives increasingly feared that China might use the Panchen Lama to impose greater control over Tibet. For this reason they considered it absolutely vital to find an immediate and amicable solution to the dispute between the Panchen Lama and the Dalai Lama. As a consequence of a series of negotiations between Weir and Lhasa, the Dalai Lama wrote to Chökyi Nyima asking him to come back to Tibet. By then, 1932, the year of the Water Monkey in the Tibetan calendar was already drawing to a close.

A letter from Chiang Kai-shek had been given to the Tibetan ruler in February 1930, on the occasion of the visit of Liu Man-ch'ing, representative of the Department of Tibetan and Mongolian

Affairs of the Nanjing government. In it, the Chinese president suggested an eight-point settlement of the Sino-Tibetan disagreements. Thubten Gyatso's answer was based on the Simla Convention of 1914 and the autonomy of Tibet.

A few months later, a new conflict resulted in bloodshed in Kham. It seems that a quarrel had broken out between two monasteries in the north of the region. The Chinese warlord Liu Wen-hui took advantage of the situation to seize control of new estates. A second front was then created further north, in the regions of Nangchen, Jyekundo and Chamdo, where Ma Pu-fang, the governor of the province of Qinghai, had penetrated into Tibetan territory. In spite of these constant Chinese incursions, a truce was signed on 10 October 1932. The Chang Jiang river was accepted as a boundary between the two countries – and remained so until the Chinese invasion of Tibet in 1949. Another truce was signed with Ma Pu-fang in June 1933, and confirmed in the months that followed.

The Panchen Lama did not give up on the possibility of receiving help from the Chinese, although, in 1930, he had refused a military escort to protect him on his return to Tibet, to avoid tarnishing his image there. But a year later, when Chiang Kai-shek had become all-powerful, he attended preparatory meetings for the revision of the Chinese constitution. Together with Zhang Hueliang, the omnipresent warlord of the north, the master of Tashilhunpo was given a place of honour. Once again Tibet was defined as Chinese territory. In 1932, Chökyi Nyima went to Beijing in a train decked with yellow hangings. He was received with full honours by the former warlords who had sided with Chiang Kai-shek, and presided over ceremonies for world peace. In all probability he had played the Chinese card. To the government of Nanjing, Chökyi Nyima was now the Peace Commissioner for the Border Provinces in the West,[12] for which he received a comfortable allowance.

In the meantime, in Lhasa, Kumbela had decide to create a crack regiment – *Trongdra* – for which he recruited from the wealthier families of the country. Although an effective political tool, the regiment did not bring happiness to those who were enrolled. It was even reported that some young soldiers wept like children when they had to have their hair cut off. Lungshar immediately sensed that Kumbela's weak point was his unpopularity. This was reflected in two street songs of the time:

> Into Trongdra regiment
> At the command of our masters we went,
> With hair like flowers in bloom
> Soon to be shorn in the barber's room.

> Chensal Kumbela, the 'favourite' they say,
> Needs the Trongdra regiment
> So here we stay
> Whether for months or only days.

The Dalai Lama's letter, written on the tenth day of the eighth month of the Water Monkey (9 October 1932), reached the Panchen Lama via the British Embassy in China. At last, formal negotiations between the master of Tashilhunpo and the Tibetan government could start in earnest. The contents of the Dalai Lama's letter were as follows:

> I wrote you twice, once in the Water-Hog Year [1923], when Your Serenity left your monastery for China and Mongolia ... and once again on the second day of the fifth month of the Fire-Tiger Year [12 June 1926] ... I hope you have received both the letters. I have had no reply to either of them.
>
> From the very beginning the relations between us, the father and the son, have been loving and affectionate ... It cannot therefore be possible that you are now acting in a way calculated to rupture this relationship. The extent of the harm which has been done by the conspiracy of some of the conscience-stricken servants is well-known to everyone. But you, naturally would not for a moment think of plunging Tibet into war, the country which is administered by the father and the son; and yet rumours are rife in Lhasa to that effect.
>
> In these days respect for religion is decreasing. It is a time when following the example of foreigners, every one is fond of black deeds [ie, war]. Nearly ten years have elapsed since you

left Tibet and while matters remain in this state I am full of anxiety as to what might happen to your life.

Moreover, if you could come back to U [Central Tibet], the relations between the teacher and the pupil would be like those between fire and the smoke. The noble tradition of our predecessors will also be maintained. Please therefore consider the matter and let me have a reply on which I can act.[13]

The Panchen Lama had never received the two letters mentioned by the Dalai Lama. However, he did send Lobsang Gyaltsen and Ngagchen Rinpoche – his most important officials – to represent him in Lhasa. They were very courteously received on 2 June 1933; they were given a private house and servants and a commission was immediately set up to discuss the conditions for Chökyi Nyima's return to Tibet.

But there remained huge differences of opinion. Chökyi Nyima not only contested the levy of revenue and taxes, but also the modernization of the country instigated by the Dalai Lama. With regard to the political system in Tibet, the Panchen Lama wished to go back to what he called an 'earlier system', in which the monastery of Tashilhunpo functioned in a fairly autonomous way. Among the conditions for his return, he asked to be allowed to possess his own armed force.

The National Assembly's written answer was read to the two emissaries, who spent several months in the monastery of Tashilhunpo before they finally left Lhasa in November 1933. On their way home, the two monks made a detour to Sikkim where, on 24 March 1934, they informed Williamson of the breakdown in negotiations with the Tibetan government. Then they abruptly left for China, where they discussed the imminent creation of a Tibetan province which, under the Panchen Lama's authority, would unite western Sichuan (eastern Kham), Qinghai (Amdo) and the north of Yunnan (principality of Djang). The Tibetan region of Tsang would be included once the Chinese were masters of the high plateau.

5

Death of the Thirteenth Dalai Lama

The thirtieth day of the year of the Water Bird ...

Shortly before his death, the Thirteenth Dalai Lama wrote: 'It is certain that we are now entering a period of oppression and terror, where days and nights will drag on in suffering.'[1] For the last few months he had felt consumed by an incurable ailment, a mixture of deep grief and constant weariness resulting from his heavy responsibilities to the Tibetans. Yet his conscience instructed him to overcome his disappointments, for he was still the symbol of the country's unity. But for how much longer?

Although suffering from a slight cold, Thubten Gyatso agreed to attend the *Mönlam Chenmo* festival (for the Tibetan New Year), so as to reassure the people, but by the end of the celebrations his health had deteriorated considerably. One day, His Holiness attended an audience with the monks of the Lower Tantric College of Gyume, but the next he was unable even to preside over the *Ganden Nachen*, the day of the anniversary of the death of Tsongkhapa, the founder of the Gelugpa lineage. This was on the twenty-fifth day of the tenth month of the year of the Water Bird (12 December 1933). That morning, as day broke over the Tibetan capital, the monks of the Upper Tantric College of Gyutö were told that the Dalai Lama would not appear at the public audience to which they had been invited, according to custom. Instead, a 'throne audience', or what the Tibetans more commonly called an 'invitation of the robe' would be held, during which prayers and incantations were said in front of the Dalai Lama's ceremonial robe, spread out on the throne.

The people of Lhasa were immediately worried by His Holiness's absence. In spite of all the precautions taken by those close to the Dalai Lama, particularly Kumbela, all sorts of rumours had been circulating. In the temple, monks were crying, and the faithful too were in tears. To appease their fears, the superior in charge of the ceremony declared that the Dalai Lama was not suffering from any illness.

Unfortunately, the truth was somewhat different. Thubten Gyatso's health had deteriorated seriously since 3 December. He had lost his appetite, and he paced up and down his room, gasping for breath and seized by fits of coughing. The physicians diagnosed serious flu, or even a simple cold. Those around him kept a careful watch on his weakening condition to assess the seriousness of his illness, for His Holiness was not one to complain. In fact, he would not have stayed in bed had it not been for their insistence.

On the twenty-ninth day of the eleventh month, after a long conversation with the servants, Thubten Kumbela called for the Nechung oracle. He also contacted the prime minister and the Kashag. On the morning of the thirtieth day, the government begged for an audience with His Holiness, which was refused. Only the very old *ganden thriba*, Jampa Chödrak, was allowed into the room, followed a few moments later by the State oracle. According to tradition, Nechung called at length upon the gods until they took possession of his body. In his first trance, he said that His Holiness should take a medicine called 'the 17 heroes for fighting colds'.[2] Kumbela himself poured the powder into a cup half-filled with water, then handed it to the Dalai Lama. Witnesses reported that the ruler refused to swallow the potion and that his favourite had to force it down his throat.

The Dalai Lama felt increasingly worse. Around noon he fell into a deep coma, interrupted only by spells of delirium. The most important lamas crowded around the dying man's bed. The Nechung oracle went into another trance. In their prayers, the lamas begged His Holiness not to leave his bodily form but to get better and go on living for a long time. As he showed no response, they asked him if he had decided to die. At that moment, Thubten Gyatso opened his eyes and gazed at them for a long time, but he did not answer their question. Then he lost consciousness again.

At 6.30 on the evening of the thirtieth day of the year of the Water Bird (17 December 1933), the Thirteenth Dalai Lama decided to leave this world. At the age of 57, he had achieved, to the letter, all he had prophesied in his political testament of a year earlier.

Tibet spent 49 days under a veil of mourning. A feeling of irreparable loss hung over the capital. In the streets of Lhasa, the Tibetans listened with great sorrow to the drum rolls from the Potala announcing the sad news. The entire population converged on the temples to pray. That night and the days that followed were dedicated to meditation. The palace was ablaze with thousands of lights and butter lamps were placed on the roof, as was the custom at funeral ceremonies or the anniversary of a death.

The country entered into a period of uncertainty, with the government not sure which way to turn. The people took the news badly, for few had known about the Dalai Lama's illness. As soon as the death of the Tibetan ruler was announced, all sorts of rumours started – about black magic, poisonings, and so forth.

At that moment, destiny decreed that the sinister shadow of Dorje Tsegyal Lungshar, the dead ruler's former counsellor, appear once again. For a long time, Lungshar, greedy for power and eager for intrigue, had been looking for a way to take revenge on Kumbela, who, in his view, had supplanted him in the pontiff's close circle. But by now, Kumbela, Thubten Gyatso's last confidant, knew that he had reached the end of his political career and, overcome with grief, he resigned from office. The most influential members of the government begged him to reconsider his decision, but to no avail. At the time when Lungshar had been plotting his revenge against Kumbela, another former favourite, Tsarong, was absent from the capital, far away from the sordid events that were about to take place.

Four days after the Thirteenth Dalai Lama passed away, the members of the government and the superiors of the monasteries of

Drepung, Ganden and Sera gathered to discuss the future of Tibet, in particular the appointment of the regent who would rule during the interregnum, until the reincarnation of the deceased was found. The prime minister, Langdün Kunga Wangchug, took charge of the affairs of the country, assisted for two months by three *kalöns*.[3]

Several Assembly members wanted to confer the regency on Kumbela, whom the Dalai Lama had most trusted. Others requested the appointment of two prime ministers – one to represent the aristocracy, one the monasteries. The majority of officials, however, thought that they should not depart from tradition and that an incarnate lama should be appointed regent as soon as possible.

While endless discussions continued within the Tibetan Assembly, an important demonstration was organized in front of the Norbu Lingka. At the instigation of Lungshar, who had constantly been telling them that it was time to act, the soldiers of the *Trongdra* demanded the immediate dissolution of their regiment. As soon as word of the demonstration reached the Assembly, the session came to a halt and the members went out to meet the rebellious soldiers, some of whom had already deserted. Langdün ordered them to disperse and reminded them that their duty was to protect the National Mint and the arsenal. But instead of going back to their barracks, the soldiers scattered throughout the capital. The National Assembly, the Kashag, had been about to support Kumbela when a surprising about turn occurred. The Assembly, which had in general been well-disposed towards Kumbela, then blamed him for the rebelliousness of his regiment.

As a master of intrigue, Lungshar used all his skills as an orator to persuade the superiors of the monasteries to immediately replace the deserters of the *Trongdra* with monks. This was a subtle trick, as a result of which, the monasteries – considered the main rivals of the aristocracy – would play a key role in future events. Some people suspected Lungshar of having instigated the military rebellion, and *kalön* Trimön overtly confronted him with this. The veteran of the 1912 war reminded the Assembly that the Kashag could not be abused so easily and that it was not up to monks to take on tasks usually performed by soldiers. He confirmed what the duties of the *Trongdra* were, and went so far as to say that anyone who tried to prevent the soldiers from acting would be fired on.

But Lungshar had not yet put all his cards on the table. He sent a petition to the Assembly calling for an explanation of the circumstances surrounding the Thirteenth Dalai Lama's death. In particular, he emphasized the fact that Kumbela had often been alone with the ruler in the moments preceding his death, and that such a situation ought to be questioned. He also recalled the fact that the ruler's health had worsened after he had taken the medicine prepared by Kumbela. Without being explicit, he aroused terrible suspicions: was the favourite responsible for Thubten Gyatso's death? Eager to avoid the interference of the Kashag, whose favour he no longer enjoyed, Lungshar asked the members of the Assembly – which he controlled, thanks to the support of the monasteries – to hold an official investigation.

Investigations duly took place. Kumbela, his close collaborators, the Nechung oracle, and Jampa Yeshe, the Dalai Lama's personal physician, were all questioned and sentenced. Kneeling before the investigating committee, which had been thoroughly manipulated by Lungshar, the Dalai Lama's counsellor had to face the most terrible insults. Lungshar demanded an exemplary punishment – death by mutilation – but Kumbela's popularity prevented Lungshar from achieving his wish. However, Kumbela's properties were confiscated and he was imprisoned in Sharcenchog, before being exiled to Demo Chamnag in Kongpo.

When prime minister Langdün and the Kashag made the decree public, a street song said:

> What is Kumbela doing now?
> He is in Sharcenchog prison.
> He may be meditating,
> But his car, alas,
> Is in Norbu Lingka, eating grass

Another asked:

> That powerful person
> Conquering all he saw,
> A favorite with the English car,
> They say that to the Gods

He was a son.
But tell me, tell me:
Where has he gone?

The Assembly's endless discussions grew more bitter by the day. Before his arrest, a supporter of Kumbela had questioned the choice of an incarnate lama as regent, pointing out that if a young and inexperienced monk were on the throne, inevitably it would be his manager who was in control, even if he were an old monk who had been granted the title of Great Treasurer and spent most of his time taking snuff.[4] Eventually the Assembly opted for a more practical regency and selected Reting Rinpoche. The Kashag agreed to this decision.

6

Rise of the Regent, Reting Rinpoche

Wolves enter the town ...

The death of the Thirteenth Dalai Lama plunged Tibet into one of the darkest periods in its history. Thubten Gyatso had been right. In the streets people sang:

> Tibet had a government yesterday:
> Lions and tigers in the fray.
> Then wolves and the foxes had their day,
> And our government was blown away.

Yet out of the confusion following Kumbela's downfall emerged a very progressive idea: the replacement of the regency by a more democratic institution. Initially the Assembly had suggested that an ordinary, but very old and learned, monk[1] be appointed, but eventually the 20-year-old *rinpoche*[2] in charge of the Reting monastery was selected. This was only the second time in the history of Tibet that a Reting had been put in charge of the State. (The first one[3] had been appointed regent in 1811, during the Eleventh Dalai Lama's minority. As the Dalai Lama passed away at a very young age, this Reting Rinpoche was appointed regent a second time, and supervised the search for the Twelfth Dalai Lama.)

Considered one of the most sacred places in Tibet, Reting lies about 40 miles north of Lhasa. It is reported that the great pundit Atisha stayed there in the middle of the eleventh century, and that his principal disciple, Dromtömpa, decided to build a monastery there in which the relics of his master could be treasured. After the political takeover of the Dalai Lamas in the seventeenth century, the Reting monastery remained under the Tibetan government's authority. At the time, the building stood between two passes, with a suspension bridge over the Rongchu leading to the monastery. The Seventh Dalai Lama entrusted the leadership of the monastery to his teacher, the first Radeng, or Reting Trichen Ngawang Chogden.

The mountainous area surrounding the Reting monastery was covered with huge juniper forests and numerous varieties of rhododendrons. In the summer, wild flowers of many colours carpeted the valley, transforming it into one of the most breathtaking sites of pilgrimage in the north of Tibet. Among the sacred artefacts belonging to the monastery were a small bronze effigy of the Buddha (brought by Atisha himself from India), numerous Tibetan scriptures and some very rare manuscripts written in Sanskrit on palm leaves. All these texts and objects testifying to the spiritual wealth of Tibet have now disappeared.

But who was the young Reting Rinpoche? In 1913, just after the Thirteenth Dalai Lama had returned to Lhasa from his second exile in India, a poor peasant family from Gyatsa, in the region of Dagpo, south-east of Lhasa, gave birth to a son who very early on showed extraordinary signs. It was reported that one day he had left a clear footprint on a stone. It was also said that he had surprised his mother by closing the opening of a clay jar with a string to prevent the boiling soup from spilling over. Another time, he had effortlessly stuck a wooden peg into a rock, declaring that visitors would need it to attach their horses. Some time later, a group of men from Reting monastery came to visit him ...

On a very cold winter's day, the child was taken to Lhasa. Unusually, large snowflakes fell from the sky. The Tibetans were happy, for they considered the rain of heavenly flowers a good omen. The child was, in fact, exceptionally fortunate. As soon as he completed his studies at the Che college of Sera, where all the

Reting Rinpoche lineage had studied, the Thirteenth Dalai Lama agreed to shave his head and give him his religious name, Jampey Yeshe Tenpe Gyaltsen. A few years later he was awarded the title of *geshe lharampa* (doctor of Buddhist philosophy), then passed a succession of qualifying exams with flying colours before returning to Reting monastery. Pilgrims visiting the area told amazing stories about the young incarnate lama: that he had, for instance, released hundreds of yaks and sheep from slaughterhouses.

Had the political circles of Lhasa not selected him as regent, Reting Rinpoche's innocent life might have continued to follow the slow pace of the seasons, with the songs of the monks echoing through the valley. In the terrible jungle he was about to enter, youth was Reting Rinpoche's unique – and sole – asset.

An unusual euphoria had taken hold of the Tibetan capital where the new regent had just been welcomed. The people recalled the Thirteenth Dalai Lama's visit to Reting monastery, the year preceding his death. Many Tibetans thought that the ruler had gone there to give Reting Rinpoche political and administrative advice, but in fact he had done nothing of the kind.

It was freezing cold in Lhasa when Reting Rinpoche crossed the town in a green palanquin carried by four uniformed men. Hardly able to contain his emotions, he entered the Potala. A religious ceremony had been organized with all the pomp due to such an occasion. The young regent was now to live on the floor just beneath the one usually occupied by the Dalai Lama, a place Tibetans called *chödzin chung* – the lower flat.

The regent's first day in Lhasa would have passed quite unremarkably had it not been for one surprising and disturbing fact: a heavy fall of snow washed away the colours of the brocade on the officials' ceremonial robes. A bad omen, said people in Lhasa.

The Thirteenth Dalai Lama had just departed for the 'realm of bliss', when Lungshar set up an underground organization called Kyicho Küntün, the 'Happy Union'. The group was composed of people who were close to Lungshar, as well as out-and-out opportunists, mostly from the nobility. This inner circle included some close friends, but Kabshöba Chögye Nyima, a member of the Finance Office and a friend of Lungshar's, had been excluded. The group's objective was simple: to establish in Tibet a republic based on an elected Assembly. Although a number of representatives from the great Gelugpa monasteries of Ganden, Drepung and Sera gave Lungshar their support, some doubt remained concerning the intentions of the former favourite. His important responsibilities and the network of influence he had created made him one of the most powerful figures in the Assembly, so it was feared that if there were to be a 'republic' he might be tempted to keep all the power for himself, turning his back on the monasteries he had used as a stepping stone. There were also strong fears among lay people: in the Kashag only old *kalön* Trimön seemed capable of opposing him.

Lungshar then launched an overtly anti-Chinese campaign – at any rate, it was more than just a display of Tibetan nationalism. Persistent rumours announced the impending return of the Ninth Panchen Lama, financially and militarily supported by China. Lungshar had played a part in the master of Tashilhunpo's escape; his return would inevitably mean a settling of old scores. Unable to confront the Panchen Lama directly, the former favourite chose instead to attack his protector, China.

Kyicho Küntün had already held several meetings when Lungshar decided to present the National Assembly with a petition suggesting numerous reforms in the Tibetan administration. For most aristocrats, whose existence depended mainly on hereditary privileges, the news was a major blow.

The Kashag immediately consulted the new regent. Anxiety seized the government, for nobody knew the exact strength of Lungshar's political party, or the reaction of the three major monasteries towards Lungshar. Tibetan society was on the verge of complete chaos. Taking advantage of the confusion, Kabshöba, who was frustrated at being excluded from Kyicho Küntün, discreetly met *kalön* Trimön in order to make a surprising revelation: that the Dalai Lama's former counsellor intended to murder Trimön, as well as other members of the Kashag.

Trimön, the hero of the 1912 war, decided to leave Lhasa at once and take refuge in Drepung, where he was very surprised to discover that the monks no longer had the slightest sympathy for Lungshar! He immediately got in touch with Sera and Ganden and explained to the superiors that if Lungshar's idea of establishing a republic in Tibet materialized, Buddhism would suffer, and that this might be fatal for traditional monastic influence. At the same time everybody kept in mind the Thirteenth Dalai Lama's political testament. Together, the religious authorities of Ganden, Sera and Drepung made a decision to support the Kashag in the fight against the former counsellor.

On 10 May 1934, the situation in Lhasa was unusually tense and rumours were rife. Reting Rinpoche summoned Lungshar to the Potala. Prime minister Langdün and several members of the Kashag were also present. Lungshar arrived with a few servants and greeted all the officials. As soon as Reting Rinpoche started to ask him very precise questions, Lungshar realized that he had been set up. He tried to escape and rushed to the door, but one of the regent's bodyguard monks grasped him roughly round the waist. The members of Lungshar's escort fled, without even attempting to save their leader.

Then Langdün came up to Lungshar and tore off his official costume, to humiliate him. When his boots were taken off, pieces of paper fell to the ground. Before the guards had time to move, Lungshar stuffed some of them into his mouth and swallowed them. However, one was left, on which was written the name of *kalön* Trimön. Undoubtedly the names of the regent and the prime minister had been written on the others. Lungshar was immediately arrested and put in jail, and then the regent arrested his main supporters. Kabshöba was also placed in custody. The Kashag had in fact hoped to get other information out of him that would have further compromised Lungshar.

Meanwhile Kyicho Küntün held a secret meeting. Emissaries were sent to Drepung, Ganden and Sera to raise support. The superiors of the three monasteries refused to support Lungshar's party, but they promised to send a delegation to Lhasa to ask that the former counsellor be freed. However, when the regent and the prime minister explained the true intentions behind Lungshar's republican slogans, the monks rallied to support Reting Rinpoche and the Kashag. Lungshar's fate now seemed decided.

On the following day, 11 May 1934, bolstered by the monasteries' support, the Kashag had eight other members of the Kyicho Küntün arrested. As if by magic, Lungshar's political party vanished in the same way as it had appeared.

In the confession wrested out of him, Kabshöba accused Lungshar of having plotted to murder ministers and a number of lay officials with the sole aim of seizing power. It was reported that Lungshar had dreamt of ruling the country once it had been transformed into a people's republic. In his confession Kabshöba also mentioned that the Thirteenth Dalai Lama's former counsellor had intended to become king of Tibet. But even today it is still impossible to distinguish between truth and fabrication in these admissions.

The regent asked that a list of Lungshar's crimes be made. Since being appointed a *tsipön* by the late ruler in 1919, Lungshar had made many enemies. Now, seeing that his end had come, they decided to come out into the open. Therefore, when Reting Rinpoche asked the National Assembly – which had for so long been dominated and manipulated by Lungshar – to give their verdict on what punishment to inflict, it was not surprising that all the members sentenced him without the slightest regret. Reting Rinpoche nevertheless reminded them that he was opposed to the death sentence, in accordance with the tradition of Tibetan Buddhism. The Assembly then arrived at their horrendous verdict: Lungshar was to be blinded with a red-hot iron, a punishment traditionally reserved for cases of high treason. To spare him too much pain, he would be allowed to take a very strong medicine, just before darkness engulfed him. In addition, Kyicho Küntün's eight senior leaders[4] were banished. The others were given only a small fine.

It was several weeks before calm returned to the capital. Then began a period of instability, for which the Tibetans would pay dearly later. In the streets of Lhasa, people sang a song which compared Lungshar with Drime Kunden, the hero of an extremely popular opera, who gave his eyes out of compassion for the suffering of humanity. But the reference requires further analysis. Numerous supporters of Kyicho Küntün had in fact become aware that it was vital to initiate major social and political changes if Tibet were to retain its independence. The idea of a republic, which had formed in Lungshar's mind while he was in Europe, might have become one of these changes had it been applied in its original form, but unfortunately Lungshar had been too greedy for power to carry it through to its successful conclusion. The Lungshar affair was a real tragedy for the Tibetans – and still represents a very controversial chapter in Tibetan history.

Reting Rinpoche emerged stronger than ever from the upheavals which had disturbed the Tibetan capital. His youthfulness made him popular, and for this reason he thought he might be able to accomplish two major tasks during his interregnum: the construction of the Thirteenth Dalai Lama's gold mausoleum and the search for the incarnate child.

But with the troubles of 1934, the *karma** of the Tibetans was once again disturbed. The pace of events quickened and negotiations for the Ninth Panchen Lama's return to Tibet, abruptly interrupted by the ruler's death, were resumed. Several meetings took place in Lhasa in the presence of Lobsang Gyaltsen, the Panchen Lama's chief secretary, and Lobsang Wangchug, one of his main counsellors, who were both still living in the private house in Lhasa allocated to them by the Kashag, with servants to assist them in their numerous tasks. It was these meetings that gave rise to new rumours suggesting an improvement in relations between the government and the master of Tashilhunpo.

Reting Rinpoche and Langdün did, in fact, send a telegram to the Panchen Lama inviting him to come back immediately to Tibet on the basis of the discussions initiated with the Thirteenth Dalai Lama. The government agreed to pay all the expenses related to the journey of His Holiness and his retinue and offered to put an escort at his disposal which would take him in due course to Tashilhunpo. The message was clear. However, the Panchen Lama hesitated. He knew about the young regent's difficulties and had been kept informed of everything that was happening in the Forbidden City. After reflecting at length, he refused to respond to the government's overtures.

In the meantime, Nanjing and London were seriously worried about the situation in Tibet, a feeling which was shared by British India. The Chinese Nationalist Party, the Kuomintang, decided to send an official mission, led by the deputy head of the Military Council, General Huang Mu-sung, to present the Chinese government's condolences to the regent and possibly re-establish diplomatic representation in Lhasa. (The Dalai Lama had expelled all the Chinese when he had proclaimed the independence of Tibet in 1913. Since then, in spite of numerous official and non-official endeavours, it had been impossible to restore any sort of lasting link between the two countries.)

A first group left China and arrived in Lhasa on 24 May 1934 in order to prepare the Chinese delegate's stay. Loaded with gifts, as custom required, the emissaries travelled by sea and then through India; General Huang Mu-sung headed a second party which reached the Tibetan capital three months later, on 28 August 1934. Meanwhile, the government of British India dispatched its own commission, led by Norbu Döndub, the Political Officer of Sikkim. His mission was to gain a better understanding of the situation and keep a discreet eye on the Kuomintang's emissaries.

Wolves had entered the town. The Tibetans very soon realized that the Chinese mission had not come solely for the purpose of expressing their condolences – although outward appearances demonstrated this to be so. Initially, General Huang Mu-sung paid his respects to Reting Rinpoche, the Kashag and various high-ranking officials, to whom he presented sumptuous gifts. He also visited several monasteries – first of all the Jokhang – in an attempt to show that the authorities of Nanjing were open to the Buddhist religion and intended to respect all Tibetan traditions. He also attended numerous ceremonies and cultural events. He honoured the most important receptions with his presence and was always careful to give sizeable donations.

When were the Tibetans' suspicions first aroused? To be precise, when General Huang Mu-sung, on behalf of the Kuomintang, made a posthumous presentation to the Dalai Lama of a jade slab symbolizing his achievements – a present the late ruler would never have accepted in his lifetime. A cautious inscription read: 'To the renowned Thirteenth Dalai Lama, who protects the living creatures of the snowy country and in whom we [the Chinese] trust as the real Buddha. This is offered by the Chinese Republican government.'[5]

Reting may have made a mistake in accepting the Chinese delegation out of a desire to maintain good relations with such a powerful neighbour but, above all, the Kashag was wrong to have agreed to political discussions with General Huang Mu-sung. When these were held on 17 September 1934 the Chinese representative made the Panchen Lama the main topic of discussion. In view of the fact that a spiritual authority had no need of weapons, Reting Rinpoche and Langdün promised that if China agreed to confiscate those of the Panchen Lama, the Tibetans would be happy to welcome back the *Panchen Erdeni,*★ whose absence remained a source of sadness and great concern to them. In turn, the government agreed to take responsibility for his security and give him back his possessions, his properties and his power. The Chinese mission's second objective was to test the resistance of the regent and his entourage. The Kuomintang wanted Tibet to resume more positive relations with the 'Motherland', and to this end said that Tibet must end all direct relations with foreign countries and accept a Chinese representative appointed by Nanjing. Not wanting to give up any part of the Thirteenth Dalai Lama's legacy, the Tibetan government decided to go no further and it put an end to the discussions.

Nevertheless, the negotiations had not been a complete failure for General Huang Mu-sung. When he left Lhasa for Nanjing at the end of November, he had in a sense half-opened the gates of the Tibetan capital. He left behind two officials in charge of a wireless unit that he had been allowed to set up on his arrival. This somewhat strange unit very quickly turned into an official Chinese mission, from where all sorts of agents operated. But on the political front, the status quo remained unchanged.

Meanwhile, the delegation from British India had also set up a wireless unit[6] and opened a clinic with a military doctor. At the same time, the Tibetan government decided to re-establish the Foreign Office created by the Dalai Lama some 20 years before. The British then used it systematically as an intermediary for their messages, but the Chinese were careful not to do so. Ignoring the existence of the official Foreign Office, they chose to bypass its authority and address the Kashag directly.

Even more shrewdly, the Kuomintang regularly sent personal gifts of money to high-ranking Tibetan officials, including Reting Rinpoche. By the end of 1934, new rumours circulating in Lhasa suggested that considerable sums from Nanjing had increased the regent's fortune. It was even reported that Reting Rinpoche had sent tradesmen to China to buy satin and china which were then sold in the Tibetan capital for his own financial gain.

7

Search for the Fourteenth
Dalai Lama

Life is a setting sun.
KELSANG GYATSO, SEVENTH DALAI LAMA

The regent was responsible for the erection of a beautiful gold tomb for the Thirteenth Dalai Lama. The Tibetans wanted it to equal, or even surpass, the tomb of the Great Fifth. Reting Rinpoche entrusted its construction to a committee headed by *kalön* Trimön. The six-storey-high edifice in the western part of the Potala, which took two long years to complete, was decorated with 18,870 gold *sang*[1] and studded with thousands of precious gems. The mausoleum was unique, so much so that the regent gave it the Tibetan name of *Gelek Dödzo*, meaning 'as virtuous and good as a miraculous cow'. The inaugural ceremony was in the style of the late Dalai Lama: simple and impressive.

The search for the reincarnated child progressed slowly. In the spring of 1935, in the year of the Wood Pig, under the pretext of a pilgrimage to Samye and Lhoka,[2] a new delegation, headed by Reting Rinpoche, *kalön* Trimön and Shakabpa, visited Chökhorgyal monastery, some ten miles from Lhamo Latso, the lake of visions. The story of their journey is full of the mystery and enchantment so beloved by the Tibetan people.

After the monks had prayed and meditated for several days on the banks of the lake, the water became cloudy. As predicted by the

69

Fifth Dalai Lama, the regent found the information he had come to seek, in the shape of three Tibetan characters (*ah*, *ka* and *ma*), a monastery with gold and green jade roofs, and a house with strangely shaped guttering. The regent recorded these indications on a piece of parchment and sealed it.

In Lhasa, the regent consulted oracles as well as high-ranking dignitaries. Once interpreted, the characters revealed that the reincarnated child should be sought in Amdo, near Kumbum monastery. Other signs pointed to the east of the country. At the time of his death, the Thirteenth Dalai Lama had been lying with his head towards the south, but it was reported that his head had twice turned towards the east during the embalming. And another very strange occurrence had taken place in the same room: one morning, while servants were bustling about the deceased, a star-shaped fungus had appeared on one of the north-east pillars.

Fortified with all these clues, the Assembly appointed three groups of monks and lay people who, during the autumn of 1935, the year of the Fire Mouse, set off in three different directions: the first group headed for Amdo in the north-east of Tibet; the second for Kham in the east; and the third towards Dagpo and Kongpo in the south-east.

By this time relations between the regent and the Panchen Lama's spokesmen deteriorated. The latter continued to seek ways to return to Tibet so that he could live among his fellow citizens in the monastery of Tashilhunpo, but without success. General Huang Mu-sung had returned to Nanjing without 'any concrete result to his credit',[3] in spite of threatening to make the Tibetan government let the Panchen Lama come back 'with the force of arms'.[4] The Kuomintang authorities did not appreciate the failure of the mission – a disappointment shared by the Panchen Lama.[5]

Shortly afterwards, the Chinese government announced the creation of a Panchen Lama Office in Xining (Qinghai), and granted him the title 'Special Cultural Commissioner for the Western Regions'. (He had already been given the title 'Peace Commissioner for the Border Provinces in the West.') Another office was to be opened in Tachienlu (Sichuan). Simultaneously, the Chinese authorities declared that His Holiness would return to

Tashilhunpo, accompanied by an official and 500 soldiers. The Tibetan government reacted immediately, aware of the danger that the arrival of armed Chinese troops in Lhasa represented. The government let it be known through its representative in Nanjing that there was no question of letting a Chinese army enter Tibet.

Disturbed by the Kuomintang's decision, the regent and prime minister Langdün asked the government of British India to intervene. New Delhi gave its agreement and dispatched the Sikkim-based official, W F Williamson, to Lhasa. As soon as he arrived in the Forbidden City, he worked hard to find a satisfactory compromise in the long-running 'religious and internal dispute' between the Panchen Lama and Reting Rinpoche's government. However, Williamson had been instructed that he was to act merely as a mediator. But the British representative in Nanjing felt even this would be an unwise line of action to take.

Although the Panchen Lama's demands were considered excessive, the government of Lhasa eventually agreed to them. In addition to the restoration of all his possessions, including his estates, the master of Tashilhunpo claimed full control of the prefectures of Nangartse, Shigatse, Namling and Penam, which had not been under his direct authority before. In their answer Lhasa refused to restore some of the Tashilhunpo estates, simply because they had been distributed to other monasteries. Surprisingly, the Panchen Lama's representatives also asked for Williamson's mediation, but Williamson fell seriously ill and died in Tibet. It is not known whether he had time to tell the Panchen Lama's representatives that their acceptance of a return to Tibet without a Chinese military escort would have brought the two parties nearer to an agreement. Williamson was replaced temporarily by Captain Battye, the trade agent from Gyantse. On 18 November 1935, when Captain Battye went to the Potala to say his farewells to the regent, the latter insistently begged him to intercede with the British government and ask it to put pressure on the Panchen Lama and force him to accept Lhasa's offer.

Since the Thirteenth Dalai Lama's death, credit for the negotiations initiated with the Panchen Lama's representatives was not entirely due to the efforts of Reting Rinpoche. The regent was fortunate in having an outstanding chamberlain, who had in particular suggested that he renovate the Jokhang and other monasteries, including Reting. He was a man of great experience who had served Reting Rinpoche's previous incarnation for many years, and he knew how to please the regent. Unfortunately some people objected to the chamberlain's influence on the regent, and they waited like wolves for their prey. Nyungne Lama and Khardo Rinpoche shared a very deep friendship with Reting Rinpoche. The regent had put the former in charge of his private secretariat, which was a commercial agency with a branch in Kalimpong in the north of India. The latter worked behind the scenes, with the regent consulting him whenever he felt the need to do so. Both men took advantage of the situation to suggest to Reting Rinpoche that he dismiss the chamberlain, on grounds of his age, and the latter retired to Reting monastery where he ended his life in peace, far away from the furore stirred up by the political manoeuvres of the regent's new entourage. Jampa Gyaltsen, the 26-year-old brother of the regent, took over as chamberlain. He was uneducated and had no interest whatsoever in politics or religion. What he liked most were horses and beautiful clothes. His appointment was a wonderful opportunity for Nyungne Lama and Khardo Rinpoche.

Reting Rinpoche worked for over a year in close collaboration with prime minister Langdün, who had already been in this post for some ten years, but then relations between the two men quickly deteriorated, with the former accusing the latter of abusing his power. One day, the regent avoided Langdün's office – and thereafter systematically forgot to consult him. This came as no great surprise to the prime minister, who had already experienced a similar situation with his uncle, the Thirteenth Dalai Lama, who had used him merely as an official liaison with the Kashag. Although, since the death of his uncle he had become the chief political figure in Tibet, he did not have the strength of character to impose his authority on the Assembly, which at the time was dominated by Lungshar. This marked the beginning of a serious blow to the power and institution of the prime minister. The regent now consulted his friends on decisions of State, taking no notice of Langdün's authority. The two men met only at religious or political ceremonies, or at the time of *Losar*.

Reting Rinpoche's greed for power was so great that, once he had reduced Langdün to the status of inefficient puppet, he decided to make a direct attack on the Kashag, whose members he found far too conservative. In effect, the latter tried not to stray too far from the political testament left by the Thirteenth Dalai Lama, especially in matters concerning relations with China. During a very stormy session at the Assembly, Reting Rinpoche compelled two ministers to resign and immediately replaced them with men of his own party. This was just the beginning.

In 1936, Sir Basil Gould, the permanent replacement for Williamson, made a conspicuous entry into Lhasa. As custom required, the British delegation brought the Tibetan authorities many presents. Within a few hours of Gould's arrival, the subject of his role as mediator in the dispute between the Panchen Lama and the government was brought up. It was later made clear that His Majesty's representative was not there to act as guarantor, but to contribute to the 'peaceful settlement of disagreements' between the parties.

Rumours that Chinese troops were about to arrive flew around Lhasa. Indeed, utter confusion reigned. The Chinese escort was supposed to comprise some 300–500 hand-picked men. Yet the Panchen Lama's attitude seemed almost ambivalent whenever the topic was mentioned. At the time of their last meeting, in 1935, the master of Tashilhunpo had told Williamson: 'The escort is not part of my request.' Sir Basil Gould also felt a change in the Tibetan government's attitude. He followed Reting Rinpoche's activities with some amusement. The man loved easy pleasures, and people liked to tell stories about him. He had learned to ride a motor bike, and had a child-like interest in photography. He loved pets and possessed, among others, a fox cub, a monkey and several pure-bred dogs. He particularly loved birds and had huge cages set up in his chambers. His collection included a mynah bird who mimicked him and a raucous magpie.

Sir Basil Gould's presents had enraptured the young regent, who seemed completely oblivious of the seriousness of the occasion and the reality of his duties. He never tired of listening to the gramophone and trying out the loudspeakers that His Majesty's representative had given him, in the presence of Sir Basil Gould and

Spencer Chapman, his private secretary. Roaring with laughter and with the volume turned up as loud as it would go, Reting Rinpoche crossed the huge reception hall to the sound of a Scottish marching tune, while his guests looked on dumbfounded. The sound was so loud that the people of Lhasa, somewhat surprised and alarmed by this kind of music, gathered below the palace. They were very surprised to hear suddenly their regent's voice, at first timidly, and then louder and louder, through the walls of the Potala! The loudspeakers had in fact been set up in front of an open window. Talking to himself, Reting Rinpoche had tremendous fun listening to the echo of his own voice and laughter.

Some time later, Sir Basil Gould heard with dismay that the regent had left for Samye, where he stayed for six weeks. Four members of the government and a Tibetan army captain acting as a photographer had gone with him. Moreover, the government could take no decision in the regent's absence. At this Sir Basil completely lost his composure. The British delegation had to face the truth: the political situation in Lhasa could not be worse; the regent was unable to rule the country and his departure to Samye was in effect an escape. Indecisive and inexperienced, although quite ambitious, and surrounded by schemers, the regent hoped that by taking this trip the crucial issues relating to the Panchen Lama would resolve themselves and thus finally absolve him of any responsibility in the matter.

There were further surprises in store for the British delegation. The Tibetan government's position regarding the Panchen Lama seemed to have softened, yet at the same time the Kashag made it known to Gould that British mediation was not wanted. The government were determined to oppose the Panchen Lama's Chinese escort with weapons, but were fearful that such a stance might lead to war with China. Other rumours circulating in the capital implied that the Chinese escort had been ordered secretly not to resist in the event of a Tibetan retaliation, but to immediately take the Panchen Lama back to the other side of the border.

In one of his reports, Sir Basil Gould explained the ambiguity of the government of Lhasa's official stand, which, according to him, was primarily due to the regent's strange behaviour. The latter was constantly exerting pressure on ministers, notably by threatening to resign. This persistent blackmail had enabled him to obtain absolute power, which he then used for purely speculative purposes. To solve the country's galloping inflation, his friends had advised him to issue a new banknote. The Thirteenth Dalai Lama had never issued a banknote worth more than seven-and-a-half *sang*, but now, for the first time in the history of the country, Reting Rinpoche had ordered 100-*sang* banknotes to be printed. This new financial policy turned out to be disastrous. The price of basic necessities rose, and the population found it hard to meet their basic needs. The standard of living for people in Lhasa fell dangerously low, but they were so afraid of Reting Rinpoche that nobody dared oppose him. He used and abused his power according to his whims, dismissing whoever made the slightest remark about him. He was violent and greedy for power, and his arrogance was sometimes unbearable. One day, he directly confronted the almost invincible influence of the lamas by deciding to appoint an abbot of his own choice at the head of a monastery of some 2,000 monks. (This abbot was entitled to a seat at the Assembly and thus played a key role in the Tibetan administration.) To this end, Reting Rinpoche summoned the abbot who was in charge and demanded his resignation. Warned of the plot, all the monks of the monastery opposed the regent and let him know that they would refuse to appoint the new abbot if he stuck to his decision. Reting Rinpoche was exceedingly angry. Nothing happened for a few weeks but, in the end, Reting had to bow to the power of the monks, whose support he most needed, and the abbot retained his post.

At that time, the monasteries considered that they represented the true essence of religion, and that the highest spiritual values were revealed in monastic life. Members of a monastic order were convinced that it was their right and duty to interfere in the country's political and economic affairs whenever they felt that the government was not acting in their interests. This attitude naturally involved them directly in the many conflicts which regularly shook the country. However, involvement in political life was strictly limited to the three great Gelugpa monasteries, Drepung, Ganden and Sera.

Monastic communities were as much like towns bustling with life as sanctuaries dedicated to spiritual studies. Monks were roughly divided into two groups: those who could read and those who could not. The former followed the normal monastic curriculum and some of these monks became scholars; those who knew only how to recite prayers usually took care of the material side of monastic life. For example, in Sera, only about a quarter of the monks could read. The others worked in the community and served tea and meals during collective prayer sessions. About 10–15 per cent of the monks were 'fighting monks' (*dobdobs*). As true weapon-carrying warriors with a very specific code of chivalry, they were the guardians of the monasteries. They regularly took part in sporting competitions highlighting their skills. These monks were usually selected for their physical aptitude rather than their spiritual inclinations.

The three major monasteries – Drepung, Ganden and Sera – included a large network of smaller monasteries scattered throughout the area. Drepung, for example, was composed of a set of semi-autonomous sub-units called colleges, or *dratsang*. Originally Drepung numbered seven colleges, of which four – Loseling, Gomang, Deyang and Ngagpa – were still active into the twentieth century. For purely strategic political reasons, the other three – Gyepa, Shagaw and Düwa – kept only an abbot. Monks belonged to a monastery by being enrolled in a college with its own administration and resources. Each college was ruled by an abbot, and divided into important residential sub-units known as *khamtsen*, which comprised the monks' quarters and cells. Each *khamtsen* had its own administrative system, and up to a certain point, autonomous resources. Colleges and *khamtsen* were allocated a particular place in the midst of the buildings and were at the centre of all the monastery's activities – ritual, educational, social and political. Each unit had its own identity and name, which had been preserved generation after generation. Men came and went, but the structure and its properties remained.

Loseling had twenty-three *khamtsen* and Gomang had sixteen. Deyang and Ngagpa had none. In a *khamtsen*, monks lived alone, in households with other monks, or in *shagtsang*. Monks in the latter formed a monastic aristocracy, with their own houses, properties and possessions. They were very influential in the administration of the colleges and were often appointed to key positions usually entrusted to lay officials. In Loseling, total control was in the hands of only three *khamtsen*. Of the 5,000 or so monks who lived there (as against only 4,000 in Gomang), 65–70 per cent were from Kham in eastern Tibet; the others came from other regions. Drepung possessed 180 estates and employed 20,000 serfs and 16,000 nomads in the monastery.[6]

In 1936, the Panchen Lama and his retinue headed for Jyekundo (Qinghai), on the Chang Jiang river. The arrival of Chökyi Nyima and his large party in one of the most prosperous towns of eastern Tibet soon had disastrous consequences on the local economy, merely because of their presence. In addition, it seemed that the winter would be particularly cold, with basic necessities scarce and inflation certain. Indeed, the Panchen Lama caught a cold and had to stay in bed. Warned about the precarious health of the master of Tashilhunpo, the official representative of the government of Lhasa, the governor of the region, sent two emissaries to the sick man's bedside to beg him to leave for the Chamdo area, where the climate was more temperate. On his counsellors' advice, the Panchen Lama declined the suggestion and explained that it was not important where he stayed as he intended to continue on to Shigatse as soon as possible. However, Chökyi Nyima did ask to be taken to a hot spring near Jyekundo, on the Chinese border.

Then an extraordinary event occurred. In February 1937, one of the three groups in charge of the search for the reincarnated child of the late Thirteenth Dalai Lama arrived in Jyekundo. The delegation, headed by Kewtsang Rinpoche, a lama of Sera monastery, was immediately received by the Panchen Lama with all the honours traditionally due to high-ranking officials of the government of Lhasa. The guests were offered Tibetan tea and a special dish of rice, while the Panchen Lama talked at length with them, answering their numerous questions and giving advice. He then granted Kewtsang Rinpoche a special audience in his room. Once he had listened carefully to the lama's stories, His Holiness gave a precise description of the place where he thought the Fourteenth Dalai Lama had been born. He depicted the circumstances of the family and described the house. Kewtsang Rinpoche hurried to this place, himself convinced that the child who had been sought and expected for so long was actually in Taktser, in the Tibetan region of Amdo, in the Chinese province of Qinghai.

The dignitaries set off towards the village indicated by the master of Tashilhunpo. Lobsang Tsewang, an ordinary monk, who carried a picture of the Ninth Panchen Lama, explained to whoever would listen that the Dalai Lamas and Panchen Lamas were of one mind and that all the differences between the government of Lhasa and the monastery of Tashilhunpo were caused by selfish men who thought only of how they could benefit from the situation. Eventually the delegation reached the village of Taktser. It was the middle of winter and very cold.

Once they had enquired about the family and the two-year-old child living there, two members of the delegation disguised themselves. Lama Kewtsang Rinpoche dressed shabbily like a servant, and Lobsang Tsewang, the ordinary monk, took on the master's role. The following is the Fourteenth Dalai Lama's account of this first meeting:

> At the gate of the house, the strangers were met by my parents, who invited Lobsang into the house, believing him to be the master, while the lama and the others were received in the servants' quarters. There they found the baby of the family, and the moment the little boy saw the lama, he went to him and wanted to sit on his lap. The lama was disguised in a cloak which was lined with lambskin, but round his neck he was wearing a rosary which had belonged to the Thirteenth Dalai Lama. The little boy seemed to recognize the rosary, and he asked to be given it. The lama promised to give it to him if he could guess who he was, and the boy replied that he was Sera-aga, which meant, in the local dialect, 'a lama of Sera'. The lama asked who the 'master' was, and the boy gave the name of Lobsang. He also knew the name of the real servant, which was Amdo Kasang ...
>
> The lama spent the whole day in watching the little boy with increasing interest, until it was time for the boy to be put to bed. All the party stayed in the house for the night, and early next morning, when they were making ready to leave, the boy got out of his bed and insisted that he wanted to go with them. I was that boy.[7]

The Panchen Lama's indications had been accurate, so Kewtsang Rinpoche decided to submit the child to further tests and his conviction was reinforced by several signs. First of all, there were the letters which the regent had seen in his vision on the banks of Lhamo Latso: *ah* meant the region of Amdo, where the delegation was, *ka* referred to the monastery of Kumbum, the major monastery in the area, and precisely the one the regent had seen; *ka* and *ma* could also refer to the monastery of Karmapa Rölpai Dorje, on the mountain overlooking the village of Taktser. A few years ago, the Thirteenth Dalai Lama had stayed there and left a pair of boots; and the monks remembered that he had looked closely for a few minutes at the house where his reincarnation was to be born.

Many years later, the man who became the Fourteenth Dalai Lama spoke about Kewtsang Rinpoche's second visit:

It is common for small children who are reincarnations to remember objects and people from their previous lives. Some can also recite the scriptures although they have not yet been taught them. All I had said to the lama had suggested to him that he might at last have discovered the reincarnation he was seeking. The whole party had come to make further tests. They brought with them two identical black rosaries, one of which had belonged to the Thirteenth Dalai Lama. When they offered them both to me, I took the one which was his and – so I am told – put it round my own neck. The same test was made with yellow rosaries. Next, they offered me two drums, a very small drum which the Dalai Lama had used for calling attendants, and a larger and much more ornate and attractive drum with golden straps. I chose the little drum, and began to beat it in the way that drums are beaten during prayers. Last they presented two walking sticks. I touched the wrong walking stick, then paused and looked at it for some time, and then I took the other, which had belonged to the Dalai Lama, and held it in my hand. And later, when they wondered at my hesitation, they found that the first walking stick had also been used at one time by the Dalai Lama, and that he had given it to a lama who in turn had given it to Kewtsang Rinpoche.[8]

Convinced that he had found the Thirteenth Dalai Lama's reincarnation, Kewtsang Rinpoche wrote all the details of his discoveries in a telegram to Lhasa. The message, of crucial importance for the history of Tibet, was written in code and sent from Xining to the capital via China and India. The answer, which reached Kewtsang Rinpoche in the same way, said that the reincarnated child was to be brought to the Potala without delay. In the meantime, Japan and China were at war. However, the Kuomintang still insisted on sending the Panchen Lama back to Tibet with a sizeable Chinese escort. It was, in fact, trying to test the Tibetan government's determination. Then a second dramatic event occurred.

The Panchen Lama again went to Jyekundo just before the beginning of winter 1937, but his health deteriorated further and he passed away in December of that same year. When told the news, the governor of eastern Tibet immediately sent two emissaries to the Panchen Lama's party, to present the government's condolences and to suggest the party went back to Tashilhunpo. This proposition divided the dead master's companions into two groups: the old and the young. The former, now that their spiritual master had passed away, saw no reason to go back to China, and wanted to follow the governor's suggestion and return to their original monastery. But power was in the hands of the younger monks who were fiercely opposed to the idea of any sort of allegiance with the government of Lhasa. They called on the Khamba tribes of the area for support. Within a few days they had amassed a large body of heavily armed troops – to protect the dead man's corpse, they said, and to replace the Chinese escort which had been called away on other duties.

The monks of Tashilhunpo then went to the monastery of Kantse, in an area ruled by the warlord, Liu Wen-hui. Despite the presence along the Sino-Tibetan border since 1927 of men belonging to Liu Wen-hui, the governor of the province of Xikang in western Sichuan, the monks seized power in Kantse. However, they failed to achieve their final aim which was to overthrow the authorities of Lhasa, who continued to have good relations with the monasteries in the area. Frustrated by this bitter failure, they attacked Liu Wen-hui's warriors and defeated them after a few days of bloody fighting.

Anxious to take advantage of the situation, the lamas of Tashilhunpo invited the Tibetans of eastern Kham to join them in chasing Liu Wen-hui out of the region for good. The governor of eastern Kham made it known to them, through two emissaries, Lobsang Damchö and Kyarsib, that an alliance was possible, provided the Panchen Lama's body was carried to Chamdo. Unfortunately, the Tibetans were not wise enough to unite for a common cause. Some of the Tashilhunpo lamas declared vociferously that they could defend Kantse on their own in the event of a Chinese attack and that, above all, they did not need the official help of the governor in bringing the Panchen Lama's corpse to Chamdo. This resolute attitude of the dignitaries of Tashilhunpo destroyed any hope of a united front against China. The governor of eastern Tibet made a few more attempts, but to no avail.

In the meantime, the armed groups from Tashilhunpo had extended their domination over large areas of Kham. The Chinese were quick to respond. One morning, Kantse found itself completely surrounded by Chinese troops. Miraculously, the lamas of Tashilhunpo managed to escape and take refuge in the region of Kokonor, in Qinghai. Although many of their number had been killed, they managed to take the body of the Ninth Panchen Lama with them.

PART II

The Tenth Panchen Lama
(1938–1989)

8

A Corrupt Regime

... a god on earth.

RIGDZIN TSANGYANG GYATSO, SIXTH DALAI LAMA

As soon as the death of Chökyi Nyima in Jyekundo was announced in Lhasa, the Kashag ordered a 49-day period of mourning, which was of course respected in Tashilhunpo, where many monks were seen in tears. Travellers visiting Lhasa described the pain of all those who had fled the country with their master. Their grief was immeasurable.

The cries of the believers, the chanting of *sutras* and the murmuring of prayers were mingled with the deep sound of conch shells, which added to the heavy atmosphere. It was reported that two believers had fainted before the gates of the monastery in which the deceased was lying. They had died on the spot shortly afterwards, their bodies whipped by a piercing gale and covered by an immaculate carpet of snowflakes. However, lamas, peasants and nomads braved the storm and the cold to pay a last tribute to Chökyi Nyima, who had died at 2.50am on 1 December 1937, at the age of 54. They brought with them numerous presents and a *khata*⋆ to leave in front of the deceased. Incense swirled around the room where the monks had lit hundreds of butter lamps. 'Living Buddhas' and abbots led the ceremonies, praising the bounty of the Ninth Panchen Lama and praying for his speedy reincarnation.

The Kuomintang itself attached great importance to the sudden passing of Chökyi Nyima. Once the authorities had worked out the

organization of the funeral, they created on 23 December a
'posthumous order' in honour of the Panchen Lama:

Member of the Nationalist Government Committee, upholder
of Buddhism as far as the borders in the west, protector of the
nation, master of great wisdom, the Panchen Erdeni was
sensitive to all things. Therefore he achieved exceptional works.
In his youth, he contributed to the unification [of China] with
numerous meritorious actions. Over the last few years [the
master] brought Buddhism to the boundaries of the west,
carefully preaching morality and virtue everywhere. The
inhabitants of the border areas thank him and express their
unanimous gratitude. As he was about to go back to Tibet,
vigorously calling for peace – exemplary behaviour for which
he will be granted everlasting respect – he died suddenly as the
result of an excess of work for his country. To express our
affectionate memory and our deep grief we hereby create a
special order in honour of the Master and confer it on the man
who protected his country so well and bestowed so much
wisdom. Therefore we give him the posthumous title of 'clear-
sighted Master'. A grant of 10,000 yuan will be allocated for
his funeral ...

Following tradition, the search for the reincarnation of the Ninth
Panchen Lama was supervised by the highest administrative
authority of Tashilhunpo, the Council of Khenpo. The Kashag was
also involved. The dignitaries of Tashilhunpo who had stayed in the
region of Kokonor were informed that they would form one
of the delegations in charge of the search. Oracles went into trances;
in the monasteries monks prayed constantly, their incantations a
plea for the speedy rebirth of their spiritual master.

In the summer 1938, a delegation headed by Bilung Rinpoche,
went to lake Lhamo Latso:

In addition to the illusions of Samsara
My limited mind is also attracted by the most illusory visions.
Or is it madness to say that the compassion of the Buddha
Can be reflected in the mirror of karmic existence?

Let me however write the following pages
For those who are inclined to believe
That the mirage of the desert can really be a lake,
For those who are enchanted by fairy tales,
For those who rejoice only in summer clouds.[1]

When the delegation reached the lake, a ceremony of offerings to the guardian of spirits was performed. Then people gathered on the banks for the ritual invocation of Palden Lhamo, an effigy of whom was thrown into the water by the lamas. Bilung Rinpoche sat on the shore, immersed in deep meditation. The account the Tibetans give of the dignitary's visit to the sacred lake is halfway between the supernatural and the phantasmagorical. Monks and lay people gathered around him and prayed, aware of the importance of their task.

The climate in that region is unpredictable and fog can sometimes hide the magnificence of the surrounding landscape for several days. On the fourth day in the early morning, when only the whisper of a mantra was heard, the wind suddenly rose and the water began to shimmer slightly. Miraculously, the morning fog suddenly vanished and the golden rays of the sun beat down on the lake, whose ripples launched a myriad of golden arrows back into space. The lake turned to sapphire; the sky was azure blue with, in the distance, white clouds encrusted like jewels.

Bilung Rinpoche joined his hands together above the water, in which his face was reflected as a shimmering image from the depths. As usual, a *geshe*★ sat beside him. He was a second witness to the extraordinary events which happened before the very eyes of the delegation.

Suddenly there was a tremendous sound like a thunderclap, completely overwhelming the men who were burning cypress and sandalwood branches on the bank as offerings to the gods. The wind blew stronger and stronger, leaving the men afraid and wondering what the gods had in store for them. The wind whipped across lake Lhamo Latso and large white clouds piled up. But as Bilung Rinpoche and the *geshe* raised their eyes towards the sky, the clouds changed, allowing a glimpse of a snow-covered mountain, a breaking wave, an ancient castle, the walls of a town, a palace, a monastery, a fierce warrior on a beautiful horse, and a dragon which sometimes brushed against their faces and sometimes roared angrily at full gallop above their heads.

As Bilung Rinpoche prostrated himself, the water of the lake changed before his eyes, assuming in turn each colour of the rainbow. Numerous scenes appeared, in the shape of a *mandala*★ or other forms. Then the water in the lake became as clear as the sky, and from its clear depths arose more images, geometric patterns, and all kinds of spectacular mirages. Eventually, the lake began to froth and changed to the colour of milk. During those few moments, everyone present witnessed the same astonishing images. Later, nobody was able to tell how long they had stayed there watching.

The men huddled up close to one another, chanting *mantras* which echoed over the lake. Then Bilung Rinpoche and the *geshe* both stood up as one, their faces aglow with intense joy. Simultaneously, the clouds disappeared, the sky turned blue again and the lake returned to its usual calm. Men hastily threw more branches into the now happily spluttering fire.

Bilung Rinpoche and the *geshe* entered the tent that the delegation had pitched near the bank and they sat cross-legged facing each other. Following tradition, the two men did not mention what they had just so vividly experienced. Two attendants simply brought them writing material: a bamboo-stick pen, and yellow paper made from tree bark, soft but thick. The other members of the delegation sat in a circle around the two men and waited patiently until they had finished writing down their visions. Once the transcriptions and drawings were completed, the leaves were sealed with a black lacquer made from a sort of mud (called *lajia* by the Tibetans), to which Bilung affixed the seal of Tashilhunpo.

This was the end of the mission for the two men and the delegation. What did the strange drawings and carefully transcribed symbols mean? It was not their responsibility to analyze, or explain them. Tradition required that, after a Panchen Lama's death, the visions observed by the delegation at the sacred lake of Lhamo Latso were presented to the Dalai Lama, or to the regent acting in his place. It was incumbent on His Holiness to decide when he would read the signs and where he would interpret them. Similarly, the Panchen Lama followed the same procedure to find the reincarnation of a deceased Dalai Lama. In this instance, since the Fourteenth Dalai Lama was only a three-year-old child and not yet officially recognized, Bilung Rinpoche handed over the two parchments to the regent, Reting Rinpoche. Several years were to elapse before the contents of the documents were read.

On his parchment Bilung Rinpoche had transcribed the image of a fierce tiger chased by three rabbits. He had also seen a very elegant woman wearing a triangular headdress opening a curtain in front of a door. The *geshe* had seen different visions: a wild lion sleeping on one of the stone stairs of the monastery of Tashilhunpo, monks' cells, and two ancient but still vigorous and upright trees.

At the time of his death, the Ninth Panchen Lama had left no indication or sign which might have been helpful in the search for his reincarnation. Therefore the dignitaries of the monastery of Tashilhunpo had to direct the search themselves, based mainly on the accounts of those who had travelled to the lake of visions. The members of the delegation noticed that Bilung Rinpoche and the *geshe* had often turned their heads towards the east in their prostrations, and this direction had been confirmed several times by the Nechung oracle in his trances.

In the meantime, the future Dalai Lama had been placed in the monastery of Kumbum, under the guidance of his elder brother who was already studying there. At the time, the region of Amdo was controlled by a Chinese Muslim governor, Ma Pu-fang. The inhabitants of the area knew him as an unscrupulous warlord who did not hesitate to put his personal interests before those of the Kuomintang. He had even transformed his province into a principality with *de facto* independence from the authorities in Nanjing. To some extent he had been able to do this because Chiang Kai-shek's attention was concentrated elsewhere, on the Sino-Japanese war. It was with the utmost caution, therefore, that Kewtsang Rinpoche begged Ma Pu-fang for his help and protection in bringing the child from Kumbum to Lhasa.

So as not to arouse the governor's suspicions, the delegation led him to believe that they had to bring to Lhasa several possible candidates for the Thirteenth Dalai Lama's reincarnation. They carefully avoided mentioning that a choice had already been made. Weeks passed and they received no answer from the governor.

Kewtsang Rinpoche's main fear was that the Kuomintang would get to hear of the selection of the child and hold him hostage. Eventually, Ma Pu-fang asked the delegation for a payment of 100,000 silver coins, which the government paid immediately. But the warlord's greed did not stop there. He tried to get more money out of the delegation – an additional 300,000 silver coins – by telling them that the monks of Kumbum wanted to be the ones who would announce the reincarnation of the Dalai Lama.

Kewtsang Rinpoche replied saying that the final choice had not yet been made and that it was a huge sum, yet he informed the government of Lhasa. To avoid the letter being intercepted, it was taken by hand to the capital. This took several months, as did the answer. The year 1938 passed. Negotiations followed one after another, but still the Chinese government refused to allow the child to be taken to Lhasa.

In the capital too, the situation was unclear. The government blamed the regent because he had discovered the Thirteenth Dalai Lama's reincarnation in a province under Chinese control, giving the Kuomintang an opportunity to take advantage of the situation by ordering that the child be taken to Lhasa under escort.

Meanwhile, Kewtsang Rinpoche found a way to satisfy Ma Pu-fang's excessive greed, with the help of Muslim traders from Xining who travelled through Amdo on the first stage of their long pilgrimage to Mecca, via India. They agreed to pay the 300,000 silver coins demanded by the warlord, provided the authorities in Lhasa reimbursed them in Indian rupees. However, Ma Pu-fang then took hostage a high-ranking dignitary, saying that he would be released, in exchange for a complete set of the Thirteenth Dalai Lama's clothes and a collection of manuscripts written in gold letters, when the reincarnated child arrived safe and sound in Lhasa. A few months later, fighting broke out in the area and the high-ranking hostage escaped and made his way back to the Tibetan capital.

The Kashag received a telegraph message from its representatives in Nanjing, with the information that the delegation and the boy could at last leave for Lhasa. This was on 21 July 1939, at the beginning of the sixth month of the year of the Earth Hare.

We set off a week after my fourth birthday, on a journey which was to last for three months and thirteen days. It was a sad moment for my parents to leave Taktser, their home, their farm, and their friends, because they still did not know what the future held for us. There were roughly 50 people and 350 horses and mules in the caravan when it started, including the members of the search party, my own family, and the party of Muslims on their even longer pilgrimage. My parents brought two of my elder brothers with them – Gyelo Thondup, who was nine, and Lobsang Samten, who by then was six. There were no wheeled carts or carriages in Tibet, and no roads for them. Samten and I rode in a carriage called a *treljam*, which is attached to two poles and carried on the back of two mules. On rough and dangerous parts of the track, the members of the search party carried me in turns. Every day, we travelled only from dawn till noon, which is the usual practice on journeys in Tibet, and every night we camped in tents, because there were very few habitations on the route. Indeed, in the early part of the journey we saw nobody for week after week, except a few nomads who came to ask me for my blessing.[2]

As the party approached the capital, the crowds increased. People prayed and shouted: 'The day of our happiness has come.' The child was taken straight to the Norbu Lingka, the summer residence of the Dalai Lamas. It was by now 8 October. At the regent's request, the astrologers immediately set to work. The day of the enthronement ceremonies[3] had to be determined as soon as possible.

Tibetan astrology was born out of the meeting of three cultural trends: the old Tibetan heritage grounded in animism and magic; Chinese astrology, introduced in the seventh century; and the Buddhist form of Indian astrology as found in the *tantra Kalachakra*, introduced in the eleventh century. From these diverse sources, lama-astrologers created the harmonious synthesis that is still in use today.

The Tibetan astrologer, or *tsipa*, is usually a religious man. In villages, he is most often a lama. His function as astrologer is sometimes complemented by another, that of seer, *mopa*. In monasteries, it is his duty to define the lunar calendar and give annual or seasonal predictions for the climate and crops. He is also the one who draws up the horoscope of a newborn baby. If necessary, he specifies rituals to ward off any planetary influences which might endanger the child's life. And it is the astrologer who, in the case of an impending marriage, studies the astrological compatibility of the man and woman and establishes their astrological profiles.

The astrologer also plays a key role at the time of death. He draws up a horoscope setting out the funerary rituals: the way the body should leave the house, which element will be involved in the funeral – air (the most common), fire, water or earth (burial). Cremations are rare in Tibet and are usually reserved for religious people. The bodies of lamas may be temporarily preserved in salt and eventually kept as relics. In the case of an air funeral, the corpse is cut into pieces and the parts of the body left for the vultures; for a water funeral the body is immersed in a river. The astrologer also prescribes rituals for the purification of the deceased in order to ensure a better rebirth.

Astrology is also influential in medicine. In effect, the physician must be able to find the best way of making medicines with plants and minerals, and the auspicious date on which to prescribe them to patients. Astrology also plays an important role in feeling the pulse and analysing urine.

In the Tibetan calendar, the astrologer gives much attention to the auspicious or inauspicious character of a day, according to the person's day of birth. Before going on a trip, the Dalai Lama will consult his personal astrologer. All Tibetans do the same in matters concerning work, travel, and so on. They believe that certain days or hours are charged with either good or evil energies, according to each individual's astrological profile.

In this way, with the agreement of the regent and the National Assembly, the date of the official presentation of the Fourteenth Dalai Lama was fixed as the fourteenth day of the first month of the year of the Iron Dragon – 22 February 1940.

The succession of religious ceremonies followed a carefully prepared procedure. Lhasa was jubilant. In the large hall, foreign representatives of China, Britain, Nepal, Bhutan and Sikkim gathered around the family of the reincarnated child, along with members of the Tibetan government, monks, incarnate lamas, and abbots from the Drepung, Ganden and Sera monasteries.

At last, the Thirteenth Dalai Lama's reincarnation entered the *Sishi Phuntso*, followed by Reting Rinpoche, now senior teacher; Taktra Rinpoche, junior teacher; members of the Kashag, the chamberlains, the Master of the Robes, the Master of Religious Ceremonies and the Master of the Table. Invocations, songs and mimes followed one after the other. Then the regent came towards the child and presented him with the *mendel tensum,* three symbolic offerings: a gold image of the Buddha of Long Life, a book of holy scriptures concerning the Buddha, and a miniature *chöten.*[4] Afterwards, Reting Rinpoche exhorted the young Dalai Lama to live a long life, both for the prosperity of the Tibetan people and for the dissemination of Buddhism. Following this there were processions to present the Golden Wheel and the White Conch, symbolizing spiritual and temporal powers. In turn, the Dalai Lama blessed the audience: 'All the seals of my office were presented to me, and there followed my first symbolic act of sovereignty: I fixed the seals on documents conveying orders to monasteries.'[5]

There is no doubt that the enthronement was one of the privileged moments of Reting Rinpoche's rule. The regent had the honour of shaving the head of the little boy from Taktser in the Jokhang temple in Lhasa and conferring on him his final name: Jampey Ngawang Lobsang Yeshe Tenzin[6] Gyatso. On that day the child, who had not yet turned five, was officially recognized as the Fourteenth Dalai Lama.

At this time,[7] corruption was rampant throughout the administration. Nyungne Lama and Khardo Rinpoche, the regent's friends, ruled the roost. In Lhasa, people were constantly appointed, dismissed, promoted and demoted; estates were given in exchange for services, or simply confiscated with no explanation. By the beginning of 1940, those close to Reting Rinpoche asked the government to present him with numerous estates as an expression of grateful thanks for the part he had played in the discovery of the young Dalai Lama. The Kashag convened an extraordinary session to discuss the issue and was about to agree to the suggestion when

Khyungram, the governor of Hor, suddenly stood up and accused those who supported the project of wanting to squander state property. Reting Rinpoche, upset because in the end he received only a few insignificant estates, made an accusation of bad administration against Khyungram, who was immediately sent into exile in Ngari, where he died some time later.

The Tibetans may have tolerated the political manoeuvres of their regent, but in no way could they accept his nocturnal affairs. In the days that followed the Dalai Lama's enthronement, posters appeared on the walls of the capital exposing the immoral conduct of Reting Rinpoche, who was thought to be too fond of drink and women, although he himself flayed lamas who kept secret mistresses. Rumours linked his name with that of a lady of Lhasa who spent her days at Reting's residence. Officially it was said that she was there to further her spiritual education; unofficially, the wagging tongues said something quite different.

During the winter of 1940, Reting Rinpoche decided to go to Samye. On his return, he consulted his astrologer, Phembo Sengge Lama, who predicted many worries if he stayed in office. Reting therefore announced his resignation as regent. As required by tradition, the Dalai Lama was consulted, even though he had not yet turned six. The child confirmed the decision of the Kashag and the Assembly, which had in fact been dictated by Reting Rinpoche himself. In complete contradiction of the rules, the Kashag, the oracles, and high-ranking lamas were not consulted about the appointment of his successor. The choice of Taktra Rinpoche, who was already over 60, was a logical one, because he was teacher to both Reting and the Dalai Lama.

Unlike Taktra Rinpoche, Reting had been very young when power was entrusted to him. This may possibly explain the immature and dissolute side of his character. His insatiable love of parties of all kinds and the most lavish of celebrations had turned Lhasa into a place of culture and happenings. Magnificent performances of *lhamo* (Tibetan opera) were organized, and the Chinese community of traders in Lhasa gave theatrical performances which sometimes lasted the whole night. To the sound of trumpets and the loud beating of drums, interspersed with the clash of gongs, a dragon chased after a celestial fire ball, to the great amusement of children and adults.

Festive Lhasa was also full of street songs. Foreign visitors were often surprised at the opulent life styles of the aristocracy. There was such a contrast between the nobility and the common people that they might have belonged to different species. Work was out of the question for the former, servants looked after them and provided for their every need. Social activities were popular: the women played badminton, and the men ma-jong and dice. When the weather was fine, the sky was streaked with multicoloured kites – Tibetans, young and old alike, and from all social classes, were very fond of them. Families challenged each other's kites in aerial combat, and the losers invited the winners for a meal.

A minority of wealthy nobles began to adopt a Western way of life. When evening fell, vestiges of modern ways appeared, and gas and Tilley lamps illuminated the darkness. Those who liked strong spirits opened bottles of Scotch whisky, Golconda wine, and liqueurs, and listened to the scratchy sounds of successful English songs such as 'Boomps-a-daisy' and 'The Palais Glide' played on the few gramophones in the capital. The cinema was a rare treat: Charlie Chaplin and Rin Tin Tin delighted aristocrats as well as the regent.

During his time of splendour, Reting Rinpoche had learned how to ride a bicycle; he also liked to play football and spent a lot of time kicking a ball around. However intense internal affairs may have been, under Reting Rinpoche's rule, Lhasa had been able to enjoy extravagant picnic parties on the banks of the rivers Khyi-chu and Tsangpo,[8] in which the regent had, of course, taken part. The English doctor from the British mission did not hesitate to give diving demonstrations to crowds of amazed Tibetans, who gathered around him, shouting, roaring with laughter and stamping their feet, so great was their enjoyment. Sometimes the doctor also made strange gestures: he ran and threw a stone in such an astonishing way that Tibetans from time to time wondered whether the Western *amchila*[9] might be suffering from a strange ailment – whereas he was just practising cricket!

On the twelfth month of the year of the Iron Dragon – in the winter of 1940 – Reting Rinpoche's resignation was officially recognized and he was relieved of his position as regent. He was replaced by Taktra Rinpoche, on the first day of the first month of the year of the Iron Snake (1941). A strange rumour circulated in the capital suggesting that the two men had agreed in secret that Taktra should resign in three years time and leave the regency once again to Reting Rinpoche. The situation involving the two regents reminded people of a certain Tibetan fable in which the tiger (*tag*) and the rabbit (*ribong*) became friends. The tiger one day killed the rabbit. In a way Taktra had indeed caught Reting and skinned him alive.

9

Selection of the Tenth Panchen Lama

... a sky filled with light and rainbows.
NGAWANG LOBSANG GYATSO, FIFTH DALAI LAMA

Reting retired to his monastery for a long period of meditation. In recognition of the great erudition of Taktra Rinpoche, the new regent, the Kashag and the National Assembly decided to confer on him the title *pandit kenting ta guo-shri*, meaning 'erudite and great teacher, glory of the country' in a mixture of Sanskrit, Tibetan and Chinese. There was nothing new in the gift of such an honorary title to a regent. At the time of the death of the Seventh Dalai Lama, the regent Demo Tulku (who was in office from 1757 to 1777) had received a similar title from the Manchu emperor Qianlong. Tibetans had maintained the tradition until the time of the Thirteenth Dalai Lama, who had wanted to put an end to this avalanche of titles because he felt that, beneath the prestige, there was a subtle implication of political subordination to the empire – although most Tibetans were undoubtedly unaware of this. To them it was first of all a mark of distinction, which they liked to show off. The title conferred on Taktra Rinpoche had in fact been granted on the basis of ancient records.

Although the regent was known mainly for his predisposition to spiritual life, he quickly revealed himself as a highly energetic man. As soon as he was appointed, he created a private secretariat ruled by his chamberlain, Jampa Tharchin. The regent's chamberlain was traditionally given the title *dzasa* and, on some occasions, he sat at the same level as the *kalön*. But eventually, the title given to Jampa Tharchin was only that of *khenchung* – a fourth-rank religious official. To the Tibetans this was an indisputable sign that Taktra Rinpoche would not stay long in the regency.

At the beginning of 1941, the regent finally came to an agreement with the dissident monks of Tashilhunpo. After a period in which the body of the ninth Panchen Lama was moved from place to place in eastern Tibet, it was eventually brought to Shigatse, where it arrived on 2 April. A *stupa*★ was built to enshrine it, so that the sublime body of the master would shine forever in immortal splendour.

Meanwhile, the State oracles confirmed that the reincarnated child of the Ninth Panchen Lama would be found in the east of the country. Several reliable persons were entrusted with the search mission, one of crucial significance for Tibet. Contact was made with the Panchen Lama's Office in Qinghai.

In the summer of 1941, the Office appointed a close supporter of the deceased – Lama Lobsang Gyentsen, Master of the Dalai Lama's Household – to supervise the search. He immediately set off in an easterly direction, towards Amdo. Some time later, the rulers of Tashilhunpo entrusted the same mission to Ngulchu Rinpoche. It was his responsibility to join the other delegation in Kumbum monastery. Once there, long negotiations began. They resulted in the formation of three groups: the first one headed by Lobsang Gyentsen, the second by the dignitary in charge of the Panchen Lama's meals, and the third by Lama Ngulchu.

As a result of the search around the cantons of Hualong and Xunhua, Ngulchu heard of a child of unusual spirituality, the son of the village chief of Wendu, in the county of Xunhua. Ngulchu went to the nearest monastery to the village and asked the elder lamas to describe the circumstances of the boy's birth; but he left the district without even visiting the parents.

Several months of exhausting and sometimes tedious search elapsed. Eventually, in the second half of 1944, the three delegations brought together ten children, all from Amdo, in Kumbum monastery and decided to submit them to a number of tests. Among them was the son of the village chief of Wendu. He had not been selected by the delegations, but his father had brought him to the monastery on the instructions of the village council.

The tests started, but seven days later the ten candidates were sent back home. A long year passed, fully devoted to prayers, chanting and divinations. Eventually the delegations recalled to Kumbum six[1] of the ten boys initially selected. All of them were from very respectable families in the area. As the list of candidates was larger than usual, the choice was particularly difficult.

While the monks recited mantras and chanted, the selection council consulted the oracles again. Tension was at its height as the forthcoming tests were most significant and no mistake could be made. The three delegations had prepared themselves with utmost care – day and night, rituals followed one after the other. At one point, a seven-year-old boy, Lungri Gyatso, was believed to be the reincarnation of the Ninth Panchen Lama. His intelligence and the fact that he was the son of Gongya Rinpoche and brother of the influential lama Chokshe of Kumbum monastery, were points in his favour. However, some doubt remained. Worried by the hesitation of a Tashilhunpo lama, the other lamas decided to make further investigations. Yet, when the child was presented with various objects, some of which had belonged to the Ninth Panchen Lama – silver bowls, five-pointed sceptres, bronze bells and a very ordinary wooden bead that His Holiness often wore – Lungri Gyatso identified them quickly. In particular he seized the wooden bead and raised it with both hands to his forehead in a devout gesture of blessing. From a purely spiritual point of view, the wooden bead is a symbol of affiliation to the lineage of Tsongkhapa, and a most precious treasure which the Panchen Lamas always wore. Unfortunately, in the following days the child fell ill and died.

Then the choice fell on Chökyong Tashi, the son of the village chief of Lede, in the district of Kumbum monastery. According to rumours, his mother had carried him for 14 months and he had shown exceptional qualities from childhood on. But as the family was preparing to become relatives of the Tenth Panchen Lama, Chökyong Tashi also died, of an unknown illness. After the child's death, the selection council focused its attention on the son of the chief of Derge. Two months later, this child also died of the after-effects of a strange illness.

Were these three deaths a coincidence? Whether they were or not, it was only then that the dignitaries decided to find out more about

Lobsang Tseten, the young peasant candidate from Wendu, in the Chinese province of Qinghai (the Tibetan Amdo). He was the son of Kongpo Tseten and Sönam Drölma, and had a deaf mute brother. Lobsang Tseten had taken part in different selections and had recognized objects that had belonged to the Ninth Panchen Lama several times. This time, in the imposing silence of the temple, under the sometimes sceptical, sometimes critical gaze of the religious people and Tibetan nobility, the child impressed everybody with his great wisdom. He behaved calmly and skilfully, answering all questions and touching the ring, the tea bowl, the jacket and the bead of the Panchen Lama. He had not been selected in the past because Lungri Gyatso had identified these objects more quickly than he had. The dignitaries who had been present at the time had then put him at the bottom of their list.

But on that day, everything was different. Lobsang Tseten suddenly noticed a man in the crowd and called out to him by his name. He was Kachen Pasang of the prefecture of Riwoche. The man had sung Tibetan opera to the Ninth Panchen Lama, though the child had, of course, never met him. Another detail was a point in his favour – at the end of the selection tests, he walked towards the personalities who were present, shook hands with some of them, nodded slightly to others and made affectionate gestures to the rest. At the time, nobody paid much attention to this, but then members of the selection council realized that the child had only greeted people who had belonged to the Ninth Panchen Lama's circle, or who had been among his servants; he had not shown much attention to those who had been strangers to him. Eventually people noticed that Lobsang Tseten talked with the same tones as the deceased, and made similar gestures. His Holiness had spoken with a slight stammer, so did the child, especially when he lost patience.

On that day, the Council of Khenpo and dignitaries of Tashilhunpo monastery were able to make a link between the child and the revelations of the lake of visions. The first two children who had been approached to become the Tenth Panchen Lama were born in the year of the Hare, and the third child in the year of the Dragon. Only Lobsang Tseten was born in the year of the Tiger. The three rabbits were thus destined to fall before the tiger. The elegant woman wearing a triangular headdress was no other than the Panchen Lama's deity, who was opening the curtain to greet His Holiness at his enthronement. In the course of their investigations, Ngulchu and his assessors discovered that the cells of Karang Bidho monastery, close to Wendu, resembled those described in the documents. And before the door of the abbot's lodgings stood two tall and vigorous trees, like those which had appeared on lake Lhamo Latso. All this proved that Lobsang Tseten was without doubt the reincarnation of the Ninth Panchen Lama.

The Tenth Panchen Lama was ordained a monk under the name of Lobsang Trinle Lhundrup Chökyi Gyaltsen. He was subject to the sole spiritual authority of the Dalai Lama but, following tradition, exercised no temporal power whatsoever.

The relation between the two reincarnations should have been quite cordial but since 1910, when the Thirteenth Dalai Lama fled to India, the Chinese, who were occupying Tibet at the time tried to cause trouble between them. They knew that by dividing the two spiritual authorities of Tibet, the Panchen Lama would in time become an easy prey. It was also true that Chökyi Nyima had not hesitated to show his ambition. When, in 1911, the Dalai Lama had secretly asked his help to fight the invaders, he had flatly refused. Later, his behaviour confirmed his greed for power and largely explained his opposition to Thubten Gyatso.[2] In 1944, seven years after the Ninth Panchen Lama's death, and eleven years after that of the Thirteenth Dalai Lama, ambiguities and divisions remained. When the Chinese arrived, the ground of understanding had thus been undermined for some time. The Kuomintang nationalists had therefore hurried to select candidates for the successor to the Ninth Panchen Lama from the region they occupied. But none of them could be officially recognized without the prior agreement of the Dalai Lama and the Tibetan government in Lhasa. This explains the unusually long time it took to confirm the reincarnation.

Meanwhile, many Tibetans in Amdo realized that many auspicious signs had accompanied the birth of Chökyi Gyaltsen, on 19 February 1938, in Wendu, a small isolated village on the banks of the Yellow River, west of the mountain of Mari. People had been celebrating *Losar*, the Tibetan New Year, as usual. As they had no radio, newspapers, schools or means of communication, the villagers were almost cut off from the world. They had no knowledge of the conflict between China and Japan, nor of the death of the Ninth Panchen Lama.

On the thirtieth day of the twelfth lunar month, the last day of the year, the villagers, like all Tibetans, had devoted the day to purification, cleaning their houses from top to bottom and washing their hair. In the nearest monastery, as in all other monastic places, monks performed the Tashi ceremony to the sombre sound of long horns. As traditionally required over generations, on the morning of Losar, the Tibetans put on new, or at least clean, clothes and tied new prayer flags to the roofs of houses and monasteries. Then the ceremonies – in which both religious and lay people took part – could start: rituals of best wishes (*mönlam**), purification of houses, sacred dances of the lamas (*tcham*), collective fasting and prayers. These would go on for a large part of the first month. On the third day of the new year, families, relatives and friends called on each other, exchanging best wishes and greetings (*tashi delek*) and sharing freshly baked biscuits (*khabse*) and Tibetan tea. The village council went to the farm of the chief of Wendu to burn mulberry branches. The astrologer lama had predicted an auspicious year, so men and women prayed for the prosperity of the community, the protection of their animals, and adequate crops.

On the morning of the fourth day, big snowflakes began to fall, but in the afternoon the sky suddenly cleared and a radiant sun appeared. The sight of the setting sun was even more magnificent; streaked with red, the sky looked as if it were radiating flames. Some elderly people, who had drunk more than was sensible, stumbled out of a house, laughing and singing. Once they had urinated, their hesitant steps led them to the edge of the village where children were playing. As they chattered away, one of the old men pointed his finger to the sky and, as if seized with sudden excitement, exclaimed: 'A rainbow! A rainbow!' 'A rainbow,' echoed the other old men.

The children stopped their games and in turn gazed at the sky. As they saw nothing, they all began to laugh and tease these men who were unable to hold their drink. Leaving his playmates, a 12-year-old boy proudly faced the strongest of the elderly people: '*Phola* [grandfather], you've drunk too much *tchang* [barley beer] and your eyes can't see anymore! Tell me where you see a rainbow.'

Another child joined in: 'No doubt you mistook those big black clouds for a rainbow!' Annoyed, the man who had been called *phola* clouted one of the children across the head and walked towards one of the houses in the middle of the village to tell his wife about his visions. He then started drinking again.[3]

The next day, the chief summoned the council to listen to the *phola* again. One of the council members, who had been on a pilgrimage to Kumbum monastery, remembered that Wendu had been the birthplace of two reincarnations, but that no rainbows had appeared in the sky on those occasions. He concluded that without doubt this must mean that a new, and more important, birth had just occurred. Wendu was one of only ten villages of the district of Xunhua inhabited by Tibetans. They were surrounded by other communities. As far back as the old people could remember, there had never been a renowned abbot in the district, or a prestigious official, or pundit or great master with any sort of influence on the life of the people of Wendu. Beyond the mountains, people did not know that thousands of Tibetans lived in Xunhua – a forgotten people, far away from the tragedies that shook the world at the time. But now Wendu was the village of the Panchen Lama.

In Lhasa, the fact that the Dalai Lama was still a minor gave rise to yet another confrontation. Since 1942, the Tibetan government had taken pains to revive the Foreign Affairs Office created by the Thirteenth Dalai Lama. However, the regent Taktra Rinpoche did not want to open up his country to the outside world, which at that time was devastated by war: the Japanese were still invading China, and British India was also threatened. Britain officially requested that arms be sent to Chiang Kai-shek's stronghold in Sichuan, via Tibet, but to no avail. Taktra stuck firmly to his isolationist position. However, the Sino-Japanese conflict increased communication between India and China by way of Tibet – to the substantial financial advantage, it must be acknowledged, of Tibetan, Nepalese and Indian traders.

On the diplomatic front, the British and Nepalese representatives enjoyed excellent relations with the Tibetan Foreign Affairs Office. Chinese troops had massed on the borders and the governors of provinces bordering on Tibet (Yunnan, Qinghai, Xikang) had even made a few incursions, but with no retaliation. However, tension between both countries was so great that a full-scale armed conflict could have broken out at any time. It was not surprising that all attempts to modernize Tibetan society failed.

In 1942, when the whole world was being ravaged by war, the Fourteenth Dalai Lama, Tenzin Gyatso, received a letter[4] from the president of the United States, Franklin D Roosevelt:

> As you know, the people of the United States, in association with those of 27 other countries, are now engaged in a war which has been thrust upon the world by nations bent on conquest who are intent on destroying freedom of thought, of religion and of action everywhere. The Allies are fighting today in defence of and for preservation of freedom, confident that we shall be victorious because our cause is just, our capacity is adequate, and our determination is unshakable.[5]

Perhaps spurred on by this, as well as by economic interests, Tibet tried once again to open up to the outside world. Because Calcutta had agreed to supply arms to the Tibetans, Taktra allowed an English school to open in Lhasa in 1944 (although it closed down soon afterwards, under pressure from the monks of Drepung and, in particular, Sera). But, in general, Taktra pursued a conservative policy which seemed completely inconsistent with the events shaking Tibet's neighbours. Nationalist China became an ally of the United States against Japan, but saw no reason to relinquish its policy of annexing Tibet. To this end, Chiang Kai-shek sent one of his counsellors, Shen Tsung-lien, to Lhasa. The British instructed Sir Basil Gould to represent them, but contacts moved no further.

At that same time, Reting Rinpoche, who had up to then maintained extremely courteous relations with his successor, began to interfere in affairs of State by trying to influence the appointment of officials. This displeased Taktra, who wanted to rule the country in his own way. Three years passed, during which the regent carried out a major reshuffle of the Tibetan administration, excluding Reting's men and replacing all those in key positions with his own supporters.

In December 1944, the Sera Che college, to which Reting

Rinpoche belonged, invited the former regent to unveil a newly renovated temple. Wild rumours flew around the town: it was reported that Taktra was about to resign, to the advantage of Reting (the secret agreement between the two men was once again mentioned) and that the country was on the brink of civil war. The confusion was made all the greater when the government welcomed Reting with all the splendour and ceremony due to a regent. After visiting the young Dalai Lama in the Potala, Reting Rinpoche had long discussions with his successor.

Reting Rinpoche's visit coincided with a series of events which brought the Che and Ngagpa colleges into conflict with the Tibetan government, and which could have plunged the whole country into violence.

It all started in the district of Lhundrup Dzong, about one day's journey north of Lhasa, and at that time ruled by secretary monks who appointed their representatives to administer the district. In 1944, Chömpel Thubten, a member of the monastic council, was elected. He then immediately commissioned his brother Chödrub Tendar to represent him in the district. The monks of the Che and Ngagpa colleges had established a system of loans on grain – at exorbitant interest rates – which had to be repaid at harvest time. The government then passed a law cancelling these debts, which in many cases had built up over the years. As crops had been extremely bad that year, the people of Lhundrup Dzong were all the more determined to refuse to give their share of crops. But the monks would hear nothing of it and, despite the law, seized not only all the grain but also the villagers' cattle and horses.

In the face of such injustice, the people formed a council and went to see the district commissionner, Chödrub Tendar, who ordered the monks of Sera to stop robbing the villagers and give them back their horses and cattle. Against all expectations, the monks refused to obey and they pounced on the district commissioner, giving him a beating. Chödrub Tendar died a few days later from his wounds.

Once informed of these events, the government of Lhasa could not leave matters alone and action had to be taken. The government appointed an investigating committee headed by the nobleman Sambo Tsewang Rigdzin, and the religious official Khenrab

Wangchug. When the committee arrived in the district, the monks had already returned to their monastery, and the investigators heard only the peasants' version of events. The report prompted the Kashag to respond immediately. They ordered the guilty monks – about 30 in number – to be handed over to Lhasa, but the abbots of the colleges involved remained deaf to the government's demands.

In 1945, the year of the Wood Bird, two days before the Tibetan New Year, the monastery was again notified of the Kashag's orders. The government requested the religious authorities of Sera to hand over the culprits before the start of *Mönlam Chenmo*. In their answer, the abbots of the Che and Ngagpa colleges expressed their surprise at the attitude of the Kashag. Deploring the fact that monks should be handed over to a civil court, they threatened not to attend the New Year ceremonies. Because their absence would have been prejudicial, the government therefore postponed the decision. Also during *Mönlam Chenmo*, Lhasa was teeming with monks on every street corner, so there was already a serious risk of trouble.

Three months later, the Kashag and the National Assembly went on the attack. They rightly thought that if the murderers of Chödrub Tendar went unpunished, similar actions might be repeated with complete impunity. A special committee was appointed and the abbots of the colleges involved were summoned. Eventually a trial took place and twenty-nine religious monks, including a Mongol (of which there were many in Sera), were found guilty, not only of the murder but also of having threatened to boycott the New Year religious ceremonies. The abbots were deposed and replaced, and the monks from Sera monastery were dismissed and their properties confiscated.

The government had managed to avoid a very serious crisis, made all the more so because, full of bitterness, Reting Rinpoche had left Sera while all this was happening. The Lhundrup Dzong incident was only a symptom of a more serious danger: some of the great monasteries, including Sera, were opposed to the regent and a rumour began to spread that Reting, with their support, would come back to power.

Meanwhile, Taktra Rinpoche had given his chamberlain nephew

the title *dzasa*, which conferred on him the same rank as members of the Kashag. The message was now clear: the regent had no intention of giving up power for quite some time. He now intervened in all matters concerning the administration, promotion and appointment of officials. In this, his chamberlain, Jampa Tharchin, was indispensable.

In Tibet, the regency has often been corrupt, and Taktra's was no exception. On his behalf, his nephew received bribes which enabled his small monastery of Talung Drag to flourish: the community increased from 20 to 115 monks, new buildings were erected and a very beautiful residence built for Taktra Rinpoche. The government, of course, had presented the regent with the estates necessary to provide for all these people. Talung Drag soon equalled Kundeling, one of the most renowned monastic institutions in the country. Distressing as it might be, the Dalai Lama was in effect supporting a completely corrupt administration, which the regent plundered throughout his rule, with the sole aim of enriching his entourage. In this respect Taktra Rinpoche's behaviour was little different from Reting Rinpoche's.

On the international scene, however, the government obtained some measure of recognition. In 1946, after World War II, a 'congratulatory mission' was sent to pay tribute to the winners of the war and a Tibetan delegation took part in the Pan-Asiatic Conference organized by the Congress Party of India, and was received by Mahatma Gandhi and Pandit Nehru in New Delhi.

After the Sera incident another series of mysterious events occurred. Reting Rinpoche returned to his monastery, but he kept a close eye on events and conspired behind the scenes. One night in 1946, as Lhalu Tsewang Dorje, Lungshar's son, was coming back late from a party at the home of his colleague Ngabo, he was set upon by gunmen. He managed to get away from his attackers, but his horse was killed.

In February 1947, at the time of the Butter Festival, when the regent and all the other high-ranking officials were due to take part in a procession through the streets of Lhasa to the Jokhang temple, all kinds of rumours circulated in the town, in particular one suggesting that there was to be a murder attempt on Taktra Rinpoche and all the dignitaries who were considered too close to him. As soon as the regent was informed, he cancelled the traditional public appearance – with good reason as it turned out, for it was later reported that an ambush had been laid for him on the way to the main temple.

Several days later a mysterious parcel arrived at the regent's secretariat. As it was unusually heavy, it was left in a corner. But when a puzzled servant wanted to open it, he heard a hissing noise. The man had just enough time to leave the room before an explosion damaged the walls and smashed the windows.

It was easy to see the hand of Reting behind these attacks. According to an investigating committee his attitude was extremely ambiguous, and he had retained close links with the Kuomintang. Although he had not been able to go to the 1946 Nanjing conference, to which he had been personally invited by Chiang Kai-shek, two delegates from the region of Kantse in eastern Kham, which was under Chinese domination, had probably spoken for him. The former regent had also sent a letter to Chiang Kai-shek requesting the Kuomintang's assistance in his plan to overthrow Taktra Rinpoche, whom he considered incapable of ruling Tibet.

When Taktra made enquiries, the British office in Lhasa and the Tibetan Bureau in Nanjing confirmed his fears: Reting was preparing a coup. On 14 April 1947, the regent, *kalön* lama Rampa, *kalön* Surkhang, Lhalu, Kabshöba and the Dalai Lama's personal chamberlain, Jampa Khenrab Tenzin, convened an extraordinary session. Immediately afterwards, Taktra Rinpoche ordered that Reting be arrested. *Kalön* Surkhang and Lhalu were assigned this terrible task. They left Lhasa that very evening, under the protection of an escort of some 60 armed men.

10

Arrival of the People's Liberation Army

Only temporarily is the strongest the best.
TENZIN GYATSO, FOURTEENTH DALAI LAMA

As the year of the Fire Pig (1947) began, the former regent Reting was arrested and imprisoned. A curfew was instituted, but every night sporadic firing disturbed the calm of the capital. Arms had been distributed to the young monks and regiments stationed in Lhasa, and the nobility became worried. Aristocrats did not hesitate to trade valuables with Nepalese traders passing through the capital, even exchanging silk and brocade robes for locally made clothes, before taking refuge in the Potala.

Lhasa became a high-risk town: shots were fired at anything that moved. On 20 April 1947, three days after Reting's arrest, the artillery was deployed and a cannon fired several times as a warning to the Sera college of Che. The monks retorted with makeshift rifles and a locally made cannon. While the soldiers of the Drapchi[1] garrison were looting houses, military reinforcements arrived from Gyantse. In town, food supplies were running out and the population feared there would be famine. The monks of Sera refused to surrender and continued to demand the liberation of Reting Rinpoche. In the meantime, the former regent's trial had begun. In his confessions, he acknowledged that he had appealed to Chiang Kai-shek to have a plane drop leaflets over Lhasa.

Eventually, one of the accused admitted conspiracy on a grand scale, including a plot to murder Taktra Rinpoche.

The government dispatched a group of 17 soldiers to keep watch over Reting Rinpoche's monastery. One night, the monks suddenly burst out of their rooms, stabbed the soldiers with daggers and killed them all. As soon as the Kashag heard the news, troops were sent to Reting monastery. The monastery was stormed and private lodgings invaded, ransacked and plundered; all the most precious and sacred artefacts were destroyed and even the golden letters were cut out of manuscripts. The soldiers set their horses loose in the monastery, and roared with laughter as they tried to scoop up thousands of Chinese silver coins which they then tried to stuff into their *chuba* (Tibetan dress). They were so heavily laden that some of them could hardly stand; their knees sagged when the officers ordered them to stand to attention. These ruffians did not even spare the fruit trees and flowers that Reting Rinpoche had so cherished. The most beautiful trees were uprooted and replanted haphazardly elsewhere. As the government had, of course, confiscated all the former regent's properties, the soldiers appropriated a heap of gold coins and some 800 silk and brocade costumes.

Only on 29 April did the monks of Sera Che show signs of weakening. They took out their protective deities and, disgusted by their failure to protect them, stripped them of their brocade robes and displayed them on the roofs of the college. They then left the monastery and fled into the hills. Some of them headed towards Reting monastery, but most of them were recaptured and shot.

Inevitably the Kashag consulted the Nechung oracle. It was suggested that the former regent should be blinded, in the same way that Lungshar had been, but Taktra Rinpoche turned down this suggestion. During a brief trance, Kutenla (another name given to the Nechung oracle) beat his breast several times and threw barley corns into the air.

Before too long, Reting Rinpoche fell seriously ill. He complained of feeling extremely cold in his gaol. Witnesses reported that inhuman cries, similar to those of wolves baying at the moon, could be heard coming from the Potala. The more sensitive said that the wails struck right at the heart of the people of Lhasa. It is also said that the Fourteenth Dalai Lama, then 12 years old, hastened to visit Reting Rinpoche.

A few days later, on 8 May 1947, the former regent, victim of a regime he had fully supported and from which he had gained so much, died in jail. A rumour spread that Reting Rinpoche had been poisoned and his genitals crushed. The following street song accuses Lungshar's son of killing Reting and being rewarded with the appointment of magistrate of Lhasa.

> It was a crime to kill Reting, but wait!
> Crime has a reward in Lhasa:
> The post of magistrate.

Theatres staged a play in which the former regent was murdered. It also featured spicy details about his taste for ephemeral pleasures, easy women, weapons and vulgar stories.

On 18 May, Taktra Rinpoche ordered that the other plotters, whose main leaders had been detained in barracks near the Norbu Lingka, be punished. Reting Rinpoche's brother was flogged in public with 250 lashes. Some 30 monks from the Sera college of Che were also beaten and then handed over to their families. Most of Reting Rinpoche's properties were sold at auction, making millions of *sang* for the Finance Office. Several weeks after Reting's death, gold dishes, brocade clothes and numerous other valuables which had been stolen by the soldiers, appeared in the markets and on every street corner in Lhasa.

Taktra Rinpoche was no better than Reting Rinpoche, the only difference being that the former was much older, although up until this time Taktra Rinpoche's advanced years had not brought him the wisdom spoken of by Gyalwa Gendün Gyatso, the Second Dalai Lama:

> A donkey cannot have horns on his head;
> Therefore, is it possible for each object to have real
>   existence?
> From the tiniest particles to the omniscient wisdom of
>   Enlightenment,
> All things are completely lacking in proper and ultimate
>   nature.
> This is the essential message of the Buddha.

This is the song of Namkhai Naldjor, the yogi of space, expressed here in Tibet, the land of calming herbs.

> You don't need reason
> To hear the whisper of wisdom,
> To understand the eternal 'Ah',
> To know that appearances are made in the mind.[2]

During his years at the Kumbum monastery in Amdo, Lobsang Tseten, the reincarnation of the Ninth Panchen Lama, shared the lively games of the other young monks of his age, which sometimes lasted for hours. One was with knucklebones, which were first dried, then polished and painted in different colours. To his young companions he sometimes said casually: 'Let us enjoy our games while we can, for I won't be here for more than two years ...' But often he would sit with the novices and say: 'Now listen, I'm going to teach you some holy scriptures ...' and launch into such lengthy discourses that even passing monks would stop to listen to him. Lobsang Tseten also made protection knots for them.[3]

The teachers would not, however, allow their disciples to play in the monks' quarters or in the *geshe*'s prayer room in this way. One day, Lobsang Tseten climbed onto the bookshelves and, just able to reach the highest, took down a very old manuscript and endlessly repeated: 'So, I'm going to teach the scriptures, I'm going to teach the scriptures ...' But at the time he couldn't even count up to 30. Although the bookshelves contained many books about spirituality, he chose a text on Tashilhunpo every time.

The dignitaries of the monastery and the young boy's parents quickly faced up to the facts: Lobsang Tseten had qualities beyond those of common people. During the selection period, he had twice visited Kumbum and had seen *tulku** Gyenag Rinpoche, who had met Chökyi Nyima, the previous Panchen Lama, several times. Gyenag Rinpoche remembered how the Panchen Lama had invited him to sit beside him at a religious ceremony, although his rank did not permit him to do that. 'You must take part in the ceremony', he had said, 'for you will have to perform it one day.' A few days later, when Chökyi Nyima left for Labrang monastery, Gyenag travelled with him. Also, when the lama had expressed his wish to go on a pilgrimage to Lhasa, Chökyi Nyima had answered: 'You do not need to go there; we will see each other again very soon.' Deeply affected by Chökyi Nyima's death, Gyenag Rinpoche again remembered those words when he was entrusted with young Lobsang Tseten.

The Fourteenth Dalai Lama, Tenzin Gyatso, spoke of his own early years as follows:

> All in all, it was not an unhappy childhood. The kindness of my teachers will always remain with me as a memory I shall cherish. They gave me the religious knowledge which has always been and will always be my greatest comfort and inspiration, and they did their best to satisfy what they regarded as a healthy curiosity in other matters. But I grew up with hardly any knowledge of worldly affairs, and it was in that state, when I was 16, that I was called upon to lead my country against the invasion of communist China.[4]

The Kuomintang declared that the final choice of the Panchen Lama had to be made official by drawing lots from the Golden Urn, according to the imperial edict promulgated by the Manchu emperor Qianlong, who had wanted to put an end to the troubles generated by the appointment of reincarnations of the Dalai Lamas, Panchen Lamas and other heirs of great Tibetan Buddhist lineages. The text comprised 29 points:

> The Dalai Lama and the Panchen Lama are the foremost disciples of Tsongkhapa. They have been ruling over the school of the 'Yellow Hats' [Gelugpa] for centuries and they are deeply respected by Mongolians and Tibetans. Latterly, the methods used to select their reincarnations have not been appropriate, thus weakening their spiritual significance. In addition personal preferences have induced members of the khan [Mongolian chiefs],[5] princely or ducal families, appointments which have become nothing but hereditary benefits. Buddhist law does not acknowledge such principles …
> … We, Protector of the 'Yellow Hats', in our wish to amend abuses, which have persisted for too long, have ordered that a

Golden Urn be made, and we have appointed officials to take it to Lhasa and put it in the Jokhang temple. When, according to the custom, an incarnation of the Dalai Lama, the Panchen Lama or any other great lama is to be found, a selection will be made among candidates showing the appropriate signs; tablets bearing the name and date of birth of each one of them, in Manchu, Mongolian and Tibetan, will be inserted in the urn. Religious services will be celebrated over seven days. Then, in front of the statue of Shakyamuni, a tablet will be drawn from the urn, in the presence of the *amban* and publicly presented to the audience; the candidate selected in this way will be the reincarnation ... If only one candidate is found, two tablets should be placed in the urn: one bearing his name, the other one with no inscription whatsoever. If the blank tablet is drawn, the child will not be able to be recognized as the reincarnation ...

Since 1944, Chökyi Nyima's circle had considered young Lobsang Tseten the reincarnation of the master of Tashilhunpo. In June 1949, when the power of the Kuomintang was faltering under the thrust of the communists, the Chinese authorities decided to take the opportunity and intervene, informing the Tibetan government that they approved of this selection. They even specified that, in accordance with Buddhist principles, they had presented Lobsang Tseten with a large quantity of gold, medicines and numerous gifts from Tibet.

The Kashag asked that the child be brought 'as soon as possible' from the province of Qinghai to the Tibetan capital, with all the other candidates. The Kashag was particularly concerned about Tseten's age. The Ninth Panchen Lama had died on 1 December 1937 and the child had been born on 19 February 1938, just two months and 18 days later. The members of the Kashag thought that a gap of at least nine months, the duration of a pregnancy, was necessary!

On the contrary, those who followed Chökyi Nyima declared that the choice of Lobsang Tseten was in accordance with Buddhist doctrine. In their view, the body may die but the mind remains immortal. Therefore, even in his lifetime, a *tulku* may be reincarnated in the body of another person, in accordance with his natural affinity to someone met in a previous life and in the best interests of the dissemination of Buddhism. There had been several cases of mystics who had chosen a pregnant woman as their future mother and begun to transfer their consciousness into the embryo before they died.

Eager to have an agent in Tibet, the nationalist government gave its full support to Lobsang Tseten. A decree of 3 June 1949 stated: 'The child from Qinghai, Lobsang Tseten, has a pure mind, full of wisdom. The investigations we made proved that he is the true reincarnation of the Ninth Panchen Lama. Therefore he will be exempted from the lottery and, by special authorization, will become the Tenth *Panchen Erdeni*.' Once again the Chinese attempted to substitute themselves for the Tibetan authorities.

As soon as the announcement was made, the Kuomintang sent a representative to Kumbum to preside over the enthronement ceremonies, which took place on 10 August of that same year in the large assembly hall of the monastery. In accordance with tradition, the shaving ceremony was performed and Lobsang Tseten was given his religious name, Chökyi Gyaltsen. The only response of the Kashag was to order the expulsion of the Chinese representative in Lhasa and of some 300–400 residents, some of whom were probably communist agents.

In China, the nationalist government was living its last moments. Chiang Kai-shek had already fled with the fabulous treasures of the Imperial Palace and, with his most faithful companions, boarded a warship headed for the island of Taiwan. At the same time, many manufacturers and bankers fled by boat to Hong Kong. As a Western journalist described it, China then began to swarm with 'tiny yellow men in green dress, walking silently in straw or rope-soled sandals in a single file, in small groups along the pavements ... Uniforms spattered with mud ... Japanese helmets ... old rifles, old machine guns, worn out sandals, faded uniforms the colour of grass juice, a guerilla army out of the remotest Chinese countryside. No lorry, no cart ...'

In September 1949, the Chinese army, met with little enthusiasm, entered Tibetan territory and seized Qinghai, and Chökyi Gyaltsen, then 11 years old. The Ninth Panchen Lama's reincarnation, imposed by the nationalists, thus became not only the youngest political hostage of communist China, but also, for the new leader of Beijing, a wonderful tool with which to blackmail and exert constant pressure on Tibet.

A few days later, Mao Tse-tung exclaimed: 'The Chinese people are standing tall.' On a pole erected for the occasion in the middle of Tiananmen Square, fluttered the red silk flag stamped with five stars. 'The East is red,' Mao also declared. He was not completely wrong: in Vietnam, at the head of his communist troops, Ho Chi Minh had freed his country from French colonialism; Dutch settlers had left Jakarta (then Batavia) and Indonesia had proclaimed independence; and a 'revolutionary' spirit stirred Korea, where a Chinese-trained communist, Kim Il Sung, was already imposing his rule on the north of the peninsula. War, bloodshed and allegedly decadent capitalism benefited the communist revolution: Lenin must have been turning jubilantly in his grave. The world was changing: India had become independent and British support was waning.

It was not long before Beijing made clear its intention to 'free Tibet'. The Panchen Lama's circle rallied to the revolutionaries and praised 'the great wisdom and courage' of Mao Tse-tung. In Tibet, there were only 8,500 men, some 50 artillery pieces, 250 mortars and 20 machine guns to face the Red Army, and within two weeks the country's main defence force was destroyed. With inadequate means of defending themselves, the Tibetans inevitably turned to the person who had been the supreme guardian of their State since the seventeenth century, the Dalai Lama.

Because of the danger posed by China, it was decided that Tenzin Gyatso should assume power before he came of age. When the regent Taktra bowed to the adolescent, his face shone with an intense light. Tenzin Gyatso leaned towards the old man, who then laid a long *khata* on his knees. The ceremony took place on 17 November 1950, the year of the Iron Tiger in the Tibetan calendar. Lhasa welcomed the new ruler with noisy celebrations.

Young Tenzin Gyatso's first political action was to appoint two strong characters – Lobsang Tashi, a monk, and Lukhangwa, a lay-man – as prime ministers. Aware of the communist threat, the two men advised the young ruler to guard against the possibility of an attack on Lhasa. The Dalai Lama had heard from his elder brother, then an abbot in Kumbum monastery, that communist troops had committed terrible crimes against monks in Amdo, so he agreed to send to Sikkim part of the Treasure, gold and silver ingots.[6]

The Dalai Lama also remembers at that time the terrible blow struck by the international community. Although the issue of Tibet had been raised at the United Nations General Assembly – at the instigation of El Salvador – and the government of Tibet was urgently asking for an investigating committee to be sent, the country received no real help. The British seemed resigned to China's rule over Tibet; India's position was uncomfortable ...

The Dalai Lama came to realize that it was impossible for a nation to survive in complete isolation, even one on the Roof of the World. The modernization programme initiated by his predecessor was now showing its limitations, because the Thirteenth Dalai Lama had not thought it necessary to become a member of the League of Nations, or to send ambassadors to various world capitals. Tibet was thus handed over to the red hordes of communist China, the very hordes that were the cause of so much bloodshed in their own country.

Tibet's isolation quickly brought the Kashag to one conclusion: the young ruler must be protected, especially since the Panchen Lama was in the hands of the Chinese communists. Tenzin Gyatso left the capital to seek refuge in Yatung, some 200 miles from Lhasa, on the border with Sikkim. He established his government in the monastery of Dunkhar, which overlooked the verdant Chumbi valley.

In Kumbum monastery, the young Panchen Lama was totally manipulated by the communists and religious dignitaries in the pay of Beijing. From then on the education of Chökyi Nyima bore the imprint of China, now under Mao Tse-tung who had taken the place of Chiang Kai-shek.

Witnesses reported that even though the Panchen Lama spent most of his time studying, he was aware of everything happening around him. In the summer of 1949 – a few weeks before the communist invasion of Tibet – nationalist agents and Ma Pu-fang frequently visited Kumbum to urge the Panchen Lama's family and the Council of Khenpo to entrust the child to Ma Pu-fang so that he could protect him and take him away to Taiwan. The meetings were held in secret, with all those taking part locked in a room without even being able to ask the servants for a cup of tea. The discussions often lasted late into the night.

The Panchen Lama, then barely 11, showed growing curiosity. Determined to know what was going on at these meetings, he burst into the room one day. A heavy silence fell around the table. Chökyi Gyaltsen sat down beside his mother and asked: 'What are you talking about?' One of his close counsellors answered: 'President Chiang wants us all to leave for Taiwan. We are discussing whether or not we should obey his order ...' 'Who must accompany Ma?' the young Panchen Lama asked. 'All of us, but mainly you', said the counsellor. Chökyi Gyaltsen suddenly stood up. He was furious. Pointing his finger at the man's nose, he told him: 'This is my concern. Why don't you discuss this with me? What gives you the right to decide in my place?'

The man, who apparently played an important part in these encounters, was astonished by this reaction. Although a close friend and protector of the young Panchen Lama, he had considered him too young to understand politics and so it had never crossed his mind to consult him on this matter.

The Panchen Lama requested that from then on, all issues relating to his future be discussed with him, otherwise he would not obey them any more. Increasingly angry, the child stammered out words that were charged with dire consequences: 'If you decide to leave with Ma, I'll stay in Kumbum monastery ... If you stay here, then I'll go with Ma ...' The child's father interfered. At first he spoke harshly: 'Sit down, Tseten. Don't be rude.' Then he affectionately drew the child to his side. From that day on, the Panchen Lama was allowed to take part in the adults' conversations, and never again did they discuss his future without his involvement.

Eventually – to escape from Ma Pu-fang, the nationalists and the communists – the Tenth Panchen Lama and his circle left Kumbum monastery in the dead of night. They moved back for the time being to Xiangride, which in 1780 had been offered by Emperor Gaozong to the Sixth Panchen Lama, just before his death.

As soon as the communists seized power in China in 1949, a telegram of congratulations was sent immediately on behalf of

Chökyi Gyaltsen, addressed to Chairman Mao of the Central People's Government, and Zhu De, commander-in-chief of the People's Liberation Army:

> The intelligence and audacity of the tactics implemented by Your Excellencies have been able to save the country and its people. The whole nation rejoiced everywhere where the Army of Justice appeared.
>
> Having received favours from China all his life, the Panchen Lama expresses his gratitude and respect.
>
> For 20 years I have fought relentlessly for the integrity of Tibetan sovereignty. I feel guilty for not having achieved my aim. Therefore I am staying in Qinghai, but I await your orders to return to Tibet.
>
> It is a good thing that under Your Excellencies' leadership, the north-west of China was liberated and the Central People's Government established. Brave and fair men will all feel encouraged. We can now look forward to peace and happiness for the people, hope for the recovery of our country and await the liberation of Tibet.
>
> On behalf of all Tibetans, the Panchen Lama wishes to remind Your Excellencies of his highest consideration and most sincere support, love and esteem.

Mao Tse-tung and the other great figure of the revolution, Zhu De, answered the message:

> We were pleased to receive your telegram dated 1 October.
>
> The Tibetan nation likes the motherland and opposes foreign invasion. Unhappy with the reactionary policy of the nationalist government, it willingly becomes part of the new united and prosperous China, in which all nationalities co-operate in equality.
>
> The Central People's Government can certainly fulfil the hopes of the Tibetan people. I hope that you will work hard, with all the Tibetans who love their motherland, to contribute to the liberation of Tibet and to union between Tibetans and Chinese Han.[7]

Some time later a report by Ngabo Ngawang Jigme, the governor of Kham in Chamdo, arrived in Lhasa. It advised negotiating with the Chinese in order to avoid an invasion, the consequences of which would be disastrous for the country. It could be said that Ngabo was a hostage of the communists, as was the young Panchen Lama, who was about to turn twelve.

Negotiations with the Chinese began in Beijing on 29 April 1951, the year of the Iron Hare. Shortly afterwards, on 23 May, under duress, the Tibetan delegation, led by Ngabo Ngawang Jigme, signed a Seventeen-Point 'Agreement', to the bottom of which a makeshift seal of the Dalai Lama had been affixed in Beijing.

When Mao heard the 'Agreement' had been signed, it is reported that he exclaimed: 'It is a victory, but it is only a first step. The second step will be to get it implemented. That will take a lot of hard work.'

The 'Agreement' handed over the whole of Tibet to China: the Land of Snows no longer existed as a sovereign nation. Some extracts of the 'Agreement' clearly set out the Chinese communists' intention: 'The Tibetan people shall be united and drive out the imperialist aggressive forces from Tibet ...' (Yet there had been no other permanent foreign presence in Tibet other than representatives of friendly nations like Nepal and Britain since 1912, when Chinese forces had been driven out of the country.) 'The Local Government of Tibet shall actively assist the People's Liberation Army to enter Tibet and consolidate the national defences' (Point 2). As for Point 8, it specified that 'Tibetan troops will be reorganized step by step into the People's Liberation Army, and become a part of the national defence forces of the Central People's Government.' And China did not forget to slip in a few empty promises, notably that they would not interfere in the 'established status, function and powers' of the Dalai Lama, and they would respect religious freedom. In matters relating to reforms they said 'there would be no compulsion on the part of the Central Authorities'.

Helpless and devoid of friends, Tibet had no option but to submit to Beijing's dictates, even though the government of Lhasa completely opposed the Seventeen-Point 'Agreement'. In August, the Dalai Lama returned to Lhasa.

Over the following months, Mao's troops settled in Tibet, a strategic area considered vital for the defence of the southern and western parts of China. They had already captured Chamdo and detained the governor of Kham, Ngabo Ngawang Jigme. On 26 October 1951, 3,000 men of the Eighteenth Army entered Lhasa. The previous year, thousands of miles away, Chinese communists had flooded Korea: the American and Allied forces, gathered under the flag of the United Nations, had been almost overwhelmed by 800,000 'volunteers' in a war that was to last three long years.

Afraid of being surrounded, Mao decided to hasten the annexation of Tibet. Simultaneously, 'counter-revolutionary' paranoia seized China: as a result hundreds of thousands were executed and over 2 million men and women being were sent to over 1,000 *laogai*, the so called 're-education through work' camps, where Mao and his accomplices confined people they considered undesirable.

11

The Panchen Lama's
Formative Years

Under escort, the Tenth Panchen Lama and his entourage eventually went back to Kumbum, where the child at last found a more suitable place for his studies. He worked under the supervision of two teachers. In the morning, after chanting and breakfast, he was instructed in the Tibetan language and guided through Buddhist scriptures. The lama who taught him grammar used the *Thirty Songs*,[1] which he wanted his pupil to learn by heart so as to receive a better understanding of the fundamentals and learn how to use them advisedly.

Chökyi Gyaltsen had no trouble whatsoever with this task, but he found it much more difficult to memorize several pages of the holy scriptures. The child preferred less austere activities: he liked to learn rather than recite parrot fashion. One day he found works by the Sixth Dalai Lama, Rigdzin Tsangyang Gyatso, and roared with laughter, alone in his room, as he read one of his poems:

> Garrulous parrot, please behave,
> You are not the thrush in the willow grove
> Only she can sing at the top of her voice.

The morning sessions were quite an ordeal because, according to Buddhist principles, teachers were allowed to criticize, scold and even beat their pupils. Even such august reincarnations as the Dalai Lama and the Panchen Lama, called the 'Sun' and the 'Moon', were not exempt from this rule – except that, before the teacher punished them, he had to bow. The Panchen Lama had never been afraid when thousands of believers bowed to him, but when one of his masters bowed, a terrible shiver ran through his body. Chökyi Gyaltsen often remembered the saying:

> Do not fear gods,
> Do not fear ghosts,
> Only fear your teachers
> When they bow to you.

A few years later, the Panchen Lama described his childhood years in the monastery of Kumbum:

> I have no memory whatsoever of my teacher ever beating me. He merely pinched my ear or sometimes slapped my shaven head when he was angry and blamed me for not being able to recite sacred texts. But the slap was not strong enough to hurt me. However, he had a very particular technique for hitting me: with his hand slightly bent, he hit with a 'wham' that sounded clear and loud. I found that funny, and sometimes I even hoped for a second slap. I could not refrain from laughing at this stupid idea, which made him all the more furious. But he was a good man. When he was angry, he lost patience and shouted, his beard was dishevelled and his eyes bulged. He sometimes brandished his fist in front of us, but I was not afraid. I even thought him extremely amusing ...

In the afternoon, calligraphy was another kind of torture for Chökyi Gyaltsen. The traditional method of learning to write Tibetan consists of transcribing words on a board made of hard, but relatively flexible wood – walnut or birch, for instance. One side is painted black and varnished. The child dusts it with white powder and then traces each line with a bamboo stick-pen, following the teacher's example. When the board is covered with signs, the child cleans it and the operation is endlessly repeated. The Panchen Lama had a young monk to help him with the cleaning of his board. The teachers were strict and Chökyi Gyaltsen spent many hours at this task. It takes two or three long years to master the method before being able to write on real paper.

Sometimes the teachers were called away on other duties. On

such occasions, when the children were left alone to get on with their calligraphy, the young Panchen Lama immediately left his board and ran down the long alleys of the monastery until he was out of breath. When he thought he was safely out of reach of teachers and parents, he slowed down and quietly explored the large rooms, temples and monks' quarters.

Sometimes he left the monastery to stroll along the village lanes and visit the shops and the Muslim bazaar. He enjoyed observing the Tibetan pilgrims turning their prayer wheels and endlessly counting the beads of their *mala*.* On these occasions, turning his back on his teachers, Chökyi Gyaltsen liked to mix with ordinary people and observe their lives. He shared with them the traditional bowl of Tibetan tea, which a woman would inevitably offer him with a bright smile, sticking out her tongue to greet him. He made conversation with ordinary monks as well as with lay people, peasants and shepherds, trying to understand their lives and their often wretched circumstances. The Tenth Panchen Lama confessed one day: 'Chatting is an art form.' But this did not prevent him from taking his studies very seriously.

In the evening, he followed the Kumbum monastery's very strict rules. But, as a distinguished guest, he did enjoy a little more freedom than the other monks. Once he had taken part in the endless rituals and eaten dinner, he was free to call on his parents and spend some time chatting with the officials of his administration. When he was just 13 years old, Chökyi Gyaltsen took part in his first significant political meeting. Prior to the signing of the Seventeen-Point 'Agreement', the Panchen Lama and his entourage – 45 people altogether – were invited to take part in the preliminary negotiations. As a result, they flew to Beijing on 27 April 1951.

According to witnesses, to start with he seemed shy and ill at ease. Clad in a saffron-yellow satin tunic, the young Panchen Lama was welcomed by Chou En-lai, who wore a dark-coloured Mao suit, and presented him with a very long silk *khata*. It is reported that they had a long conversation about the Chinese revolution, the future of Tibet, the imminent peace conference, the visit in Beijing, unity between the Tibetan and Han people and relations between the Dalai Lama and the Panchen Lama. The Chinese leader even discussed with the young boy the trivialities of everyday life. Gradually Chökyi Gyaltsen relaxed and with his smile and wisdom, brightened up the encounter with his communist hosts.

At the table, Chou En-lai proved to be a lively and refined man, explaining to Chökyi Gyaltsen the gastronomic features of the various dishes. When the interpreter could not find the Tibetan equivalent of a culinary term, Chou En-lai changed the subject, emphasizing with roars of laughter, that the interpreter was in more trouble than they were. At one stage, the communist leader suddenly stopped talking and exclaimed: 'I suggest we keep silent for a while, to give our interpreter companion time to eat.'

Unfortunately, the communists had only one thing in mind: the manipulation of one of Tibet's religious leaders. The first encounter between the Panchen Lama and Mao Tse-tung took place during this same visit to Beijing. On the evening of 23 May, Mao gave a banquet to celebrate the signing of the Seventeen-Point 'Agreement', and made a short speech. Afterwards the Panchen Lama was pushed onto the stage to make a toast and deliver his first political speech: 'The issue of nationality in China and the Tibetan issue, left in abeyance for so many years, have been successfully solved under the leadership of Chairman Mao. The liberation of Tibet is a happy event in the great multiracial family of China ...'

Chökyi Gyaltsen left Beijing with his escort on 2 June. They arrived back in the monastery of Kumbum in Qinghai on 26 June.

That night, in his bedroom, the Panchen Lama may have been inspired by this text by the Third Dalai Lama, Sönam Gyatso:

So many people believe that a master should be venerated only if he displays obvious qualities. They say: 'I follow him to listen to his teaching of the Dharma, and not because of him', or 'I do not see anything extraordinary about him, so why should I revere him?' What nonsense! Surely, even though our parents may be ordinary people, we must recognize their goodness, for it is a source of great benefit. But if we do not value them, we generate only pain and confusion. The same applies to our attitude towards a guru.[2]

In Lhasa, 1952, the year of the Water Dragon, began with great anxiety for the Dalai Lama, for Taktra Rinpoche had just died. The Dalai Lama presided over a ceremony attended by thousands of monks, and consecrated the funerary *stupa* of his old teacher. On the political front, Tenzin Gyatso did not approve of the speech the Panchen Lama had made in Beijing after the signing of the Seventeen-Point 'Agreement', but he understood very well the difficult situation in which Chökyi Gyaltsen was placed at the time:

> I sincerely regretted those old differences, and I still do. I do not think he was allowed to forget them entirely, because of his continuous Chinese teaching. If he and his followers had done so, Tibet's disaster might have been less complete. The Chinese were trying to do in our generation exactly what they had failed to do in the last; and this time, it has certainly been an advantage to them to have a Tibetan religious leader in whose name they can make their proclamations. But the Panchen Lama cannot be personally blamed. No boy who grew up under such concentrated, constant alien influence could possibly retain his own free will.[3]

He had sent him a telegram dated 19 July 1951:

> Auspicious divinations have assured me that the previous Panchen Lama has been truly reincarnated in you. Therefore I have made up my mind to announce that you will settle in the monastery of Tashilhunpo. We wish you a speedy return and beg you to inform us of the route you are planning to take.

On 5 September, Tenzin Gyatso informed the Panchen Lama that he was sending lay emissaries and high-ranking religious dignitaries from Drepung, Ganden and Sera to meet him and that he eagerly wished to welcome him in the Potala. The delegation reached Kumbum in December; the Council of Khenpo was immediately given notice that people all the way from Kumbum to Lhasa were liable to be asked to do unpaid work (corvée). In effect the villagers were forced to undertake the transportation of people and the goods of trade caravans and travellers. On 19 December the Panchen

Lama left Kumbum for the Tibetan capital, where he arrived after a particularly painful four-month journey.

Lhasa welcomed the 14-year-old adolescent with great fervour. Monks crowded the route taken by the caravan. Chökyi Gyaltsen was accompanied by an escort of numerous Chinese officials and the senior leaders of the Council of Khenpo. His first encounter with the Dalai Lama, his senior by three years, was particularly tense. There is no doubt that the Chinese would have preferred the Panchen Lama to sit at the same level as the Dalai Lama, but Chökyi Gyaltsen felt a very deep respect for Buddhist traditions. In the course of an informal meeting, the two reincarnations tackled the differences which had brought their predecessors into conflict, and resolved to base their relations on new ground. Unfortunately, at the end of the Tenth Panchen Lama's stay, his retinue and counsellors prevented the traditional exchange of silk scarves (khata). Just before his departure, the Panchen Lama somehow managed to exchange a few more words with Tenzin Gyatso in his residence, the Norbu Lingka.

Chökyi Gyaltsen left Lhasa on 6 June 1952 and headed for the monastery of Tashilhunpo, which he reached 17 days later. The monks welcomed their master with great enthusiasm. He had only just settled in when the Council of Khenpo appointed a new teacher, Ngulchu Rinpoche, who was entrusted with the important task of furthering Chökyi Gyaltsen's education, which until then had been somewhat interrupted.

Ngulchu Rinpoche was very different from the Panchen Lama's two previous teachers. His great charisma attracted the respect of all the monks of Tashilhunpo. But the carefree days when Chökyi Gyaltsen was able to run away from the monastery were at an end. His time was now fully dedicated to the study of sacred texts, prayers, meditation, long exercises in calligraphy and recitations.

The atmosphere in Tashilhunpo was completely different from Kumbum. Chinese civilian or military officials frequently called on the young Panchen Lama to discuss with him the future of Tibet. Sometimes he attended meetings of the Shigatse Work Division Committee.

Tenzin Gyatso, meanwhile, was completing his spiritual training, alongside his temporal duties. They both involved the study of *Dharma*.*

> Masters of present times, lineage of gurus, Three Jewels,[4] peaceful or angry gods and goddesses of meditation, all the protectors of Buddhist Law, and guardians of Truth, I call for you in my prayer. Come forward in a cloud of deep wisdom and great compassion. Teach the Law like the growling of a dragon. Let your power transform into a stream of mystical realizations. May your blessings inspire my thoughts, and may I mature to achieve spiritual freedom.[5]

The Dalai Lama also initiated a number of reforms. The young ruler considered that Buddhism was totally incompatible with the unequal sharing out of riches. To put his plan into action, Tenzin Gyatso set up a 50-member committee to examine a series of propositions which would be presented to the National Assembly.

In Tibet, most land belonged to the State and peasants received a plot in return for a lease. To pay their rent, some peasants gave part of their crops to the government and this formed the main source of State stocks for the monasteries; others gave their labour. Neither the taxes nor the corvée system were unfair; furthermore, because the land belonged to the State, it could be passed on to succeeding generations. Peasants were also allowed to rent, mortgage or sell their plot, but this seldom happened.

The first reforms the Dalai Lama intended to tackle concerned privately owned properties, or land that had become private property when it had long ago been allotted to families of the Tibetan aristocracy or to monasteries. Tenzin Gyatso planned to requisition these estates, in return for compensation, and turn them into new State properties which would then be redistributed to peasants, mainly to State farmers, to achieve greater social equality; but the young Dalai Lama would not have time to both implement and experiment. However, he did decide to tackle the issue of taxes. From time immemorial the Tibetan State had determined the contribution of each province. In addition, also from time immemorial, the provincial authorities had levied additional unofficial taxes to meet their expenses. No legal mechanism existed in Tibet to determine precisely how much these deductions should amount to, let alone to abolish them. After consulting with the Kashag and the reform committee, the young ruler prohibited such unfair practices. This was met with great dissatisfaction, but Tenzin Gyatso had no intention of stopping there.

Over a number of years, the Tibetan government had been granting loans to peasants who were having difficulties. But a minority had taken advantage of the system to increase their riches by way of subtle embezzlement. When Tenzin Gyatso got to hear of these abuses he first defined three categories of loan beneficiaries: those who could pay back neither the capital nor the interest; those whose annual income was too low to reimburse the interest but who could possibly repay the capital, at least by instalments; and, finally, those who had grown rich through uncontrolled loans, who were to repay both the capital and the interest.

To Tenzin Gyatso, these reforms were essential, for they would enable Tibetans to enter into the modern age and give them more equality and a fairer life. But the sudden arrival of the communists upset all these plans.

In 1954, the Chinese government invited the Dalai Lama and the Panchen Lama to Beijing, just after Tenzin Gyatso had received his full ordination during the *Mönlam* festival of the year of the Wood Horse. The ceremony had taken place in the temple of Jokhang, in front of the statue of Chenrezig. When the people of Lhasa heard of his imminent departure, many rumours circulated. The Tibetans were extremely worried and openly opposed the departure, but to no avail. Tenzin Gyatso attended a great farewell ceremony on the banks of the river Khyi-Chu, in the presence of all the members of the government. Many thousands of believers prayed. In Shigatse, too, similar ceremonies took place. Because the master of Tashilhunpo had been away from his land for such a long time, the people, especially the monks, were afraid they would never see him return.

The Dalai Lama left Lhasa on 11 July, with an escort of Chinese troops led by General Zhang Jingwu. The Panchen Lama set off five days later, escorted by General Fan Ming and his men. The two lamas met in Shanxi on 1 September. There they boarded a special train to Beijing, where Vice-President Zhu De and Chou En-lai were waiting for them. To prevent unsupervised communication between the two lamas, Tenzin Gyatso and his retinue were accommodated close to the bridge of the Imperial River, while the Panchen Lama and his circle were put up at the Palace of the Unencumbered View. On the evening of their arrival, a banquet was given in their honour, presided over by Zhu De. The welcome speech left no doubt whatsoever about China's views on Tibet. Although Zhu De's speech was extremely courteous, he rejoiced at the return of Tibetans to 'the motherland'.

The first encounter with Mao Tse-tung took place on 11 September. The interpreter, a Tibetan from Kham, was communist Phütso Wangye, who had worked in the Chinese educational services in Lhasa before being dismissed. At the time he had been an influential member of the Liberation Committee of Chamdo.

In the course of the meeting, the Great Helmsman expressed his joy in welcoming the emanation of Chenrezig, the *bodhisattva* of compassion, and that of Amithaba, the Buddha of Infinite Light. He was all the more delighted, he said, because he himself was an emanation of *boddhisattva* Manjushri.* A considerable claim! It also hinted at Mao's desire to assume the cloak of imperial authority.

The visit to Beijing thus got off to a positive start, but the Dalai Lama soon became disillusioned:

> During the course of it [our first meeting], he told me that he had come to the conclusion that it was too early to implement all the clauses of the Seventeen-Point 'Agreement'. One of them in particular he felt could safely be ignored for the time being. This was the one that concerned the establishment of a Military Affairs Commission in Tibet whereby the country would be governed effectively by the PLA. 'It would be better to establish a Preparatory Committee for the "Autonomous Region" of Tibet,' he said. This organization would see to it that the pace of reform was dictated by the wishes of the Tibetan People themselves. He was most insistent that the terms of the 'Agreement' were put into effect as slowly as we ourselves judged necessary.[6]

Tenzin Gyatso and Chökyi Gyaltsen were happy to meet the other foreign personalities who were visiting the Chinese capital, but this did not please the Chinese officials. They then set off on a trip lasting several months, through China to Manchuria and Inner Mongolia. In the course of this journey, the Dalai Lama's mother (*amala**) fell seriously ill. For several days her condition gave cause for grave concern, but thanks to the efficient care of *amchila* (doctor) Tenzin Chödrak, she was able to resume the tour of the 'wonders of Chinese communism'.

On one of their last visits to Mao before they returned to Tibet, the Great Helmsman had come up close to the Dalai Lama and said: 'Religion is poison. Firstly, it limits the population, because monks and nuns remain celibate; secondly, it takes no interest whatsoever in development ...' On the previous day, obviously very irritated, Mao had lit a cigarette and inhaled deeply. Then exhaling the smoke through his mouth, he had said to both lamas: 'I explained yesterday to the Dalai Lama that I receive a modest salary, but that I have a lot of expenses: I smoke, I drink tea and I need to buy a lot of books; therefore I have very little money left. Now that you are leaving, I cannot give you a present. I can only leave you these few words: unity, progress and future development ...'

In fact, within a year, Beijing gave the Panchen Lama a political importance that none of his predecessors had ever enjoyed. The Chinese authorities even granted the Council of Khenpo political authority over the western part of the country, similar to that enjoyed by the Liberation Committee of Chamdo in the east.

The Preparatory Committee for the Autonomous Region of Tibet (PCART) gathered for the first time on 6 May 1956. The Dalai Lama was appointed chairman, and the Panchen Lama one of the vice-chairmen. The former governor of Kham, Ngabo Ngawang Jigme, now reinstated after a period of 're-education', was appointed secretary-general. At the time, the PCART had 51 members, 15 of whom represented the Local Government of Tibet, that is to say, the centre of the country, 10 the Shigatse Council of Khenpo, 10 the Chamdo People's Liberation Committee, 5 the Central Committee for Work in Tibet, plus 11 prominent Tibetan personalities. The structure of PCART clearly indicated Beijing's intention to block all the initiatives of the Dalai Lama and his government, effectively reducing it to the status of a Local Government.

In Kham the Chinese had not waited for Beijing's instructions before embarking on the destruction of local traditions. In their inflexible determination to transform Tibetan society, the Chinese government first of all provoked uprisings in the provinces of Kham and Amdo, and this then set ablaze the whole of Tibet.

12

The Tibetan People Rebel

A sword cannot sever itself ...

Communist China initiated a terrible policy of repression in Tibet. The end of the war with Korea, in July 1953, was without doubt one of the main reasons for their abrupt change of policy. In effect, Beijing feared that Tibetan diplomatic endeavours and the uprising of the Khamba tribes[1] in the eastern part of the country might rapidly result in the political and military involvement of the United States. President Truman did not deny such a possibility but he did stipulate that the Dalai Lama must reject the Seventeen-Point 'Agreement'.

It seems that the Dalai Lama did express a desire to go to Washington, but was probably dissuaded from doing so both by influential lamas and the Nechung oracle. Various considerations ruled out international intervention in support of the Dalai Lama. The United States neither wanted nor felt able to give him overt support, for fear of increasing tensions in Asia after the Korean war. India's position was ambiguous: Nehru looked unfavourably on the arrival of the Chinese army in Tibet, but on the other hand he had to be realistic since some border areas (Aksai Chin, North-East Frontier Agency) were already being contested by Beijing. The threat of war pushed Nehru to normalize relations between India and China. In April 1954, in a treaty signed by both countries, India recognized Tibet as a 'Chinese region'. India's non-alignment received the support of Chou En-lai at the Bandung conference one year later. In any event, China gained control of Tibet.

To put down the uprising in Kham, Beijing committed many atrocities. For instance in the little town of Doi, in Amdo, 300–500 villagers were killed by a bullet to the neck, to serve as an example to the other inhabitants gathered together in the town square for a collective criticism session (*thamzing*★).

In 1955 fighting broke out in Litang, Batang, Derge, Chamdo and Kantse. Supported by the people, tens of thousands of Khamba horsemen bravely fought against Chinese troops, sometimes at altitudes of over 1,500 feet and in temperatures as low as -40°C. In 1956, Beijing accepted the truce negotiated by the Dalai Lama's emissaries in eastern Tibet, but it transpired that they were only playing for time so that they could re-organize their troops who were trapped in the mountains. Almost immediately, the communists broke the agreement and again attacked villages and monasteries.

On 1 June 1956, in retaliation for a major Tibetan offensive, the Chinese army bombed the monastery of Litang after a two-month siege and destroyed it completely. In 1980, when a Tibetan delegation, sent by the Dalai Lama at the Chinese government's request, was finally able to visit the area, only a sad pile of ruins and ashes stood where the monastery had been. The governor of Litang had been tortured to death in the town square, and hundreds of monks and nuns had been subjected to the most horrendous torture and shameful humiliations before being killed. Among the atrocities recorded by an international commission set up by the United Nations, witnesses reported that they saw religious people buried alive in a common grave. Camps for the refugees and nomads were bombed by planes bearing the colours of Beijing, and pilots did not hesitate to open fire on both children and herds of yak.

At the time, ever more fearful of open conflict with his powerful neighbour, the prime minister of India, Nehru, systematically censored information from Tibet about Chinese atrocities. He then turned his attention to Pakistan. His refusal to denounce the Chinese occupation of Tibet was eventually to result in an endless series of difficulties, the least of which was the expensive problem of protecting border areas in north India.

In 1956, Marshall Chen Yi, deputy prime minister of the People's Republic, was dispatched to Lhasa for the inauguration of the

PCART – a demonstration of how important the Tibetan issue was to the Central Committee. A reinforcement of 40,000 troops was another indication of Beijing's intention to put down the uprisings in Kham and Amdo as quickly as possible. The bloody fighting between Tibetans and Chinese eventually led Mao Tse-tung to order a six-year adjournment of the reforms mentioned in the Seventeen-Point 'Agreement'. In the meantime, Chen Yi was to persuade the Dalai Lama and the government of Lhasa to join with Beijing in their efforts radically to transform Tibetan society, culture and traditions.

According to Chinese sources, the Panchen Lama, the Council of Khenpo and the district of Chamdo had called for a more rapid implementation of reforms. Chökyi Gyaltsen, said Beijing, had even advocated that Shigatse become an experimental area if political circumstances did not make it possible to apply reforms to the whole of Tibet. Young cadres, who had trained in Beijing and joined the Communist Party, presented the Dalai Lama with a petition requesting an immediate implementation of the communist programme.

Chen Yi met the Panchen Lama several times in Tashilhunpo on the pretext of persuading him not to oppose the government of Lhasa. China, though, was a sly fox when it came to political strategy. The Panchen Lama's youth and naïvety enabled the marshall to convince him that the implementation of the Seventeen-Point 'Agreement' and the social reforms planned by the Great Helmsman could only benefit the country's development: not only would the life of working people be improved, but conditions would be better for both the spiritual institutions and the Kashag.

During those negotiations, an encounter took place between Chen Yi and the Dalai Lama, then just over 20 years old, at the Norbu Lingka. 'Don't be worried,' said the former, 'although the reforms have been adjourned for six years, we can still discuss them. The well-being of the Tibetan people is at stake. When we "expropriated" the properties of capitalists in China, their lives were totally unaffected. Personally, I had many capitalist friends when I was the mayor of Shanghai and Nanjing; they were all very rich and possessed numerous factories and shops. We bought their companies and achieved a peaceful transformation of society. The capitalists, the working people and the motherland all benefited from this action.'

Dressed in a superb green uniform and sporting all his decorations, Chen Yi marched up and down the audience room, pounding the pale red carpet. Suddenly he planted himself in front of the *kalön* gathered around Tenzin Gyatso for the occasion: 'What does "expropriate" mean? It means that the State will buy up all your farms and pastures and give them to poor serfs. Their lives will be transformed.'

Clenching his fists, Chen Yi then proudly beat his chest: 'I am a marshall of the People's Liberation Army and the deputy prime minister of the Republic. I tell the truth. The State will take care of everything, from politics to everyday life. The country is poor now, but we have the necessary funds for a far-reaching transformation of Tibet. If we talk now of reforms, it is because the ancient system is bad. Everything that is backward, obsolete and detrimental to the social development of the people will be eliminated ... On a purely personal level, we will be able to remain friends after the liberation. You will be allowed to become the country's executives and to work in the Preparatory Committee for the Autonomy of Tibet, or in various government departments. What is there to be afraid of? I am your friend. I advise you to act in full awareness of this and to let the interests of the people and the motherland come first ...'

At that stage, Chen Yi called on the Dalai Lama as witness. Joining his hands, as if to implore him, he said with an ironic smile, 'Am I not right?' Tenzin Gyatso only nodded. A terribly sad smile briefly lit his face. The Chinese leader walked across the room and again addressed the *kalön*: 'I hope you will report my words to your friends, your family, the nobility of this country and all the religious dignitaries. Let us relax and stop making imaginary problems and worrying unnecessarily. Under the leadership of Chairman Mao, our government, the Dalai Lama and the Panchen Lama, let us unite and combine our efforts so that we can work together for the progress of Tibet ...'

Some communist sources declare that Marshall Chen Yi had been very impressed by the Potala and by the treasures of Tibetan culture kept there: 'A major site of Buddhism ...' However, when he met the Dalai Lama or visited the Panchen Lama in

1 Tenzin Gyatso, the Fourteenth Dalai Lama *(left)* and Chokyi Gyaltsen, the Tenth Panchen Lama *(right)*, are received in Beijing by Chairman Mao in 1954.

2 *(from left to right, front row)*, the Tenth Panchen Lama, the Fourteenth Dalai Lama, Chou En-lai, Nehru, and Indira Gandhi – New Dehli 1956.

3 The Fourteenth Dalai Lama and the Tenth Panchen Lama are received in New Delhi in 1956, on the 2,500th anniversary of the birth

4 Nehru receives the traditional offering of a *khata,*
a white silk scarf, from the Tenth Panchen Lama.

5 The Tenth Panchen Lama
(left) and the Fourteenth
Dalai Lama *(right)* in
New Delhi 1956.

6 Front *row (from left)*, Gyalyum Chenmo (the mother of the Fourteenth Dalai Lama), Indira Gandhi, and Sonam Drolma (the mother of the Panchen Lama); standing behind them are the Panchen Lama and the Dalai Lama.

7 The Tenth Panchen Lama blesses Tibetan refugees during an audience at Kotah House, New Delhi.

The Tenth Panchen Lama is accused by representatives of the Chinese people during a session of public criticism *(thamzing)*. Chairman Mao watches on from his portrait behind the Panchen Lama.

9 The Panchen Lama bows to 'acknowledge his mistakes'.

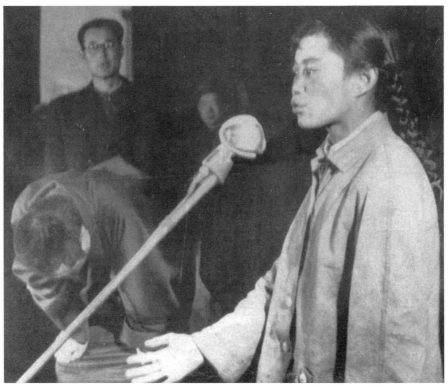

10 The Tenth Panchen Lama in his residence in Beijing after his release by the Chinese authorities, and appointment by the People's National Congress as vice-chairman of the Autonomous Region of Tibet.

11 Oracles act as mediums between the spirit and earthly realms. The Nechung oracle is a state oracle and, as such, is asked for advice about any important state affairs. One of his roles is to help interpret signs during the search for the reincarnation of a Panchen Lama. The picture shows the Nechung oracle in a trance.

12 *(above and below)* Lhamo Latso, the lake of visions. A visit to the lake is an essential
tep in the search for the reincarnations of Dalai Lamas and Panchen Lamas. During the
search for the Tenth Panchen Lama, the lake is said to have turned each colour of the
rainbow, and many different patterns and images appeared on its surface.

13 Chinese army truck crossing New Square in front the Potala.

14 The Potala, the Dalai Lama's palace in Lhasa, at dawn.

5 The monastery of Tashilhunpo, near Shigatse in the south of Tibet, 1996. It was founded by the First Dalai Lama, Gendün Drub, in 1447, and since then has been the temporal home of the Panchen Lamas.

6 Chadrel Rinpoche, Abbot of Tashilhunpo monastery, 1994. He was appointed by Beijing to lead the search for the successor to the Tenth Panchen Lama. However, the abbot and his secretary were detained following the anouncement that the Dalai Lama had recognised the incarnation of the Panchen Lama. They were accused of having been in secret communication with the Dalai Lama.

17,18 Following the declaration of martial law in 1989, there were widespread demonstrations: (*left*) an injured demonstrator is arrested by a Chinese soldier; (*right*) a Chinese official interrogates a Tibetan nun.

19 Drapchi Prison: Lhasa's main prison. In 1995 Beijing admitted that there were 200 prisoners held for 'counter-revolutionary offences'. There were also an estimated 1,000–2,000 held in 'administrative detention'.

20 His Holiness the Fourteenth Dalai Lama holding a photograph of the Eleventh Panchen Lama.

21 The family of the Eleventh Panchen Lama.

Tashilhunpo, he frequently pointed out to them that Tibet was in need of 'a number of cadres specialized in economy, culture, education, science and the arts'. These cadres should also have 'extensive political training, so they can be permanently in touch with the masses …' He also stated that 'considering the work that remains to be accomplished, the number of Tibetan cadres is not enough …'

There were three phases in the Chinese seizure of Tibet: between 1950 and 1951, China's main aim was to 'liberate' the country; then followed, from 1952 to 1954, a phase of stabilization; finally, a phase of consolidation began in 1955, ending with the institution of the Preparatory Committee for the Autonomous Region of Tibet. Communist troops were deployed on Tibetan territory, setting up bases in the main towns of the country – Lhasa, Shigatse, Gyantse, Yatung, Gartok – and in certain strategic areas along the border with India.

Even to this day, very little information is known about the life of the Tenth Panchen Lama. Beijing has the deplorable habit of turning historical facts to its own advantage: Chökyi Gyaltsen's life is no exception. Tibetan sources living in Tashilhunpo at the time stated that the young Panchen Lama, then 18, was hindered in his studies because of the political disturbances, but he received some instruction from a hermit called Kachen Ang Nyima, from Dzonga in the south of Tibet, and Gyenag Rinpoche was able to pass on to him all the spiritual teachings of Tashilhunpo. After the death of Ang Nyima, he received a sound knowledge of Buddhist texts from his teacher Ngulchu Rinpoche. Chökyi Gyaltsen said he had been aware of a terrible pressure in Tashilhunpo monastery, which he had not felt in Kumbum. He often met and learned from prominent scholars and members of the Council of Khenpo, as well as lamas trained in the monasteries of Drepung, Ganden and Sera.

One day in Ganden, Chökyi Gyaltsen had taken part in a debate on 'the fundamental canon of Mahayana Buddhism'.[2] In accordance with tradition, the *geshe* presiding over the session had begged the Panchen Lama to sit in the place of honour, as befitting his rank. At the end of the session, as Chökyi Gyaltsen had been about to leave the room, the scholar asked him, pointing to two religious men: 'Panchen Rinpoche, which of these two lamas has the better knowledge of the scriptures?' According to witnesses' reports, this is when Chökyi Gyaltsen suddenly realized that his knowledge was too superficial. Resolving in his heart of hearts to remedy the situation, he evaded the question by answering: 'They both manage pretty well.'

It is reported that at this time Chökyi Gyaltsen began to learn Chinese, from a party member who had been appointed for that purpose. He was accommodated in Tashilhunpo, not far from His Holiness's quarters. He naturally taught the language through the study of works giving the communist version of China's history. It is said that the Panchen Lama's very first lesson was called 'The East is red'.

Chökyi Gyaltsen devoted the rest of his time to various political and spiritual matters. He welcomed numerous believers and often met Chinese authorities, particularly representatives of the People's Liberation Army.

A rumour went around Lhasa, as well as several other towns, that the Panchen Lama was supporting the occupying forces' policy. It was reported that Chökyi Gyaltsen was 'a Han lama', 'a red lama' who was working for the Han. 'There was no room for the Tibetans in his heart', it was said. Events seemed to confirm these words. In 1956, the Panchen Lama opened a technical school in Shigatse where Tibetan, Hindi and Chinese were taught to some 300 students from the most prominent families of the Tsang region. The school also offered training in such diverse subjects as photography, driving, riding, surveillance and shooting, as well as various other military activities.

Meanwhile, Maharajah Kumar of Sikkim, president of the Buddhist Society of the Indian subcontinent, had sent a message to Tenzin Gyatso and Chökyi Gyaltsen inviting them both to the Buddha Jayanti festival celebrating the 2,500th anniversary of the birth of the Buddha. After endless negotiations with the Chinese authorities, the Dalai Lama eventually left the Potala in November 1956. First he joined the Panchen Lama in Tashilhunpo for a few days, then the convoy of Tibetan dignitaries and their Chinese escort set off slowly for India, via Yatung.

The Indian government arranged for a special train to take the delegation all over India, stopping at the main religious sites – Sanchi, Ajanta, Benares, Bodh Gaya – places with a strange and subtle beauty. Everywhere, the Dalai Lama and the Panchen Lama were welcomed as official guests, but the Chinese officials' constant surveillance spoilt what should have been a time of deep spirituality and hope for the Tibetan people. It was almost impossible for Tenzin Gyatso and Chökyi Gyaltsen to be alone and talk in complete freedom. They were constrained by very strict protocol.

Most of the Chinese officials taking part in the journey had held posts in Lhasa, and thus had a good knowledge of Tibetan. The Dalai Lama's younger sister, Jetsun Pema, was one of the party. Her testimony is quite clear:

When I was younger, I had not been able to understand clearly what was happening in Tibet, but I had instinctively rejected the Chinese because they prevented my niece and nephew and me from going to Lhasa during the school holidays. We knew that they were to blame and we did not forgive them for the long months spent without seeing our parents. We also knew that if we were to return to Tibet, they would not hesitate to send us to China to undergo Communist education and indoctrination there. Moreover, I had learnt that many of my friends had been sent in this way to Beijing ...

During the journey, I met the Panchen Lama for the first time. Although the Dalai Lama expressed his thoughts easily, the Panchen Lama seemed rather an introvert. He did not often smile and I found him very intimidating.

The Panchen Lama's mother was also of peasant origin. She came to our compartment whenever she could and spoke at length with Amala and Tsering Dolma, touching on everyday subjects such as embroidery, knitting or cooking. They were relatively unaffected by this strange atmosphere of mistrust, with its absence of free expression.[3]

The Tibetan delegation travelled untiringly across India by train for three months, attending first-class performances of traditional dancing and concerts of Indian music in honour of the Dalai Lama, the Panchen Lama and the other guests of the government of Delhi.

During the day, they visited numerous temples and Tenzin Gyatso and Chökyi Gyaltsen also met influential political figures. However, the Tibetan ruler was very disappointed by these meetings. Nehru had actually declared that India could be of no assistance to him, yet he promised the Dalai Lama that he would come to Lhasa as soon as possible.

Against the advice of Tibetans who had already taken refuge in India, the Dalai Lama and the Panchen Lama returned to Tibet, where the situation was deteriorating day by day. Armed resistance had spread throughout the whole country. People fought desperately against the communist troops who had committed such terrible crimes over the last few months. Religious people and villagers alike were the victims of retaliations organized by the PLA.

As the year of the Earth Pig, 1959, arrived, the Dalai Lama realized that Tibet was heading for disaster. But he had promised his tutors that he would sit his last monastic exams during the ceremonies of *Mönlam*. At the time he stated:

> ... the Preparatory Committee continued to meet on a regular basis to discuss meaningless policy amendments. It was extraordinary to what lengths the Chinese authorities went to provide a façade behind which they could carry on their abominations elsewhere in the country. I felt powerless. Yet it was certain that if I resigned (which I did consider doing) or opposed the Chinese directly, the consequences would be devastating. And I could not allow Lhasa and those areas of Tibet that were not so far engulfed in bloodshed to succumb as well. Already there were at least eight divisions of the PLA operating in the east: over 150,000 trained men with sophisticated battlefield technology confronting an irregular band of horsemen and mountain warriors. The more I thought about the future, the less hope I felt. It seemed that no matter what I or my people did, sooner or later all of Tibet would be turned into a mere vassal state in the new Chinese Empire without religion or cultural freedom, let alone that of free speech.[4]

March 1959 marked a decisive turn in Tibetan history. The Dalai

Lama passed his exams and returned to the Norbu Lingka, his summer palace, where a huge crowd gathered. Everywhere in town, posters had been put up demanding the departure of the Chinese and the denunciation of the Seventeen-Point 'Agreement'. On 10 March, it was the women's turn to rebel. Tenzin Gyatso consulted the Nechung oracle and, in agreement with his entourage, took the decision to leave Lhasa as soon as possible. On 17 March, two shells fell in the gardens of the Norbu Lingka.

At nightfall, I went for the last time to the shrine dedicated to Mahakala, my personal protector divinity. As I entered the room through its heavy, creaking door, I paused for a moment to take in what I saw before me. A number of monks sat chanting prayers at the base of the large statue of the Protector. There was no electric light in the room, only the glow of dozens of butter votive lamps, set in rows of golden and silver dishes ... A small offering of *tsampa*★ sat on a plate on the altar. ... One of the monks took up his cymbals, whilst another put a horn to his lips and blew a long, mournful note. The cymbals clashed together and were held, vibrating. Its sound was so comforting ... For a moment, I lingered in silent prayer ... Before leaving the room, I sat down for a few minutes and read from the Buddha's sutras, stopping at the one which talks of the need to develop confidence and courage.[5]

Later that night, Tenzin Gyatso, the Fourteenth Dalai Lama, left Lhasa to go into exile. We can only imagine his thoughts and his infinite sadness.

The Tenth Panchen Lama did not hear about what had happened in Lhasa until 20 March. Hu Bing, the assistant secretary of the Work Division Committee, and Zhang Dingyi, the assistant director of the United Front Department of Work and the Chinese teacher of the Panchen Lama, were careful not to reveal the exact truth. They told him that, on Beijing's order, a counter-revolution hatched by the Kashag had been quelled by the People's Army. Chökyi Gyaltsen asked to be told everything in detail. Aware of the extreme gravity of the situation, he also asked for news of the Dalai Lama. Hu Bing answered: 'According to the radio message we received, he has been abducted by counter-revolutionaries and his whereabouts are unknown. He may be heading towards Lhoka ...'

Chökyi Gyaltsen was unable to conceal his intense distress. Slowly pacing up and down the room, he repeated twice in a low voice: 'His whereabouts are not known ...' Then he addressed the two Chinese: 'Will the kidnappers kill Kundun?[6] What is the central government doing? Where will they take him? ...' Hu Bing refused to answer on the pretext that he did not have precise information. The Panchen Lama was then heard to say in a muffled voice: 'May the Buddha look after him, and may he soon come back to Lhasa!'

Hu Bing took advantage of Chökyi Nyima's distress to impose a number of conditions: 'Should the government of Lhasa and the Tibetan army initiate a rebellion, we would order our troops to immediately disarm the soldiers stationed in Tsang, to avoid any further trouble ... In accordance with the Seventeen-Point Agreement, the Tibetan army must join the People's Army. Now that rebellion has started, there is no other way out. In addition, we are also going to seize the *kyidzong*[7] and subdue the religious authorities of Shigatse appointed by Lhasa ...'

In a threatening voice, Hu Bing warned the Panchen Lama against any attempt at insubordination: 'We hope that the monastery of Tashilhunpo will not help the rebels. If this were to be the case, I am afraid that you would no longer be able to control the situation. We want you to instruct the Council of Khenpo, the monks and your police force [approximately 500 men] not to cause any trouble ...'

Chökyi Gyaltsen promised to pass on these orders very soon and asked Hu Bing to do all he could to avoid bloodshed and armed confrontation. 'We can solve the issue of the soldiers peacefully. I am ready to help you by meeting them.' The Panchen Lama received no answer from Hu Bing, who simply turned his back on him and purposefully headed for the door. Chökyi Gyaltsen caught up with him and, taking his arm, said to him with touching seriousness: 'As soon as you receive any news from Kundun, I want you to tell me ... May he be safe and sound.'

13

'Democratic Reforms'

Wedding of blood: tears of mourning.

The Dalai Lama, Tenzin Gyatso, reached the border with Assam on 30 March 1959; at this time he also announced the creation of a government in exile, news which was broadcast around the world by All-India Radio. Nehru sent him a message of welcome. A few weeks later the Dalai Lama denounced the Seventeen-Point 'Agreement' which had been signed in 1951.[1]

Shortly after the Tibetan ruler's escape, the technical school created by the Panchen Lama acquired 96 horses, thus increasing the number of its cavalry to 150. The monastery of Tashilhunpo decided to put these horsemen at the disposal of the People's Liberation Army, to help it eliminate any remaining pockets of resistance. By the end of April, Chökyi Gyaltsen announced in a dispatch that 'rebellion had been quelled in Tibet, order had been restored and democratic reforms could now be implemented ...', whereas in reality, in spite of the Dalai Lama's call for an end to the fighting, resistance had been reorganized in Kham. The Tibetan area of Mustang, in Nepal, was soon to become one of the last strongholds.

By way of 'democratic reforms', the Chinese continued to confiscate estates and agricultural equipment and redistribute them to the underprivileged. This agrarian policy was accompanied by a wave of arrests. Many so-called 'enemies of the people' – that is, landowners and rich people – were labelled 'reactionaries' and they abruptly disappeared or were executed without trial.

Discontent, initially limited to Kham where 'reforms' had been applied as early as 1954, spread throughout the entire population of Tibet. The Chinese authorities decided to reinforce their control over the people. Using the excuse that they suspected certain Tibetans of harbouring anti-Chinese feelings, they launched a massive purge. To escape mass arrests, many men and women resorted to suicide by hanging or drowning themselves.

After 'democratic reforms' and repression, the communists turned their attention once again to helping the disadvantaged, this time on an ideological basis: correcting their distorted thinking and politics, awakening class consciousness, and reappraising history and economics. They redistributed land by establishing people's communes and agricultural cooperatives, but were unable to achieve their objectives due to a shortage of agricultural equipment. And, in spite of the promises, there was no seed. In the streets of towns and villages, people sang:

> At first the Chinese made us laugh,
> Then they made us cry ...

In 1962, communes similar to those which had been created in China between 1958 and 1960, appeared in various parts of Tibet. Experimental centres opened in Lhasa, Shigatse and Lhoka, backed up by propaganda praising their virtues. Middle and lower class peasants were told they could better themselves by becoming chairmen (*turing*) or foremen (*dhutang*) – provided, of course, they denounce 'reactionaries'. When they refused to collaborate, they were submitted to a public trial (*thamzing*), during which they were cruelly tortured.

Leaders were trained in the communes and then sent to other areas to create new ones. Because volunteers were rare, people were made to gather in the village square and, under duress, vote by a show of hands or by signing a petition, in favour of the Chinese system. Tibetans chosen in this way were compelled to go along with this propaganda because they knew that their families would suffer if they refused. Those who became chairmen and foremen received favours from the occupying forces.

According to the Chinese government, the Tibetans were at last entering into the modern age and, through a system of communes, would acquire a certain amount of autonomy and, where necessary, would be able to help other developing communes. In reality, living conditions in the communes were deplorable. The annual output of grain was divided into five parts, the smallest of which went to the peasants, who were in danger of starving if they did not ration it out carefully. In Taktse,[2] the communists had introduced a system called 'imitating Tachai', a town in the province of Shanxi in China, where peasants were supposed to have turned almost barren land into fertile ground through their hard work. We now know that the State gave generous help and that the output figures were exaggerated. In any case, an extensive propaganda campaign was launched in China and Tibet. Not only were the peasants grossly overworked by the authorities, but their output was controlled by officials who took advantage of the situation to levy a number of new taxes and revenues at harvest time.

Not content with 'democratic reforms', the Chinese imposed strict rationing on the peasants: about 30lb – 30 *gyama* – of food per person per month, though this did not include elderly people or those unable to work. Before 1959, whether rich or poor, farmers had always had enough oil, butter and meat to provide for the needs of all members of their family, both young or old. With the social policies and rationing introduced by China, Tibetans had to be content with *tsampa* and black tea all year round, whereas Chinese employees received 30–35lb of rice and flour, and 31–32lb of oil per person per month. Rationing and the need to work longer hours eventually exhausted the population.

The nomads were another target of the Chinese. They formed more than 20 per cent of the population and, more importantly, made up its less controllable portion. Under the pretext of turning them into civilized people, the communist government forced them to enrole in people's communes and confiscated their herds. But in spite of all Chinese efforts – seduction or repression – the nomads refused to pay taxes and overtly opposed the occupying force. This attempt to settle the nomads was one of the main causes of the famine which is still widespread in Tibet today.

Before 1950, barley, from which *tsampa* is derived, formed the basis of the Tibetan diet. The Chinese replaced it with a type of wheat which was not suitable for the climate of the country – it wouldn't ripen and most crops froze in the ground before they could be cut. Before the invasion, part of the land was intentionally left fallow and served as pasture for yak herds. Following the Chinese requirement that all land be cultivated, former pastures were turned into ploughed fields and vast expanses of wheat. As a result, entire herds of yak died and, without their manure, the rough ground gradually became impoverished.

Tibetan farmers and nomads appealed directly to the Chinese authorities, but without success. Famine broke out in 1960 and rapidly spread throughout the country. In agricultural areas, such as Kantse and Dragyab in the east, people were reduced to begging and had to leave their homes to look for food. Those in urban areas were not spared either. To control towns, the Chinese created so-called work and solidarity committees in various strategic areas. Composed of 50–60 men, most of them soldiers, these committees made arrests and organized the confiscation of property. All inhabitants had to attend political meetings praising the merits of the revolution which had put an end to feudal society. Every morning, under the supervision of committee members, representatives of the three classes considered 'enemies of the people' cleaned the streets. In the afternoon they watered the young trees which had been planted along the lanes, and in the evening attended public self-criticism sessions. After the meetings, if they still had some free time, the work and solidarity committees found yet more tasks for them to do.

In 1961, a committee was created to settle the issue of trade. The stores and properties of 'large-scale traders who were the enemies of the people' were seized and redistributed to 'small shopkeepers'. Those who owned middle-sized stores were compelled to sell their establishments because of ever-increasing taxes. If they were unable to pay these taxes, they could be jailed and subjected to *thamzing* sessions – for non-payment demonstrated a 'counter-revolutionary' lack of goodwill. As for small shopkeepers, now reduced to a minority, their slightest misdemeanour exposed them to regular public criticisms and beatings.

However, Chinese-owned establishments were regularly supplied, but most Tibetans were not authorized to shop there. Only those on the list supplied by the authorities were allowed to do so.

After the administration was purged in 1959, all cadres were members of the Communist Party. Recruited in factories, offices and schools, they collaborated completely with the occupying forces but, cut off from the masses, they were unable to infiltrate the Tibetan resistance. Some of them were very suspicious of Chinese policy, but they had also been very critical of Tibetan society before 1959. Other cadres came from poor families; few overtly opposed the Chinese policy and they were badly organized and without any real political training – most of them ended up in jail. But no one – peasant, nomad, trader or manager – escaped the weekly *thamzing* session, where the accused stood for hours in front of family, children and friends, who were forced to take part. As well as self-criticism, the accused had to endure the insults, beatings and spitting of relatives. Frequently, men and women who had been humiliated and held up to ridicule, confessed to being reactionaries and enemies of the people and begged for a quick death.

The already dramatic situation worsened during the Cultural Revolution of 1966–76, which claimed its first victims in Lhasa in the summer of 1966. The Chinese oppression of the Tibetan people was then extended to all aspects of life. Religious practice, which had already been severely restricted, was now forbidden. The Tibetans' private lives were closely watched by Chinese officials: traditional costume and headdresses were denounced as remnants of feudal times; couples living together without official sanction were publicly humiliated. Under the pretext of taking a census of the population, people were counted and their movement was either strictly controlled, or forbidden.

Lhasa became a town of 'frightened and hungry women'. Those who belonged – even distantly – to the nobility or to anyone who, in the view of the Chinese, supported it, were sent to labour camps. Suspicion became so great that people feared even casual conversations with friends – there was always the possibility they might choose to collaborate in order to release a relative from jail. Lorries loaded with children regularly passed through the capital on their way to unknown destinations. At the end of their journey, death usually awaited them. Macabre stories from this period clearly demonstrate the cruelty of the occupying forces. The Chinese sent nine- and ten-year-old children to catch birds. If they did not bring back enough, both parents and children were severely punished, the former for having produced 'reactionary offspring'. Again, these barbaric actions had only one objective: the destruction of Tibetan culture, within which Buddhism and its respect for all forms of life was omnipresent.

Red Guards travelled up and down the country, pillaging, raping, plundering and destroying everything that was in any way related to the cultural heritage of Tibet. Those who survived these atrocities spoke of bodies piled up in common graves, with the earth so hastily thrown over them that arms and legs could be seen sticking up from the frozen ground. Others had seen heaps of entangled corpses, which the Chinese eventually set on fire.

During that time, Tibet, like China, fell prey to the young people who had been cleverly manipulated by Mao Tse-tung and Lin Biao. Altogether, millions of prisoners disappeared in camps. Survivors, historians and researchers agree that the Chinese concentration camps were comparable to those of World War II. In Tibet, new camps were added to those which had already been operating since the early 1950s. In these hells Tibetans were chained, beaten to death, forced to work in the freezing cold and subjected to public self-criticism sessions. Besides corporal punishment, there was also the mental torture of daily indoctrination and brainwashing: beaten, humiliated and tortured, prisoners thanked their torturers and, once released, remained grateful for all the atrocities and humiliations they had endured. It is easy to compare the methods applied by Chinese communists with those used in Dachau and Auschwitz, but with one major difference: the atrocities initiated in 1950 are still being perpetrated today.

Before 1950, religious people and monasteries in Central Tibet had for the most part been spared. There were 600,000 monks in Tibet before 1950; in the following years most of them renounced their vows and many were arrested, put in jail or murdered. The few great monasteries around Lhasa and in Amdo and Kham that were not destroyed – including Derge, Chamdo and Batang – were literally emptied of all their occupants and sacred artefacts and blown up with dynamite. Their works of art were then sold in trade centres such as Hong Kong in order to finance the further destruction of Tibetan culture and religion.

After the Dalai Lama's escape, the Tenth Panchen Lama, Chökyi Gyaltsen, was appointed acting chairman of PCART. In 1960, the Chinese made him vice-president of the People's Congress, in the hope that they would be able to use him as a spokesman for their policy in Tibet. In this capacity he visited several regions of the country, but everywhere saw only misery and desolation.

In 1962, the Panchen Lama met Westerners in Lhasa and, despite his very limited freedom, expressed his intention to follow two courses of action: 'to accomplish his revolutionary duty to the people' and 'to lead the life of a good Buddhist', for he had 'to consider his next incarnation'. Strangely, he told them that Buddhism was in part responsible for the serfdom and exploitation of the Tibetans. Yet he thought that this was not in the true nature of Buddhism. His words testified to an awkward liaison between two aspects of his training: the spiritual (Buddhist) and the materialistic (communist). According to him, Buddhist ethics permitted the theft of neither 'a thread nor a needle', to quote the very words of one of the main communist slogans in use since the time of the Long March. He explained, with good reason, that the feudal serfdom of Tibet had been created by men whose views were far removed from their religion. He added: 'Communist theory says that the State will eventually disappear. Similarly, in Buddhism, religion will no longer be necessary when human beings become perfect.' Perhaps he himself was reassured by these words summarizing faith and ideology.

In 1962, the year of the Water Tiger in the Tibetan calendar, the Panchen Lama was summoned to Beijing by Mao Tse-tung. Crowds of destitute Tibetans lined his route, imploring Panchen Rinpoche to bring to an end their suffering and the hardships they endured under the occupation. Once in Beijing, he personally appealed to the Great Helmsman to stop the atrocities against his people, to increase food rations, to provide care for the elderly and disabled, and to respect religious freedom. Mao replied politely, but nothing changed in Tibet.

On his return to Tashilhunpo, Panchen Lama Chökyi Gyaltsen realized that the situation had deteriorated considerably within his own monastery. He heard, for instance, that several *tulku* had been gathered together in a room and subjected to long sessions of *thamzing*. The Panchen Lama was not happy about the fact that the instigators of the persecutions had selected poor monks as their targets. He asked to be given a detailed account of what had happened in his absence. It turned out that a Chinese dance group had been accommodated at the monastery. As some of its members did not like to remain idle, they had spent all their mornings practising their singing exercises, in which both men and women took part. The young singers were naturally rather noisy. Shocked by these goings on, the older lamas accused the artists of defiling holy places, corrupting the spirit of Buddhism and disturbing faith-related activities. In accordance with the rules of the monastery, they asked the women to leave. The story of what happened had become somewhat distorted by the time it reached the Chinese authorities, who took advantage of the situation to punish some of the monks as an example to the others. Several monks hung themselves to escape punishment.

In order to appease the monks and lamas, Kyikhang Khenpo, a pro-communist cadre in charge of the Religious Affairs Committee of Shigatse, intervened. He explained to the Chinese that the *tulku* were not opposed to reforms; they had simply requested that the women leave. He went on to suggest that the authorities postpone the arrival of another group of dancers or singers. He also asked them to reduce the size of the work team based in Tashilhunpo, as some of the monks found such a prominent presence disturbing.

This report was also distorted, and very soon Kyikhang Khenpo was regarded as the instigator of the troubles. He was made to undergo a terrible session of *thamzing*, in the course of which he was humiliated before all the monks of the monastery. He went on hunger strike, but a member of the work committee came every day to force him to swallow food, saying that 'he was supporting the counter-revolutionaries with his odious attitude'. One day Kyikhang Khenpo seized a dagger and cut his own throat. His life was saved just in time, but the deep wound had severed his vocal cords. Despite the injury, he was dragged several times to public *thamzing* sessions where he was blamed for having 'moved away from the people' and called 'a martyr to reactionary serfdom'.

Unable to speak, Kyikhang Khenpo wrote about the hardships he had endured in a letter to the Panchen Lama: 'Following your orders, I took part in revolutionary tasks after the liberation. Over the last seven years, I have followed the Communist Party's instructions and worked for it. I supported and was actively involved in democratic reforms. Never would I have imagined that a mere suggestion would provoke such an attack and such persecution. Now it is not easy for me to live or to die ...'

When the Panchen Lama read the contents of the letter it is said that he could hardly contain his anger. Too many tragic errors had been committed on behalf of communist liberation. The people were suffering, monasteries were being ransacked and the monks who had not been killed were mostly forced to lead a secular life. In some regions the occupying forces even forced monks and nuns to marry and then watched them have sexual intercourse.

At this time, monasteries were accused of all sorts of wrong doings: encouraging the exploitation of the people, murder, reactionary resistance, and defending feudal superstitions detrimental to the population's right way of thinking. Chinese documents described monasteries as 'the source of the disasters happening in Tibet', and said that: 'Monks and monasteries must be totally eliminated.' Every day the *tulku* had to endure terrible sessions of *thamzing* during which they had to denounce the parasitic life of monks in Tashilhunpo as well as in the rest of Tibet. The Chinese authorities, of course, forbade their troops to beat the accused – they saw that other monks took care of that, and if these monks did not strike hard enough, they in turn were subjected to the same humiliations.

Chökyi Gyaltsen wrote a report (the Seventy-Thousand Characters) in which he expressed his understanding of the situation, including his awareness that violence was explicable during a revolution and was sometimes, as history had shown, fair and inevitable. However, it was not taken seriously by the Chinese. In answer, the leaders of the work committee of Shigatse only advised him to read the first volume of the Tibetan translation of Mao Tse-tung's *Collected Papers* and to study more seriously the correct way to manage mass revolutionary movements, as set out by Mao in his 'Investigative Report on the Peasant Movement in Hunan'. They also expressed their intention to 'stimulate and educate' the Panchen Lama with the aid of Mao's aphorisms, which would help him understand certain concrete realities:

Revolution is not a dinner party. Neither is it the same as writing an essay, painting a picture or doing embroidery. It cannot be as delicate, quiet, elegant, refined, mild, kind, polite, restrained and magnanimous. Revolution is a riot. It is a violent action by means of which one class overthrows another. A rural revolution is a revolution in which peasants overthrow the feudal power of the landowning class. If the peasants do not make good use of all their strengths, they cannot overthrow an ancestral authority which is so deeply engrained in the mind.

However, a noticeable gap remained between Tibet and the rest of communist China after the period of 'liberation' and 'democratization' in Tibet. The orders of Beijing, published in official documents, always mentioned Tibet and Taiwan in brackets. To the officials and soldiers stationed in Tibet, this was an insult, and it partially explained their eagerness to 'develop' the country and bring it up to the level of the 'motherland'. Some of them were heard to say that they would not leave the country as long as the brackets remained in these documents, even in the face of death. They had lost patience and their revolutionary feelings had become exaggerated. Their ardour was significantly intensified in 1958, at the time of the Great Leap Forward, in a desire to 'catch up' with neighbouring annexed provinces, or even those in China. In order to reach their goal, they intended to accomplish 'the work of 20 years in a day'. Consequently, 'the principle of cautiousness and gradual progress' no longer applied. According to them, the human factor was an essential element of successful reforms and revolutionary zeal could change everything. They thought that the high plateaux of Tibet should serve as 'satellites' for further undertakings and that any opinion different from theirs should immediately be opposed as a manifestation of right-wing conservatism, retaliation and 'counter-revolutionary sabotage'.

These Chinese officials made extensive use of the media to promote their argument for a Great Tibetan Leap Forward – a dynamic move from feudal serfdom to socialism and communism through democratic reforms. According to them, within a few years, 'Tibet would take the lead over its neighbours' and the central government would achieve 'an unprecedented miracle in human history' on the Roof of the World. But by 1960, tens of thousands of Tibetans had left the country to join their spiritual and temporal leader, the Dalai Lama, and to flee from their torturers.

The Panchen Lama became increasingly worried about the deterioration of the situation in Tibet. In the Dalai Lama's absence, and as the second spiritual authority in the country, he felt he had to intervene whenever he had an opportunity to do so. In 1958, he had been terribly shocked when he had visited his own birthplace. Most inhabitants of Qinghai were either Salar or Tibetan, but there were also Hui, Han, Dongxiang, Baonan, Mongols, Tus and Manchus. They had all suffered the exactions of the barbarian warlord, Ma Pu-fang, as well as those of the communist reforms.

Most of the people from Wendu and its neighbouring villages belonged to communes where agricultural cooperatives had been set up. Thanks to land reforms, these cooperatives had rapidly flourished, thus immediately producing a violent reaction from some thousands of people who had nothing. In Wendu, taking advantage of an occasion when the villagers were gathered together for the ritual burning of mulberry branches, a group of 200 Tibetans armed with spears, bows and daggers, led by Gyanpal Rinpoche (one of Chökyi Gyaltsen's first teachers) and Nuri Pönpo (an opponent of the reforms imposed by the occupying forces), attacked the work committee of the province and killed its leader. Plundering the cooperatives, they redistributed grain to the starving peasants. Gyanpal Rinpoche stayed at the monastery of Wendu, where he was arrested and put in custody. Nuri Pönpo called on all the forces available in the region in an attempt to free the *tulku*, but without success. The People's Liberation Army intervened and put an end to the Tibetan rebellion. As an example to others, once the uprising had been suppressed the Chinese communists in Wendu and the neighbouring villages murdered over 500 innocents, who were armed only with their *malas* and prayer wheels. In the space of one afternoon 2,500 people were arrested and transferred to labour camps – Gyanpal Rinpoche committed suicide. These events brought to an end the famous 'counter-revolutionary uprising of Xunhua' – or 'the incident of Xunhua' according to the local Chinese authorities.

At the time, a report was written on these events and submitted to the central powers. The provincial committee drew from it a political lesson which was then implemented throughout the whole nation:

> Class conflict remains the main conflict we have to face in this intermediary period. In politics, the party must remain watchful, so as to be able to triumph permanently over the paralyzing ideology of the extreme right and to fight all class enemies ...

Beijing simply added this surprising comment: 'The ethnic issue is fundamentally a class issue.' This crucial remark was later closely linked with a series of controversies surrounding the 'Seventy-Thousand Characters', a report which the Panchen Lama handed to Mao Tse-tung on 18 May 1962 (*see* chapters 14 and 15), but which remained secret for a long time afterwards. Witnesses say that Mao Tse-tung went into a thundering rage when he read it.

14

The Seventy-Thousand Characters (1)

As soon as the Dalai Lama arrived in India, he set up a government as well as various organizations to welcome the streams of refugees and take care of their needs. Thanks to the Indian government, which put land at the disposal of the Tibetans, colonies were formed in the hope that one day the settlers might return to their motherland. On his visits to these first settlements between 1960 and 1965, Tenzin Gyatso exhorted his fellow countrymen to do all they could to preserve their culture and traditions.

The Commission (later Assembly) of Tibetan People's Deputies was founded on 2 September 1960. By the time it entered its second term of office it was working on the basis of a temporary constitution drafted in 1961. Shortly afterwards it opened bureaux in Kathmandu, London, Zurich, Tokyo and Washington. Yet further representations followed,[1] thus facilitating contacts with the outside world. In Tibet, lay and religious people tried all possible means to flee from Chinese oppression. Risking their lives, thousands crossed the Himalayas to join the Dalai Lama and his government in Dharamsala, on the southern foothills.

In the spring of 1962, the failure of the Great Leap Forward that might have put China on the path to prosperity could no longer be hidden. Criticisms of the country's leaders remained moderate, although the economic disaster affected the whole country. Following the habit established after the Republican Revolution of 1911, once it was in power the communist government clearly demonstrated its firm intention to preserve the 'union of the five races – Han, Manchus, Mongols, Tibetans and Muslims'. Despite the political upheavals, China remained composed of 'different nationalities'. A symposium on work for those of different nationalities under Chinese rule took place in Beijing in 1962. It was attended by Tibetan delegates from Qinghai, Sichuan, Yunnan and Gansu. The Panchen Lama was also present, but he said little. With him was Sherab Gyatso, a *rinpoche* of great erudition.

Normally this type of meeting was not a very lively affair, and attachment to the motherland would be referred to using conventional language and current phraseology. But suddenly Sherab Gyatso began a long speech, addressed mainly to minister Li Weihan, one of the signatories of the Seventeen-Point 'Agreement' and who, in his capacity as leader of the Nationalities Committee, was considered a specialist within the Communist Party on ethnic issues:

> We are here to talk about the situation of our people ... We should all be concerned by the rise and fall of our country. The Communist Party is the mainspring of our adventure, but our country is not a communist country. Neither is it the country of Mao Tse-tung, Chou En-lai, or even you, minister Li; the country belongs to our people and to all the nationalities. Our great family numbers 54 brothers ... Rise and fall, glory and disgrace are entirely related to the fate of this great family ...

Although tinged with defiance, his talk covered all the Chinese leaders' favourite topics. Sherab Gyatso took a pencil and tapped on the microphone; a loud crackle echoed throughout the room, followed by a heavy silence:

> I am a simple monk and I would not wish it otherwise. I am like an incense stick; whether I rise or fall, I am still an incense stick. I am not like you lay people who want to get married and have children in order to honour your ancestors, do good to your offspring and become immortal. When faced with a problem, I do not look back 300 years, nor do I look around me 10,000 miles. I have not the slightest fear. I can be lit or all of a sudden blown out ...
>
> I love my country, my religion and the Communist Party. The nationalist government and Chiang Kai-shek treated me well. They appointed me vice-president of the Committee for

Mongolian and Tibetan Affairs and gave me a salary. In 1949, they invited me to follow them to Taiwan. I stayed in China because I knew that the nationalist government and Chiang Kai-shek were scoundrels. They sought the help of foreign imperialists and oppressed people of all nationalities within the country. There were corrupt officials at all levels of the institutions. This is why they lost power and the support of the people and were forced to flee to Taiwan ...

Even if Sherab Gyatso had not been totally convincing in the justification of his role in the government of Nanjing, his criticisms against Chiang Kai-shek were relatively well-founded: it was after all true that Chiang Kai-shek had betrayed China by embracing the Protestant faith and forming an alliance with the United States. He continued vehemently:

However, let me tell you what I really think. I believe that you too lost the people's support with some of your methods. You did things that even Chiang Kai-shek and Ma Pu-fang, the governor of Qinghai, never dared do. The Communist Party employs 'three great methods' to triumph over its enemies. One of them involves criticizing others as well as self-criticism. You do not seem to have made much use of the latter over the last few years. You criticized other people, but you did not criticize yourselves ...

His audience listened in silence.

Some people said that the 'three, six and nine' could not be contested. You advocated the 'three red flags' when work went according to your wishes and was fruitful, but when faced with criticisms you intimidated the people with your 'six political norms', which overburdened the people more surely than a high mountain. And when output declined and the flaws and errors of the system could be clearly seen, you asked us to make a difference between 'nine fingers and one', between the norm and the arbitrary, between Xenan and Xian. Who made these mistakes? Who was responsible? ...

Then the monk held Li Weihan's icy glare for some time before he calmly went on:

> Minister Li, some people have said that another of your strategies involved luring the snake out of its nest. You should come clean about what happened during the 1957 campaign against the right. You became left-wing at the time; you took part in this campaign and were thus able to kill two birds with one stone.

This was a serious accusation. At the end of 1956, Mao Tse-tung had launched a 'rectification campaign' (*zhengfeng*) calling on the Chinese to criticize the Party and its agents. The Great Helmsman's aim was to turn any blame that might have been directed at him onto other people, and to recover the ground he had lost with the failure of his previous policy. The movement surpassed all his expectations and quickly ran out of control. In the spring of 1957 and during the summer that followed, Mao led a campaign of harsh repression against his detractors, whom he accused of being 'rightist bourgeois' who had used the 'rectification campaign' to question the basis of communist policy. It had been necessary to find scapegoats among government members, and Li Weihan was one of those who had felt he was in danger. In order to escape the re-education camps where some 400,000 Chinese had been imprisoned, former opponents of the Chinese authorities had become fervent right-wingers. Sherab Gyatso was in fact accusing the Chinese official of being an opportunist, someone who knew how to adapt to prevailing circumstances to retain power. He continued on the same line:

> I do not know if you are now using a different strategy. I have no fear. Everything I say today stems from one wish: that the Communist Party's Central Committee and the State Council – as Chairman Mao, President Liu Shaoqi and Prime Minister Chou En-lai have declared several times – assess the experiment and the lessons we drew from these few years in order to improve our future work. I have no other wish, absolutely none. My only wish is that our country becomes strong and rich so that its people may lead a happy and stable

life and Buddhism may prosper. May the founder of Buddhism testify to my loyalty and compassion! ...

Some people in the room applauded, but most participants were torn between feelings of hope and fear. The wrath of the authorities could have come down on Sherab Gyatso at any time. Li faced the monk and told him:

Master, I do not know whether you are left-wing or not, but you have always been a friend of the Party, and a longtime patriot who should be respected. You have advocated patriotism within religious circles as well as within the different ethnic groups. You have an open and clear mind. I respect you ...

Sherab Gyatso made no reply to this compliment. The lama and the minister continued the discussion later in the afternoon in a small conference room, before very few witnesses. The Panchen Lama was present but, curiously, he insisted on remaining silent. Sherab Gyatso went on:

It does not matter whether I am right- or left-wing. You can even say that I am right-wing. What does it matter, provided our work is well done, conditions for the people improve, culture is protected and promoted, and religious freedom truly respected. I understand that this is for the good of the country and of Tibetan people, and of all other nationalities in all areas where the Communist Party of China and the people's government have initiated 'democratic reforms', suppressed rebellions and opposed separatism.

Tibet had indeed been one of the first victims of Chinese policy. In spite of conciliatory speeches and freedoms guaranteed by the Constitution, the religious people of the high plateau had died in their thousands and religion, if not exactly forbidden, was at least violently suppressed. The results of these reforms had been tragic: thousands of deaths, the transfer of large numbers of the population, and general impoverishment.

The monk continued tactfully:

We share the same vision on these points. The problem is that you go too quickly, you want to take too big a step in just a few years. You want problems which require dozens of years, centuries, or even several generations, to be solved in very little time ... You want to become a Buddha during this lifetime. But it does not matter, for this shows good intentions, and we are both inexperienced. You said that I was angry, and in truth I am, because you refuse to accept that there are problems and mistakes, or you simply shift the responsibility onto other people ...

Sherab Gyatso's interpreter, a Chinaman called Chen, was understandably very uncomfortable with this situation. In Tibetan, he begged the lama several times to stop his accusations. In effect Chen thought that in confronting Li Weihan the lama was committing suicide. But he met with no success. To hide his fear, the interpreter nervously touched his lips with his tea cup. At times his hands were seized by a slight tremor and he began to stammer. Aware of the panic that had taken hold of the interpreter, Li offered to replace him. Without the slightest hesitation, Chen accepted, but this did not stop Sherab Gyatso from talking:

You avoid practical matters, but you love to play with figures: one way, two barracks, three flags, four great freedoms, five principles, six norms, seven investigations, the eight-character charter, nine fingers ... You also used many numbers in your speech: 'If you support one side, the other one may fall; spend 90 per cent of your time studying Mao's works and 10 per cent studying those of Marx and Lenin ...'

He then delivered the final blow:

Let me follow your example and use figures to illustrate the mistakes you have made over the last few years: first of all, you lie; second, you refuse to acknowledge your wrongdoings; third, you attack the people iniquitously; fourth, you do not have a Buddhist heart and you have no regard for humankind ...

The lama fingered his *mala* nervously as he brought the meeting to a close:

Essentially, all your failures result from your great haste, be it in Tibet or in Han regions ...

A few days later, Sherab Gyatso handed a report of his speech to Chen, who was also acting as his secretary during this visit. Chen told the monk:

You are an erudite and respected Buddhist scholar, but you know nothing about politics, least of all about the history of the Han. Bear this in mind: 'Emperors are always right. A subject must be executed if he makes the slightest mistake' ... In times past, emperors never admitted that they were wrong. The situation now is absolutely the same: only subordinates have the right to make mistakes. Never do the authorities make any mistakes and the central power is always right. Had I known that you would talk so imprudently, even transferring responsibility onto Chairman Mao, I would not have agreed to be your translator. Offending a leader will cost you your life. Today, you have been able to express everything you feel; but from tomorrow on, do not say anything more ...

Chen had made a good summary of Chinese politics: the emperors of the past had made way for a new 'red emperor', Mao Tse-tung. Nothing had fundamentally changed and the Son of Heaven still ruled over the country. All those who dared oppose the established order were in great danger.

Sherab Gyatso looked with great tenderness at this man who was so worried about what would become of him. He took his hands and pressed them very hard:

I know that you feel very concerned about me, but how can I turn away from the suffering of the Tibetan people and the sabotage of Buddhism? Chairman Mao, Prime Minister Chou En-lai and Minister Li Weihan have declared on numerous occasions that they want us to express our opinions openly so as to promote democracy, combine our strengths and our wisdom and face the crisis with one heart. If we report only good news, hide the bad, and always tell the central powers that the situation is auspicious and hopeful, how can they know the truth about Tibet and correct past mistakes?

Sherab Gyatso then quoted one of Mao's oft-repeated maxims: 'Marxists do not fear criticism.' Either unconsciously or out of unreasoned optimism, he had forgotten that the country's recent history had shown just how dangerous some criticisms could be.

Chen, without forewarning the lama, prepared a document he called 'Sherab Gyatso's Speech at the Symposium on Nationality' and took it to Li Weihan's secretariat:

Here is the official manuscript of Master Sherab Gyatso's speech. His other remarks were not official; he was merely talking casually about this and that and those remarks should not be taken into account. I hope, comrade minister, that you will not report them ...

To explain Sherab Gyatso's behaviour, Chen reminded them of the reading groups which had been organized since 1960 in the schools of the Party so that people could discuss things freely and speak from the heart. One day, amidst noisy laughter, Mao Tse-tung had said that those who took part in the groups must apply a certain method: three meals a day, two of substantial food and one of nothing. They should pour out their anger during the day and listen to people's dramas in the evening. Their stomachs would feel better if they could talk, work off their bad moods, and fart as much as they want ... Mao had added: 'We committed insane deeds. We have no other choice but to continue to listen to the accusations of those who are angry.'

Sherab Gyatso's speech was evidence of a protest movement which, without resorting to arms, was beginning to stir in Tibetan circles close to the Chinese government. The Panchen Lama,

Chökyi Gyaltsen, was not to be outdone. One day, during a trip with Li Weihan and other personalities, he talked to them at length:

People say 'The United Front is just one more banquet ... but I do not need you to invite me for dinner or to take me on a sightseeing tour.'

These criticisms of the United Front, which set out to combine Chinese communist and nationalist forces in the fight against imperialist powers, certainly made the communist officials tremble. The Panchen Lama continued, in a half-threatening, half-submissive tone:

I hope that you will seriously examine the issues related to the United Front and draw conclusions from the work that has been achieved with the different nationalities over the last few years. Did not Chairman Mao himself say that the Communist Party promoted 'seriousness'? I only hope that you will take my advice seriously and finally solve the problems faced by Tibet and the Tibetans ...

Back in Beijing, Li Weihan told Mao about his conversations with the Panchen Lama. According to Li, these long talks, thirteen altogether, had enabled him to gain a clear impression of the Tibetan situation. He had written an account entitled 'Report of Conversations Between Comrade Li Weihan and Vice-President Panchen Lama'.

As early as 1961, Panchen Lama Chökyi Gyaltsen had started to write a text known as 'The Seventy-Thousand Characters'. He had done so for a more serious purpose than simply venting his personal anger. The report he was preparing was a veritable accusation against Tibet's communist invaders and a declaration of their failure. His criticisms were based on what he had seen on his visits to hunger-stricken Tibetan provinces ravaged by bloody persecutions.

At the beginning of 1962, the Panchen Lama inspected the Tibetan areas of Qinghai, Sichuan and Yunnan; later on he visited Gansu and Xinjiang. In many of these places, Chökyi Gyaltsen felt that the instructions of the central government, Mao Tse-tung, Chou En-lai and even the Party were often distorted for personal gain. Everywhere conditions had continued to deteriorate. In Qinghai, the poverty was so extreme that people were deprived of virtually everything; the Panchen Lama met people who hadn't even a bowl to eat from, whereas in the past such an item would have been available to everybody, rich or poor. Angry, Chökyi Gyaltsen ordered that bowls be bought and distributed to the people. He even went so far as to criticize openly the party activists of the area, in both towns and villages. He banged his fist on the table, hardly able to contain his exasperation:

> In the past, lay people gave donations to monks and offerings to *tulku*. Never did we hear of *tulku* buying bowls for lay people. In the old society, even beggars owned at least one bowl. Under the rule of Chiang Kai-shek or even Ma Pu-fang, which lasted several years, people were not so poor they could not afford to buy a bowl ...

Spoken in the heat of the moment, these words were later to become 'the instruments of his crime'.

In Sichuan, the Panchen Lama dared question the report made by local authorities. He thought that its content was untrue and that it depicted too optimistic a picture of conditions in Kantse and Ngaba, two autonomous Tibetan prefectures in the former East Kham:

> The conditions you describe do not match the truth in any way. Kantse and Ngaba are the two regions where the anti-reform movement began. The rebels have been suppressed for five or six years, yet there are still rebellions today ... These have spread alarmingly throughout the whole population. Ordinary people, cadres and simple workers, who were all innocent, have been arrested and accused of being 'rebels'; all these people have disappeared ... Besides, both living conditions for the masses and production are not as good as you claim. A large number of men, women and children have died of starvation. At the time of the implementation of

'democratic reforms', many monasteries were destroyed, lamas were forced to lead a secular life, and freedom of religion was neither respected nor protected; you have always held up the people to ridicule ... The party often accuses me of addressing only issues related to nationality and religion at meetings. Is that not logical and natural for a *tulku* and a Tibetan? You are all members of the Communist Party, are you not? You're all Party cadres, and doesn't the Party aim to serve the people wholeheartedly? So why don't you speak up for the people? Why don't you report the actual situation to the government? Why do you close your eyes to people's misery? ...

It was the first time that the Panchen Lama had talked publicly about the massive rebellion in Kham. In the mid 1950s, in a brave but desperate struggle, the Khambas had taken up arms against Chinese rule and the disastrous reforms imposed upon them.

Chökyi Gyaltsen continued in a serious tone:

As cadres and representatives of minorities, it is our duty to report their misfortunes to the Central Committee of the Party and to the State Council. We should not raise a wall between the Party and the masses. On the contrary, we should act as a bridge ...

The Panchen Lama made a vague gesture with his hand, then after a moment's silence, he added:

It is a heavy task to build a bridge on which people may come and go, for we ourselves must suffer and carry the burden. Yet it is in the interests of the people and the future of the Party. If we stand like a wall between the masses and the Party, we are detrimental to the interests of both ...

Pointing to the secretary of the autonomous prefecture, he concluded:

As members of the Communist Party and especially as party cadres, you should be the first to set an example, so that people can at last follow you!

This trip had been a turning point for Chökyi Gyaltsen. His criticism had been directed not at the communist ideal but at its implementation, which had been so disastrous in Tibet as well as everywhere in China. Noticing the apathy of those he spent time with, the Panchen Lama decided to write a text in which he could explain to Chairman Mao Tse-tung himself the situation in Tibet, as he had observed it during his trips around the country. He was just 24 at the time.

When he wrote the first lines of the 'Seventy-Thousand Characters', Chökyi Gyaltsen first had to face the hostility of his entourage. His teacher, Ngulchu Rinpoche, attempted to dissuade him. Memories of the horrors of repression, torture, and *thamzing* sessions were still too vivid in his mind. And to him, the moment was ill-chosen, for China was facing serious economic problems and even the Party cadres were suffering as a result of strict food rationing. The failures accumulated by Mao, especially that of the Great Leap Forward, had reduced the country to a state of extreme poverty.

If some cadres had managed to come out of the political struggles unharmed, or even to benefit from them, others had certainly taken it to heart that they should set an example of solidarity with the people. One day, Marshall Chen Yi, the Minister of Foreign Affairs, together with other influential members of the Party, paid a courtesy visit to the Panchen Lama. On the table of the audience room stood a beautiful dish of mouth-watering apples. Chökyi Gyaltsen offered them to his Chinese visitors, but they ceremoniously stared at them without making the slightest move. Noticing their covetous looks, the Panchen Lama himself served the apples to his guests, who ate them with obvious delight. 'Delicious. It has been such a long time since I last ate an apple,' let out Chen Yi. Surprised, the Panchen Lama could not refrain from asking him why. 'Really, you don't know?' said Chen Yi. 'In difficult times, we do not have enough food; so how could we find fruit?' The Panchen Lama was even more surprised: 'But you are the Minister of Foreign Affairs. Don't you have fruit every day for your guests?' Chen Yi replied: 'The fruit in effect is intended for them, not for us. Several thousands of people work at the Foreign Office. I am their boss. If I were the first one to break the rules, how could I control my subordinates?'

In the course of another important meeting, one of his guests asked Chökyi Gyaltsen for permission to smoke. He took a cigarette and a lighter out of his pocket, but despite several attempts, was unable to light up. 'No lighter fuel? Ask the driver to give you some,' suggested the Panchen Lama. 'Maybe the flint is worn down', answered the guest. 'Then why don't you just get another one?' said the Panchen Lama. In the end, exasperated, the man, who was a commander, slipped the lighter back into his pocket. Chen Yi asked one of the servants to find a box of matches which he handed over: 'Better be a patriot and use local products!', he laughed. The Panchen Lama gave a wry smile: 'Comrade Chen Yi, it was easy to find flints in Tibet before trade stopped between China and India. Why didn't you ask earlier? ...' and, addressing the servants, he asked them whether they had flints for lighters. They all laughed and walked towards the commander to offer him their Tibetan lighters. 'Are these enough?' asked the Panchen Lama ironically. The guest seemed embarrassed. In an attempt to save face, Chen Yi said: 'Our comrade's tactics are very simple, master. The more lighters there are, the better.' 'This commander,' he went on in a mock severe tone, 'is a great tactician in the Party. He really is terrible; he leaves no stone unturned, even in the master's house!'

Despite these trivial incidents, which sometimes made people smile, Chen Yi was a major figure in Lhasa at the time. The Panchen Lama therefore decided to make his intentions known to him. Once he had listened carefully, Chen Yi answered: 'State everything you know and tell it unreservedly ...'

Reassured, Chökyi Gyaltsen set to work with increased dedication and fervour.

15

The Seventy-Thousand Characters (2)

The Panchen Lama completed his report in Beijing. He shut himself up in his residence at 23 Dong Jiao Street, a simple one-storey building a few steps away from the Chinese Academy of Social Sciences. Invariably there would be a group of Tibetan and Mongolian believers waiting patiently beyond the huge metal gate in the hope of catching a glimpse of their spiritual master at work.

Visitors were usually shown into the Panchen Lama's small study, where he sat behind an almost bare wooden table on which stood an old black Panasonic radio. Distinguished guests were often invited for dinner – perhaps a leg of lamb from Amdo – in the large room opposite the study. The bookshelves were full of sacred works and on the walls hung *thankas** representing the complete Panchen Lama lineage and an impressive photograph of Mount Kailas.[1] Chökyi Gyaltsen often spent time contemplating this image of what is undoubtedly the most sacred mountain in the world. For him and for all Tibetans, Mount Kailas was an icon of eternal Tibet.

The Panchen Lama spent his days and nights covering sheets of paper with writing, often tearing them up and starting again. He had only one aim in mind: to denounce the atrocities committed by the Chinese occupying forces in Tibet. Apart from his meetings with the Foreign Office minister Marshall Chen Yi, and Marshall He Long, famous mainly for his taste in cigars, he avoided all the social and political activities to which the central powers regularly invited him.

When the first draft of the manuscript was completed, he showed it to Ngabo Ngawang Jigme, who was secretary-general of PCART at the time, and to Sherab Gyatso and some close friends. Ngabo gave him useful advice on the way he should present the text, but he mainly suggested that he replace the written petition with a clear and more moderate verbal report to the Central Committee. It was a tactful way of telling the Panchen Lama not to hand over his report.

Sherab Gyatso reacted more as a linguist and judged the Panchen Lama's writing very severely. Busy with his duties at the Buddhist Association of China, he had had no time to write comments. When he gave the manuscript back to Chökyi Gyaltsen, Sherab Gyatso only said: 'Your writing is unreadable. I was confused by it. I found numerous pages hard to understand. In some parts of the text, your words lack precision and fluency. I think you should read more, study calligraphy and complete your cultural training ...' In saying this he was making an acknowledgement that the Panchen Lama had received no traditional training whatsoever; the Chinese had seen to that.

The Panchen Lama's teacher, Ngulchu Rinpoche, who was also present at the meeting, volunteered to rewrite the manuscript himself. He duly set to work and wrote the Tibetan version of the document prepared by his pupil. It took him two months, deliberating over each word and sentence. He made no changes to the content, however, for he was not sufficiently aware of political and social issues.

One evening in mid-May 1962, Ngulchu Rinpoche entered the temple which had been set up on the premises where the Panchen Lama was staying. He lit the butter lamps and incense sticks and laid out offerings on the altar, thus creating a solemn and sacred atmosphere. Then he sat cross-legged and prayed. One hour later, he summoned the Panchen Lama. As Chökyi Gyatsen walked into the temple, Ngulchu Rinpoche begged him to sit in the place of honour. Chökyi Gyaltsen could not imagine what was on the mind of his teacher, who looked at him sternly.

Once the Panchen Lama was seated, Ngulchu Rinpoche dismissed the servants and the other monks. He adjusted his robes and respectfully prostrated himself three times before the statue of the Buddha. Then he turned back and bowed for a long time before his pupil. Never before had Ngulchu Rinpoche behaved in such a way. Chökyi Gyaltsen motioned his teacher to stand up. The latter prostrated himself twice more. At this point the Panchen Lama suddenly recalled his childhood. A shiver ran through him: 'Do not fear gods, do not fear ghosts, just fear your teachers when they bow before you.' As a child, he had always been afraid of those moments preceding physical punishment, but he could not believe that his teacher would beat him now that he was an adult. Furthermore, never had Ngulchu Rinpoche raised his hand to him since he had taken this post in 1954. A strange silence reigned. 'What have I done to deserve his anger?', wondered Chökyi Gyaltsen. The heavy silence was worse than a slap.

Eventually, Ngulchu Rinpoche came and sat beside him. Only then did he break the silence. He urged him not to present the petition to the Chinese government. Chökyi Gyaltsen did not understand his teacher's sudden opposition. The year before, Ngulchu and Ngabo had insisted that he give up the idea, but Ngulchu had told him that if he persevered with his intention, he should at least attend to the writing, for it was essential to present the report in a fluid and precise language.

'What you have to say you have already said several times to most of the Party leaders', said Ngulchu Rinpoche. 'The central powers have appointed investigation committees which regularly send detailed reports on the situation in Tibet. In the course of the last two plenary sessions, I heard two delegates mention the problem of our country and people. Their view of the situation and the mistakes that were made is exhaustive enough. If they intend to correct them and solve our problems at last, they will do so. If they have no such intention, you can write all the petitions you like but they will take no notice.' The religious man made one thing absolutely clear: in the end, only a few men in Beijing make the decisions.

The Panchen Lama did not share his teacher's opinion, and told him so quite frankly: 'The situation in Tibet is very complex. If the central government receives only incomplete information and has no overall understanding, it will not pay attention to the overall problem of Tibet; and it will do nothing ...'

Ngulchu Rinpoche was not convinced. Chökyi Gyaltsen tried to reassure him by explaining that this was the right time to hand over such a document because the central powers had announced new directives, possibly a sign that they were easing up on their reform policy.

This did nothing to reduce his teacher's fear. He was convinced that 'something bad would happen'. He had in fact consulted the oracle several times and the outcome had not been encouraging. Ngulchu Rinpoche reminded his pupil that in politics things change as quickly as the summer weather in China. 'Today,' he said, 'we follow the policy of the "three prohibitions" and the "three me's". Tomorrow, it will be the policy of the "three understandings" and the "three struggles".' His enumeration of real and imaginary slogans illustrated the reality of Chinese politics over the last few years: hesitations and about-turns had made the situation extremely unstable.

'No, that is not true,' repeated the Panchen Lama. He knew that it would serve no purpose to go against the instructions of Mao Tse-tung, Chou En-lai and Li Weihan, yet if he handed them the document, more attention might be focused on what was happening in his country.

Ngulchu Rinpoche refused to give in to his pupil's arguments: 'The Dalai Lama had to flee our country,' he recalled, and in a prophetic tone added: 'If misfortune befell you, it would affect not only you. Our monastery of Tashilhunpo, our region of Tsang, and the political and religious life of the whole of Tibet would also suffer. Millions of Tibetans would feel isolated and abandoned ...'

The teacher could hold back his tears no longer. The Panchen Lama, very aware of his love and concern, hesitated to contradict him but was even less happy about the idea of betraying his conscience and letting his personal safety come before the future of his country. He explained at length to Ngulchu Rinpoche that he had taken the decision only after mature reflection on what would be the best for Tibet and the prosperity of Buddhism. The conversation continued long into the night, but neither of them gave way.

When the report was at last completed in Tibetan, the translation into Chinese began. Again, because the Panchen Lama wanted the text to be as precise as possible, he invited the Ninth Panchen Lama's interpreter back from Sichuan to assist his own translators. Eventually, he chose the cautious title: 'Report on the Suffering of the People of Tibet and the Tibetan regions and Propositions for the Future Work of the Central Committee Under the Respectful Supervision of Prime Minister Chou En-lai.' The Chinese version of the text numbered 70,000 characters, and thus its length became its title.

The petition was handed over to Chou En-lai on 18 May 1962. It comprised eight sections:

1 The struggle to quell rebellions;
2 Democratic reforms;
3 The raising of livestock, agricultural output and the life of the masses;
4 The work of the United Front;
5 Democratic centralism;
6 Dictatorship of the proletariat;
7 Religious issues;
8 Nationalities.

Chökyi Gyaltsen asked the central powers to accept the petition in the spirit in which it had been written. It merely aimed to find a solution to the social, economic and cultural difficulties of the country. He wrote:

After the introduction of reforms, Buddhism received a serious blow, and is now about to disappear ... Many prisoners died in a distressing way when the dictatorship of the proletariat was introduced. Over the last few years, the population of Tibet has been greatly reduced ... the majority of able-bodied and intelligent men from the Tibetan regions of Qinghai, Gansu, Sichuan and Yunnan have been imprisoned ...

The 120-page document gave a detailed account of the situation in the Tibetan regions which the Panchen Lama had visited on his investigative journey in 1961 and 1962. One of his main criticisms concerned the excessive punishment imposed by the authorities in retaliation for the 1959 uprising in Tibet.

We have absolutely no means of knowing how many people were arrested. There were at least 10,000 arrests in each region. Good or evil, innocents or guilty, all were arrested, in contravention of any legal system anywhere in the world ...

In some areas, most of the men have been imprisoned, leaving only women, elderly people and children to carry on the work ...

The Panchen Lama denounced categorically a punishment policy that was based on collective responsibility. Under this policy it was permissible to execute Tibetans if members of their family had been involved in any way in the struggle against the Chinese. He accused officials of having deliberately kept political prisoners in extremely harsh conditions, which had resulted in a great number of unjustifiable deaths. The Panchen Lama continued, hoping – somewhat naïvely – that he could persuade Beijing to discontinue its policy of people's communes:

> You must first of all make sure that the people do not starve. In numerous regions of Tibet, people died of hunger ... In some areas entire families died and the death rate was extremely high. This is utterly unacceptable, terrible and serious. Tibet may have lived in a dark age of barbarous feudalism in the past, but there were never such food shortages, especially after the blossoming of Buddhism. In Tibetan regions, the masses now live in such destitution that elderly people and children die of starvation ... or they are so weak that they have no resistance to disease and consequently die ...

Chökyi Gyaltsen also pointed out that some of Beijing's decisions had had tragic, and unforeseen results. For instance, in order to give everybody a meal, they had forced people to eat in canteens. But the sole result of this was that the Tibetan population became even hungrier, for they received a daily ration of only about 5oz of grain mixed with grass, leaves and tree bark. The Tibetan dignitary wrote bitterly:

> This horrible pittance is not enough to sustain the life of anybody; people are hungry all the time. Also, once prisoners have completed their time in jail, always in very harsh conditions, they are made to carry out extremely hard tasks.

Never have such things happened before in the history of Tibet. People could never have imagined such terrible famine, not even in their worst nightmares. In some areas, if someone even catches a cold, he inevitably contaminates hundreds of people and most of them die ...

Further into the text, the Panchen Lama denounced official policy as the reason for all the deaths – not natural disasters, as Mao Tse-tung had declared to foreign guests.

In Tibet, most activities related to agriculture and raising livestock stopped for two years, from 1959 to 1961. The nomads have no grain, and the farmers no meat, butter, or salt. It is forbidden to transport food or materials. Ordinary people are not allowed to travel, and their *tsampa* bags have been confiscated ...

Thirty-eight years after the Panchen Lama's plea, it remains difficult to assess accurately the consequences of the Chinese policy imposed on Tibet and on the neighbouring areas inhabited by Tibetans since 1950. However, the many testimonies gathered by the Tibetan government in exile, or by independent organizations such as the International Commission of Jurists appointed by the United Nations in 1959, demonstrate the scale of human and cultural tragedy endured by the Tibetans.

As the Panchen Lama pointed out, the land reforms and people's communes resulted in thousands of deaths. Villages disappeared, valleys were emptied of their inhabitants and some ethnic groups almost wiped out. The exchange of produce between nomads (meat and dairy products) and farmers (vegetables and grain) became impossible because of the transfer of populations and the loss of high pastures to cultivation. The change of diet and the obligation to grow varieties of grain that were inappropriate for the climate also contributed to the slaughter. Chökyi Gyaltsen recalled that famine had been unknown in the past. Ancient documents do mention shortages of food, but the populations concerned did not hesitate to move to find better land, with the agreement – and even the financial support – of the lord for whom they worked.

Health was an issue. In Tibet, there had been endemic diseases such as smallpox, which had affected the Thirteenth Dalai Lama. In the event of an epidemic, the local authorities barred all access to the valleys affected, to prevent the illness spreading, then doctors and healers did their best to cure the afflicted. With the massive influx of Chinese people came new diseases, against which the indigenous population had no adequate defence. Antiquated industries and mines caused work-related illnesses and, more frequently, cardiovascular and respiratory problems as a result of the pollution. The outcome of this was disastrous and the deterioration in living standards had seriously detrimental results. The Chinese authorities acknowledge that the population decreased by approximately 7.5 per cent between 1951 and 1959. The consequences of their policies and the discrimination against Tibetans are still visible today. In the Autonomous Region of Tibet, life expectancy is 40 years, whereas in China it is 71 years. The infant death rate is reported to have reached 150 per 1,000, compared with only 32 per 1,000 in China and around 7 per 1,000 in the West.

Moreover, the transfer of population mentioned by the Panchen Lama in 'The Seventy-Thousand Characters' reveals a policy of assimilation. Before the 1949 invasion, the population of Tibet totalled approximately 6 million people. Over 1.2 million Tibetans disappeared during the period of terror following the 1959 uprising and the '20-year war'. 1987 statistics estimated the Tibetan population at 5.2 million. Statistics published in 1990 assessed it at 4.59 million. As early as 1962, the Panchen Lama expressed his concern:

The population of Tibet has seriously dwindled. Not only is this detrimental to the prosperity of the Tibetan race; it is also a great danger to its very existence, possibly bringing it to the brink of extinction.

Nowadays Lhasa is a Chinese town, with only one third of its 135,000 inhabitants being Tibetan. It is the same in all Tibetan towns and some of them have even been erased from maps to leave room for typically Chinese cities, inhabited only by settlers.

The poor state of health of the Tibetan people denounced by the Panchen Lama is partly explained by the fact that most of the Chinese doctors sent to Tibet were those who had failed their exams, and these were the ones who then trained Tibetan doctors. For a long time, traditional Tibetan medicine was regarded as mere superstition. Under these circumstances, public health declined and there were numerous cases of disability, or even death, caused by inappropriate prescribing. As the number of hospital beds was insufficient, Tibetans and Chinese were segregated, to the advantage of the latter. Even now, the hospital of Lhasa does not provide the level of healthcare that might be expected from a modern establishment; for any delicate operation it is necessary to go to Chengdu, in Sichuan, or another large Chinese city.

Before 1959, tobacco was strictly forbidden in Tibet, and several reasons were put forward to justify its prohibition. According to one, the blood of a female devil, killed during a fight with the gods, continued to nourish the subtle life of the plant; smoking, therefore, was equated with absorbing bad energy! But tobacco had always been smuggled, and the end of traditional structures freed its consumption. Its use was also promoted by Chinese soldiers, along with the consumption of strong spirits. Nowadays, through idleness and the lack of a spiritual inner life, more people use and abuse these products. Their low price, at least as far as spirits are concerned, is certainly an incentive to do so. The Chinese administration makes a handsome profit from them: it is easier to subdue a people which is to an extent anaesthetizied.

Some sources indicate that there were forced abortions in Tibet as early as 1955, though at this time they were limited to certain areas of Qinghai. But in 1960, a few months after the Lhasa uprising, refugees testified that such measures had spread throughout the whole territory. Since 1963, the Chinese authorities have been advising Tibetan men under 30 and Tibetan women under 25 not to marry, but they have encouraged mixed marriages between Tibetans and Chinese.

To limit the Tibetan birth rate, the Chinese sterilized vast numbers of women or forced them to have abortions, sometimes as late as eight-and-a-half months into the pregnancy. Young girls, sometimes only 12 or so, and women up to the age of 45, were rounded up in the village square, where a medical tent had been pitched. Armed soldiers guarded the site. These 'volunteers' were taken care of after the operation, but other women were not so lucky. Foetuses were stacked at the entrance of the tent, where they could be seen by the young Tibetan women waiting their turn. Some women suffered terrible injuries as a result of these operations; others did not survive them at all and died on the spot.

The population was subjected to constant controls, notably the unannounced search of their homes. It was, of course, compulsory to declare any pregnancy. If doctors thought that a family was not respecting the policy of the Party, they immediately proceeded with sterilization or abortion. These same doctors received bonuses based on the number of operations they performed.

From 1964, the Chinese used the Tibetans as guinea pigs. Young women in particular were forcibly taken to undergo surgical operations. The bodies of those who died were then cut into pieces and thrown to birds of prey – 'to respect Buddhist tradition' said the Chinese; 'so that they could not be recognized' added the Tibetans. When the Chinese doctors departed, they left behind only a pile of bloody bandages and surgical instruments, often forgotten amongst the remains of the corpses.

The policy of forced sterilization and birth control still goes on. According to the Chinese authorities, they are only injecting high-risk Tibetan women against syphilis! There is also a very high death rate of children aged between one and six, and Chinese doctors 'put to sleep' newborn babies by giving them injections of pure alcohol in the head. Children are also smothered with devices specially designed for this purpose. Such practices are still carried out and their perpetrators still receive bonuses.

By submitting to the demands of the Chinese administration, Tibetan women have lost all their rights, including those over their own bodies. From the moment of conception, Tibetan children were, and still are, in the same position. The State appropriates them and decides who will be born and who will live. Today in Tibet, Beijing still has the right to kill a Tibetan child whose only crime was to be born without the consent of the occupying administration.

The Panchen Lama did not hesitate for one moment in his violent attack on Beijing, and in particular on their prohibition of religious practice: 'When a nationality is deprived of its language, traditional dress and customs, then it disappears and transforms into another nationality. How can we guarantee that the Tibetans will not be transformed into another race?' At the same time he criticized the religious policy of the Chinese communists. Indeed, the central powers considered this point the most dangerous part of his document. The Panchen Lama fully supported attempts to reform the monasteries, but on the one hand he accused local 'leftists' (who disregarded the government's instructions) of all manner of abuses, and on the other feared that the Chinese Communist Party might be tempted to eradicate any form of religion. For him, religious freedom was an absolute right; any attempt to forbid it would have serious consequences.

'Of the 2,500 monasteries existing in the past [in what is now called the Autonomous Region of Tibet], only 70 remain, and 93 per cent of the monks have been forced to leave their monasteries,' he wrote, four years *before* the Cultural Revolution, although this is usually cited as the reason for the closure and destruction of monasteries in Tibet. 'The Buddhist religion, whose only aim is Enlightenment, has up to now flourished in Tibet. It now seems to be on the verge of annihilation, under our very eyes. Neither I nor 90 per cent of my fellow Tibetans can tolerate this.'

Since then, over 8,000 monasteries and cultural centres have been ransacked and destroyed. The Chinese are now faced with a dilemma. If they were to grant true religious freedom, monasteries and nunneries would spring up all over the country; if they were to prohibit or curtail religious freedom, they would inevitably be faced with further difficulties in the country, for religion and national identity go together in Tibet. For young Tibetans, monasteries are their only chance to receive an education in line with the values and traditions of their country. Therefore, the more limitations the Chinese impose on the monasteries, the greater the Tibetans' bitterness and their desire to resist.

16

Imprisonment and Rehabilitation

Can it be darker than darkness?

In 1964, the year of the Wood Dragon, the sky grew ever darker over Tibet. The Panchen Lama had continued to attract the anger of the Chinese leaders over the last two years. Mao Tse-tung now referred to him as 'the enemy of our class'. It was said that the Chinese premier Chou En-lai had admitted that mistakes had been made in the past, but not that he had ever tried to exterminate the Tibetan race, religion and culture. Yet the report of the International Commission of Jurists proved the opposite and the United Nations twice denounced China for its policy in Tibet.

Chökyi Gyaltsen met the authorities of Beijing several more times. Chou En-lai even commented on 'The Seventy-Thousand Characters':

You were able to write this document in record time. This is an extraordinary feat. You have managed to combine our views on social classes, nationalities, patriotism and the people. Our policy consists in getting rid of counter-revolutionary actions and correcting past mistakes. Wherever there is a rebellion, we must quell it without thinking. Up to now, reforms and the suppression of rebellions have saved the Tibetan religion and race, which were on the brink of annihilation ... I hope that you will be able to suggest ways of improving agriculture, raising livestock and trade, by applying our methods, which have borne fruit in other regions of China. The resolutions concerning the lives of the most destitute people should also be taken into account ... We are absolutely convinced that Comrade Panchen Lama and Comrades Ngabo, Phagpala and Che Jigme are opposed to imperialism. As patriots, they acknowledge the leadership of the Party and follow socialist principles. It is necessary to trust in our comrades on the Work Committee, whose aim is quite simply to fulfil their mission in Tibet, not to destroy the race and the religion of the country ...

As usual, a great number of monks gathered for the *Mönlam* celebrations that year, but everywhere, armed soldiers watched for the slightest sign of protest, and pro-Chinese informers mingled with the crowds around the Jokhang and the other temples of the town. Faithful to their sacred rituals, the Tibetans put on their best clothes, cleaned their houses and repainted the façades. New prayer flags were tied to the roofs of houses and monasteries. However, both religious and lay people felt increasingly uncomfortable about the Chinese occupation. As they sent their good wishes to the Panchen Lama for a long life, their thoughts and prayers went also to the Dalai Lama, who they knew was now settled in Dharamsala. In spite of everything, he was still their spiritual guide and temporal leader.

During the New Year celebrations, Chökyi Gyaltsen decided to address the population of the capital, who had massed before his Shugtri Lingka residence for the occasion. Surrounded by prominent Chinese personalities, Chökyi Gyaltsen embarked on a long speech accusing the occupying forces and making frequent references to 'The Seventy-Thousand Characters'. Lamas had begun their sacred dances (*tcham*) as he approached the end of his speech saying: 'I want you to know that I consider His Holiness the Fourteenth Dalai Lama as my refuge in this life as well as in the next ...' His final words were 'Long live the Dalai Lama!', which Beijing took as an insult.

The die was cast. A few days later, Chökyi Gyaltsen went back to Shigatse, but Beijing had already taken a decision: from then on Tibetans were forbidden to go on pilgrimage to Tashilhunpo monastery. One August morning, Chinese troops suddenly surrounded the place and armoured cars aimed their guns at the *stupas*. The Panchen Lama was arrested, as were dozens of monks who tried to defend their master. His teacher, Ngulchu Rinpoche, and a high dignitary called Dzasa Tsethong met the same fate.

Chökyi Gyaltsen's trial lasted 17 days. He was accused of being an obstacle in the way of socialism and of having supported underground guerrillas whose aim was to drive the occupying forces out of Tibet. Every day, the Chinese forced his closest assistants, including Phagpala Gelek Namgyal, Yeshe Tsultrim and Trantsa Tamdrin Gyelpo, to accuse him of the most odious crimes during *thamzing* sessions in front of monks and lay people. Informing became an everyday occurrence and a terrible political tool. The communists' aim now was to humiliate the Panchen Lama, a man who had been continuously manipulated from a very young age.

On 17 December, in Beijing, the central powers removed the Dalai Lama from the chairmanship of PCART. He was described as 'an incorrigible stray dog in the pay of reactionary and imperialist foreigners' and accused of having created 'a fake government and constitution'. Four days later Chou En-lai made a public speech offering the Panchen Lama 'a last chance to repent'. The Panchen Lama refused and was put under house arrest. Several sessions of *thamzing* followed, in the course of which he was subjected to the worst possible humiliations.

His chances deteriorated with the arrival of the Cultural Revolution. After Red Guards appeared in Lhasa, it was no longer possible for communists to make pacifying speeches about Tibet. The Panchen Lama was taken to Qincheng jail in Beijing, from where he was not released until 1977. The Dalai Lama describes this period with great restraint:

And when the people rose in revolt, which they did on several different occasions after 1959, whole villages were razed, their inhabitants murdered, whilst tens of thousands of the remaining population were put into prison. There they were kept under the most vile conditions, with forced labour by day, *thamzing* sessions until late at night, and only starvation rations to nourish them. I myself have since spoken to a number of people who were prisoners of the Chinese. One of them was Dr Tenzin Chödrak, who had been appointed my junior personal physician in the late 1950s. When the first fact-finding mission went to Beijing, I requested that they ask the authorities there that he be released and allowed to join me in exile.

Nothing came of this at first, but a year later he was finally freed and, at the end of 1980, he came to Dharamsala. The stories of cruelty and degradation he brought with him were almost unbelievable. Many times over the twenty years of his incarceration he had been close to death from starvation. He told me of how he and his fellow prisoners were forced to consume their own clothing for food and how one inmate with whom he was in hospital at one time, was so desperate that when he passed a worm in his meagre stool, he washed it and ate it.[1]

After the death of Mao Tse-tung in 1976, the year of the Fire Dragon, people believed that they saw some signs from China of willingness to open up and engage in dialogue. In 1977, Chairman Li Xinnian made more conciliatory speeches and even expressed regrets about the excesses of the Cultural Revolution. The trial of the 'Gang of Four' presented an opportunity to promote a new image of China, far removed from the abuses of previous years. At that same time, Ngabo Ngawang Jigme, who was by now something of a notable in the Communist Party, announced in a speech that Beijing wished the Dalai Lama to return to Lhasa. In November 1978, the release of 34 prisoners, all former members of the Tibetan administration, was given massive publicity.

A few months later, the Chinese dissident Wei Jingsheng, in a 20-page text dated 3 March 1979, described life in the prison of Qincheng, which had been so unbearable that, like many other political prisoners, the Panchen Lama had tried several times to commit suicide, notably by refusing to eat. On several occasions Chökyi Gyaltsen had asked his gaolers to let him die. 'You will be able to take my corpse to the Central Committee', he told Wei Jingsheng.

As for the Chinese re-education camps, the infamous *laogai*, 50 million[2] prisoners have disappeared there since the communists arrived in power. Since 1949, over 1.2 million people[3] – one Tibetan in five – have been victims of genocide. In these camps, people whose work output is considered insufficient are still being starved, tortured, left to die, or executed. Men, women and children still die without knowing why. Their corpses are part of a thriving industry – which is condoned by hospitals, doctors and transplant recipients. Ninety per cent of the transplants sold by China are from executed prisoners, women who died in childbirth and 'illegal' children. The recipients are in Singapore and Macao as well as some Western countries. Since 1949, Western countries have continued, in the interests of trade and profit, to turn a blind eye to a country which continues to kill, murder and torture on behalf of communist ideology.

Wei Jingsheng wrote much later:

... Just as the two of us passed by the village the bright sunlight shone on the green weeds growing through the cracks in the mud walls ... Later, at a gathering at a friend's home, I heard stories of how villagers had exchanged their babies with each other as food. I felt I could practically see, looming up from the weeds in the cracks of those mud walls, the pained expression of parents chewing the flesh of children they had received in exchange for their own babies. Were the children happily catching butterflies in the fields nearby reincarnations of those children who had been eaten? I felt sorry for them, and even sorrier for their parents. Who had made them do this? Who had made them swallow, amidst the tears and misery of other parents, the one thing that they had never imagined they would taste, human flesh.

By now I could make out the face of the executioner quite clearly. He was a man of the kind that appears, as the saying goes, only 'once every few centuries worldwide, and once in several millennia in China.'[4] That was Mao Tse-tung. It was Mao and his followers who had used their most evil systems and policies to force those parents, starved beyond reason, to give up their own flesh and blood to feed others in exchange for flesh to feed themselves. It was Mao Tse-tung who, in order to make up for his crime of smothering democracy[5] and carrying out the 'Great Leap Forward', had driven millions of dazed peasants to take up their hoes and strike down their neighbours and eat the flesh of people just like themselves to save their own lives. They were not the executioners; Mao Tse-tung and his followers were. Only then did I understand where Peng Dehuai[6] had found the strength to attack the Mao-led Party Central Committee. Only then did I understand why the peasants so bitterly hated 'communism', and why they could not comprehend why Liu Shaoqi's policy of calling for more private plots and enterprises and fixed output quotas had been overturned. It was because never again did they want to be forced to give up their own flesh and blood for others to devour, and to lose all reason and kill their neighbours for food just to go on living. This was a much stronger reason than any 'ism'.[7]

In spite of the tortures and the endless sessions of *thamzing* he endured, the Panchen Lama survived, simply because being alive would allow him to testify on behalf of Tibet, his country, and of the Tibetans, his people. He was reminded constantly of this text by Gyalwa Gendün Gyatso:

The cycle of existence is a burning chain of suffering, birth, illness, old age and death pours down on us like rain. Is there anything more insane than knowing this and not fighting for ultimate liberation? When illness strikes us, we find it difficult to endure the pain beyond a few days. Just imagine what we would do if we were reborn in hell? We should avoid evil behaviour, and nurture the ways of goodness.[8]

On 1 February 1979, the United States officially recognized China. In 1978 the Panchen Lama had been rehabilitated and appointed vice-chairman of the Autonomous Region of Tibet. Restored to his position as vice-chairman of the People's National Congress, he immediately asked the Chinese authorities for permission to go to Tibet; they granted this but managed to make it impossible for him to get in touch with certain people who were 'not very commendable'.

At this time, three delegations of Tibetans in exile were allowed to go to Tibet, via Beijing, on investigative missions. The first delegation confirmed the suffering of an entire people, mass destruction and famine; the second one, composed mainly of young people, had to go back to India very quickly; the third, led by Jetsun Pema, the younger sister of the Dalai Lama, looked into education. Jetsun Pema secretly met Dr Tenzin Chödrak, who later rejoined the Dalai Lama in Dharamsala and took up his old position as his personal physician.

In Lhasa we saw 30,000 of our countrymen. The visits followed one another in an exhausting rhythm, from five in the morning until two the following morning. It took all our energy not to leave anyone out so that we could listen to all those who wanted to talk to us. We divided the work. At night some of us remained in our rooms while the others visited the inhabitants. Two small girls served as our messengers, bringing us letters for His Holiness. Both of them knew the mantras very well and recited them with me. Although I, of course, remember them very well, I cannot mention their names because this would place their lives in danger.

The day of our arrival in the capital was very moving. We approached from the direction of Shigatse, then, on turning a corner, we suddenly caught sight of the Potala. The building was as extraordinarily beautiful as ever. The delegation settled into an inn and, as soon as I could, I looked out of the window. The Potala stood majestically on a hill in the moonlight. The sight of a small light flickering made me feel nostalgic. Later, I learnt that, apart from a caretaker in one room, no one now lived in the immense empty palace. Remembering my childhood and my visits to His Holiness, I was unable to hold back my tears.[9]

Only in 1982 was the Panchen Lama eventually allowed to leave Beijing. On his arrival in Lhasa, on 6 July, over 20,000 people came to welcome him in front of the Tsuklakhang. He declared:[10]

Tibet is my birthplace and I feel particular concern for the country. I have not spent the last 18 years here, but my heart has always been at one with that of the Tibetan people. I always missed Tibet and the Tibetan people and I always thought about the interests of the people ...

Some time later, Chökyi Gyaltsen made another speech:

Young people should take advantage of their youth to study hard, and particularly to study Tibetan culture, so as to raise the level of the whole nation and help it to take its place among the developed nations ...

On 24 July, over 500 monks welcomed Panchen Rinpoche to Tashilhunpo. The ceremonies were impressive and the place was filled with a strange fervour. The Chinese kept constant watch over Chökyi Gyaktsen, but this did not prevent him from declaring his attachment to Tibet.

In 1985, the year of the Wood Ox in the Tibetan calendar, during the *Mönlam* festival, the Panchen Lama again addressed the Tibetans:

The friendship I share with His Holiness the Dalai Lama is of a spiritual nature. In that way there is no difference between His Holiness and me. Some people try to sow discord between us. But they will not succeed.

Two years later, in the year of the Fire Hare, during the People's National Congress in Beijing, the Panchen Lama again very firmly criticized Chinese policies concerning education, economic development, population transfers and discrimination against Tibetans in Tibet.

Chökyi Gyaltsen, the Tenth Panchen Lama, arrived in Shigatse on 9 January 1989 to consecrate the renovated mausoleums of the Fifth, Sixth, Seventh, Eighth and Ninth Panchen Lamas, which had been destroyed during the Cultural Revolution. The celebrations took place on 24 January. Chökyi Gyaltsen took advantage of the occasion to declare that the Chinese occupation of Tibet had brought more destruction than benefit to the Tibetan people. He had perhaps gone too far. Four days later he died, in mysterious circumstances.

After the death of Chökyi Gyaltsen, the communists painted a posthumous picture of the Tenth Panchen Lama, in the light of their atheist views. According to them, he was an outstanding spiritual master in Tibetan Buddhism, a great 'patriot' and an efficient statesman. They said that the Tenth Panchen Lama, as vice-chairman of the People's National Congress Permanent Committee, the highest political organization in the People's Republic of China, and honorary chairman of the Buddhist Association of China for many years, had opposed the 'separatists' led by the Dalai Lama and his clique, thus significantly contributing to the unification of the 'motherland', to the happiness of the Tibetan people, to the expansion of Buddhism and to world peace. And, by constantly working for the advancement of Tibet, he had promised to be reborn so as to be able to pursue his significant task. This was the official picture, with no mention of Chökyi Gyaltsen's anti-Chinese stance in 1962, his imprisonment or his 're-education'.

The authorities in Beijing also had their own version of the circumstances surrounding the Tenth Panchen Lama's death. This is their account of events. He left Lhasa for the monastery of Tashilhunpo on 13 January 1989. On 22 January, he consecrated a *stupa* containing the relics of five of his predecessors, collected from the ruins of the tombs dynamited by Red Guards during the Cultural Revolution. He also presided over several religious ceremonies. Overworked, he suffered a heart attack and the central government immediately dispatched high-ranking officials and heart specialists to Shigatse to assist the Panchen Lama's personal physicians, but all treatment was in vain. Chökyi Gyaltsen left this world on 28 January 1989, at 8.16pm.

To the Tibetans in exile, relying on eyewitness accounts, it looked more like a poisoning organized by Beijing, provoked by the Panchen Lama's speech after consecrating the *stupa*, in the course of which he had expressed pro-independence sentiments.

Regarding the issue of his reincarnation, local communist officials said that, four days before his death, the Panchen Lama had gathered around him high-ranking lamas from the provinces of Qinghai, Gansu, Sichuan and Yunnan and said to them: 'First choose three candidates, then draw lots from the Golden Urn, which should be placed in front of the statue of Shakyamuni.' It is of course now impossible to confirm the accuracy of these words.

In order to respect the alleged wishes of the Panchen Lama and Tibetan tradition, the authorities in Beijing ordered a 49-day period of mourning and invited all Chinese Buddhists as well as Tibetans to pray for the man whom they now praised as a national hero, after having mistreated him for some 15 years. The funeral was scheduled for 30 January. The People's Government of the Autonomous Region of Tibet and the Democratic Management Committee of Tashilhunpo were made responsible for the building of a *stupa* and a memorial in honour of Panchen Chökyi Gyaltsen; both were to be erected in the monastery itself 'so that future generations may honour the memory of the man who accrued so much patriotic and Buddhist merit'.

At the same time, a committee was appointed to take charge of the communist search for the reincarnation of the deceased, under the overall responsibility of the Democratic Management Committee of Tashilhunpo, who could if necessary call for the assistance of the Buddhist Association of China and its branch in Tibet. These measures – warmly welcomed in Tibetan Buddhist circles, according to the authorities in Beijing – were made public by Li Peng himself, at that time the premier of the People's Republic of China.

PART III

The Eleventh Panchen Lama
(1989–)

17

Puppet of Beijing

B eijing allotted a subsidy of 77.41 million yuans[1] for the building of a *stupa* (inaugurated on 4 September 1993), the preservation of relics and for the funding of its search for the reincarnation of the Tenth Panchen Lama.

On 31 January 1989, Beijing appointed Chadrel Rinpoche to set up a 'search committee' to find the reincarnated child. A few days later, the Chinese premier, Li Peng, declared that from then on 'strangers would not be allowed to interfere with the selection'.

In August, the Chinese authorities made public a five-stage project for the search, selection and recognition of the Panchen Lama, which was the result of a compromise with the religious authorities of Tashilhunpo. The first three stages followed the Tibetan tradition, the other two were Chinese additions:

1   The questioning of mystical signs to find suitable children as candidates;
2   The setting of traditional tests to differentiate between candidates, such as asking the children to choose objects which had belonged to the Panchen Lama;
3   The use of oracles and divination to confirm the best candidates;
4   The drawing of lots by a Chinese official to select the reincarnation;
5   The approval of the final decision by the authorities in Beijing.

Since the government of the People's Republic of China, whose doctrine was atheism, supported the spiritual procedures involved in the search, ulterior motives were suspected. The political authorities in Beijing ordered that ceremonies conforming to Tibetan Buddhist traditional rituals should be performed regularly in the monasteries of China as well as those of occupied Tibet. Between December 1990 and July 1993, the monks of monasteries in Qinghai, Gansu, Sichuan and Yunnan – that is, in areas inhabited by Tibetans – each day recited 23 sacred texts from *Kangyur* and *Tengyur*. Some *sutras* were even chanted over 5 million times to support the search for the reincarnation.

One delegation, headed by one of the Tenth Panchen Lama's teachers and advised – not to say watched over – by Zhao Puchu, chairman of the Buddhist Association of China, and Phagpala Gelek Namgyal, vice-chairman of the same association and honorary chairman of its Tibetan branch, went twice to the lake of Lhamo Latso.

As soon as he arrived in this mystical place, the Tenth Panchen Lama's teacher, with the assistance of several spiritual masters, made an offering to the guardian of the spirits who opens the gates of the sacred site. After several days of chanting, the water of the lake suddenly changed before their very eyes. All the colours of the rainbow appeared in turn in their splendour. Vivid scenes unfolded, which the teacher dutifully noted down. They included *mandalas*, geometric patterns and spectacular images. The water then turned a milky colour and began to bubble. The magical qualities of the lake of Lhamo Latso were revealed only to those whose minds had remained pure.

Back at their monastery in Shigatse, the members of the delegations met several times. The lake had, in effect, revealed secrets; and because the Tenth Panchen Lama had faced north-east at the time of his death, they concluded that his reincarnation was probably born east or north-east of Tashilhunpo, in the year of the Snake, Horse or Sheep in the Tibetan calendar.

On 24 February 1994, three search groups were secretly dispatched to particular areas of the country. Over the following year, 28 children were selected in 46 counties in the provinces of Qinghai, Gansu, Sichuan and Yunnan, as well as in the Autonomous Region of Tibet. The lamas went once more to the lake of Lhamo Latso, where they waited some days for more visions. Once the clues gathered by the three search groups and the new secrets revealed by the lake had all been closely examined, the delegation decided to retain 8 of the 28 candidates. Their selection brought to an end the first stage of the search for the reincarnation of the Tenth Panchen Lama.

According to Beijing, the search had so far proceeded without incident. But soon the Chinese government declared that the Dalai Lama was trying to sabotage the search and that his declarations and actions were putting at risk investigations which were China's 'sole' responsibility. By saying this, not only was China disregarding the centuries-old relationship between the Dalai Lama and the Panchen Lama, but it had once again appropriated a spiritual issue, despite the country's ideological materialism. The Chinese government denounced the 'manoeuvres' of Tenzin Gyatso who, they said, had as early as December 1993 sent spies to Tashilhunpo to get in touch with 'separatists' and 'traitors', such as Chadrel Rinpoche. According to the Chinese authorities, the latter had taken advantage of his responsibilities as superior of Tashilhunpo and chairman of the search committee appointed by Beijing to delay the proceedings and, in particular, to hand secretly to the Dalai Lama the list of candidates for the succession of the Panchen Lama.

Meanwhile, China was still deliberating over its candidate, who was to be chosen by the drawing of lots from a Golden Urn when, on 14 May 1995, in accordance with Tibetan tradition, Tenzin Gyatso, the Dalai Lama, officially recognized Gendün Chökyi Nyima, a six-year old boy from the village of Lhari, in the province of Nagchu, as the Eleventh Panchen Lama. Once again, conflict between the Dalai Lama and the People's Republic of China was only too obvious.

The communists had been bypassed by the man they considered as a 'bandit' and as one of the most dangerous opponents of the People's Republic of China. An official condemnation of the Dalai Lama's decision was made by Sengchen Lobsang Gyaltsen, honorary chairman of the Democratic Management Committee of the monastery of Tashilhunpo, who explained that this 'plot', organized in the monastery itself, could only be detrimental to Tibet. In effect, he felt that the Dalai Lama's choice was totally illegal and not in accordance with historical conventions linking Tibet to China.

In his speech, he reminded people that the selection of the Panchen Lama had to be made by drawing lots from a Golden Urn, and then be confirmed by the central government of the People's Republic of China. He also stressed that the parents of Gendün Chökyi Nyima, who were entirely in the pay of the Dalai Lama and his 'clique', had lied and pretended that their son was born at the end of April 1989. They had falsified his date of birth so that it was in line with that of a possible reincarnation. Finally, Sengchen Lobsang Gyaltsen declared: 'In any case, the child presumptuously appointed by the Dalai Lama cannot take part in the Golden Urn lottery. The search committee, the Democratic Management Committee and the ordinary monks of the monastery of Tashilhunpo will never accept his candidature.'

As faithful heirs of a centralized policy taken to the extreme, the Chinese authorities *now* believe that their right to control the selection of the most significant reincarnations of Tibetan Buddhism goes back to the Ming (1368–1644) and Qing (1644–1911) dynasties. The following letter, although written after the Golden Urn ceremony, sets out the background to this belief. It was written by Cai Fangbo, the Chinese ambassador in Paris, in answer to a letter about the selection and fate of Gendün Chökyi Nyima which had been sent to him by Louis de Broissia, the French Deputy for Côte-d'Or and Chairman of the Parliamentary Group for Tibet in the National Assembly, and Claude Huriet, Senator for Meurthe-et-Moselle and Chairman of the Association of Friends of Tibet in the Senate:

I received your letter of 29 May 1996. Its reading prompts me to inform you of my disagreement with the appointment of Chökyi Nyima as the successor of the Tenth Panchen Lama. In fact, the Dalai Lama's confirmation of the alleged reincarnated child of the Tenth Panchen Lama is illegal, null and void. To enable you to know more about the procedures, Tibetan religious rituals and historical rules governing the search for a reincarnated child of the Living Buddha, I would like to present them briefly to you, in the hope that this will help you to form an unprejudiced opinion on the issue.

The finding of a reincarnated child as successor to the deceased Living Buddha is specific to Tibetan Buddhism. Under the Yuan dynasty (in the 12th century) a system was established, and still remains in use, according to which the central government officially confers on the reincarnated child the title of Living Buddha. During the Ming and Qing dynasties, all the activities related to the succession of Living Buddhas gradually became subject to the control of the imperial authorities and ruled by the law and regulations of the State. As a result, the lottery and the central government's approval of the selection represent historical rules for identifying and confirming the reincarnations of great Living Buddhas, including those of the Panchen and Dalai Lamas. Moreover, Tibetan Buddhist circles are very much attached to these historical rules. Therefore it is clear that official confirmation of their reincarnations and titles by the central government is essential if the Dalai Lama and the Panchen Erdeni are to be legal and effective authorities in Tibetan Buddhism.

To assert his supreme authority, to preserve national unity and to prevent fraudulent activities in the search for the reincarnated child, the Qing dynasty instigated a lottery system. In effect, in 1793, Emperor Qianlong, of the Qing dynasty, promulgated a 29-article 'Ordinance for the More Efficient Governing of Tibet'. The first article stipulated methods and procedures governing the search for reincarnated children of the Dalai Lama and Panchen Lama. The lottery system was established by this document. To ensure its implementation, Emperor Qianlong ordered that two golden vases be specially made: one to be kept in the monastery of Jokhang for use in the search for the reincarnated children of the Dalai Lama, Panchen Lama and other great Tibetan Living Buddhas; the other to be placed in the Lama temple in Beijing to be used in the search for successors of great Living Buddhas of the Mongolian region.

According to religious rituals, it was first necessary to find children who were likely candidates for the reincarnation and then to inform the emperor and ask for his authorization to confirm one of them by means of a lottery. Then, with the emperor's approval, on an auspicious day, tablets bearing the names and dates of birth of the children were inserted in the golden vase. Then, in front of the statue of Shakyamuni and before the whole audience, the emperor's representative in Tibet drew lots to select the reincarnated child.

It should be emphasized that, since the time of Emperor Qianlong of the Qing dynasty, in accordance with administrative procedures, the local government of Tibet must always report faithfully and exhaustively to the central government everything related to the search, confirmation and enthronement of the reincarnations of the Dalai Lama and the Panchen Lama. The power to ratify this belongs solely to the central government. Consequently, the central government of the Kuomintang ratified the enthronement of the present Fourteenth Dalai Lama. Furthermore, the chairman of the central government Committee for Mongolian and Tibetan Affairs came specially to Lhasa to preside over his enthronement. As for the Tenth Panchen Lama, his title was conferred on him by Li Zhongren, acting chairman of the central government of the time. His enthronement ceremony took place in the monastery of Taer in Xining,[2] presided over by the chairman of the central government Committee for Mongolian and Tibetan Affairs.

The procedures concerning the search, confirmation and enthronement of the Eleventh Panchen Lama were in perfect accordance with religious rituals and historical rules: 1 A search party composed mainly of Living Buddhas and high-ranking monks from the monastery of Tashilhunpo was formed; 2 The reincarnated child was searched for according to religious rituals and established procedures; 3 The central government was informed of the discovery of children likely to be the reincarnation, so that the lottery could be authorized; 4 Lots were drawn in the presence of a central government representative; 5 Once the reincarnated child had been selected by lottery, the central government's official ratification was sought to enable the reincarnated child to be given his title of Panchen; 6 The enthronement ceremony was organized and again presided over by a central government representative. Several ceremonies took place after the lottery and the approval of the selection by the central government: at the first the title of Eleventh Panchen Lama was conferred on the reincarnated child; at the second he was enthroned; and at the third he received the Buddhist precepts. At that point, as the successor of the Tenth Panchen Lama, the Eleventh Panchen Lama can enjoy the full authority of the monks and believers in Tibetan Buddhism, who have complete trust in him.

All this demonstrates that it is the central government that has the power to ratify the reincarnated child's access to his title and that there is no way in which the Dalai Lama might presume to have this right. Yet, on 14 May 1995, before the lottery took place, and on his own initiative, the Dalai Lama suddenly announced in India the discovery of the alleged reincarnated child of the Panchen Lama. This sabotages religious rituals and goes against historical rules. It was a fraudulent move and a trick. This action denies the central government's supreme authority over the succession of the Panchen Lama. It is therefore illegal, null and void. The Dalai Lama tries by all means to exploit the issue of the succession of the Panchen Lama with the aim of changing the historical tradition observed by all Panchen Lamas who, one after the other, have always demonstrated their patriotism and spiritual authority in Tibetan Buddhism. In fact, the Dalai Lama's evil purpose is to create disorder in Tibet and bring about secession from China. As for the fate of the alleged reincarnated child confirmed by the Dalai Lama, I can tell you that the life and security of the child and his family are being taken care of. Therefore, we do not see any need for members of the French parliament to come and meet the child and his family in China.[3]

Beijing also makes reference to statistics, published by the Board for the Affairs of National Minorities, about the Qing dynasty: between the end of Emperor Qianlong's rule (1735–96) and the thirtieth year of Emperor Guangxu's rule (1904), 39 *tulku*, including the Tenth, Eleventh and Twelfth Panchen Lamas, were selected by lottery. According to the Chinese ambassador in Paris, for over 200 years in China, governments kept to this tradition, with the support of Tibetan Buddhists, making it an immutable convention for the reincarnations of Dalai Lamas and Panchen Lamas. Consequently, the central powers think that this is an essential procedure for the selection of the reincarnation of the Tenth Panchen Lama. However, they specify that an exemption might be granted in circumstances previously determined with the authorities concerned.

The ambassador of the People's Republic of China gave a very good summary of the Chinese conception of relations between his country and Tibet. It is based on a centralized view which consciously leaves aside certain historical truths. Unfortunately, in the West, because of a poor knowledge of Tibetan history, there have been many false assumptions about Sino-Tibetan relations, but the historical arguments put forward by the Chinese diplomat do not stand close and objective analysis. When monastic structures began to develop in the twelfth century, the abbots and religious leaders of the Tibetan high plateau looked for patrons among the most powerful families. This was in accordance with an important concept in Buddhism which links a person dedicated to spiritual life with his benefactor. The former prays for the latter and the latter ensures the material comfort of the former.

As the economic and political implications of monastic networks became more obvious, it became necessary to have ever more powerful protectors. The Tibetans turned to the Mongols, rulers over the north of Asia. Once the Mongols became masters of China, the religious men of the high plateau continued more than ever to maintain their links with the new Yuan dynasty (1271–1368). The Mongolian emperors recognized the authority of the Sakyapa lineage in Tibet and set up political structures. In exchange, the Sakyapa religious men ruled over Buddhist affairs in the whole empire. It was therefore a relation between equals: 'The religious personality guarantees spiritual life ... and the patron as benefactor enables the religion to flourish.'[4] It was also a relation between individuals and not between States. The relation persisted in spite of changes in dynasties, because the successive rulers of China always found great political advantage in being the protectors of Tibetan religious people, whose influence spread throughout the Chinese empire, with only little or ineffective control imposed on it by the imperial authorities.

Emperor Qianlong, whom the ambassador mentions, was

undoubtedly one of the most striking figures in the long history of China. His armies intervened twice in Tibet: once against Dzungarian Mongols (1751), then against the Gurkhas (1791). The regulations he promulgated in 1793 aimed to restore order in Tibetan political life, though most of them were never implemented. The Golden Urn was seldom used and, when it was, it was more of a symbol, as the Tibetan hierarchs had already been chosen according to tradition. As a disciple careful to revere his spiritual masters – including the Sixth Panchen Lama, Lobsang Palden Yeshe, to whom he was indebted – Qianlong upheld his position as protector. At that time political and spiritual masters remained equals.

This protective duty almost completely disappeared in the nineteenth century, when the Tibetan government had to face two invasions on its own. After that Tibet declared itself a tributary, not of China which was then in a state of decay, but of Nepal (1856). When Tibet was threatened and later invaded by Anglo-Indian troops in 1903 and 1904, China did not make a move. Once more the protector had failed in its duties.

The stand taken by the ambassador reveals a presumption inherited from the empire which has survived both republican and communist revolutions. The emperor of China, whatever his dynasty, was always the 'Son of Heaven', to whom everyone was subject. In this way the Qing emperors thought of Western rulers as their vassals. This feeling of natural superiority over the rest of the world, and mainly over Asia, continued to be held by the regimes which succeeded the empire. In the case of Tibet, which restated its independence in 1913 – as Mongolia had done two years earlier – the Chinese authorities attempted, but without success, to take on the emperor's role of protector. Contrary to what the ambassador of the People's Republic of China wrote in his letter, the delegate of the Kuomintang, Wu Zhunqing, who attended the enthronement of the Fourteenth Dalai Lama in 1940, had no particular status; the Chinese delegate was on the same footing as those from Britain, Nepal, Bhutan or Sikkim.

With all due respect to the Chinese diplomat, Tibet has never been a Chinese region. The regime in Beijing, and this is a tragic paradox, insists on following in the footsteps of the emperors in only one respect: convinced of their rights, the Chinese impose their views wherever they can. This was why Tibet was forced to sign the 1951 'Agreement' and why Tibetans are now obliged to accept Beijing's interference, even in spiritual matters. The abduction of the Eleventh Panchen Lama is an indication that this conviction continues.

It was with this justification that the communists did not hesitate to declare that the Tenth Panchen Lama wished his reincarnation to be confirmed by the drawing of lots from the Golden Urn. According to them, most prominent personalities in Tibetan Buddhism were in favour of this system. After the death of the Tenth Panchen Lama, Ngabo Ngawang Jigme[5] and one of Chökyi Gyaltsen's first teachers had suggested – the former in February 1989, the latter in August 1990 – that the ceremony take place in the temple of Jokhang. *Rinpoche* and lamas attending various sessions of the National People's Congress and the Chinese People's Political Consultative Conference allegedly confirmed the Panchen Lama's request and emphasized that this was without doubt the fairest mode of selection.

The ceremony finally took place on 29 November 1995 – the eighth day of the tenth month of the year of the Wood Pig in the Tibetan calendar – considered by astrologers to be an auspicious day. The Jokhang opened for prayers at dawn. Thousands of butter lamps had been lit, transforming the place with a mysterious play of shadows and light. But the day before, several hundreds of heavily armed soldiers had been posted in strategic areas of the Tibetan capital, and dozens of armoured cars had constantly patrolled through the town.

After the opening speeches, Gyaltsen Norbu, the representative of the State Council and governor of the Autonomous Region of Tibet, officially opened the celebrations. He said, in Chinese and Tibetan: 'The ceremony of the lottery for the appointment of the reincarnation of the Tenth Panchen Lama will now begin!'

At the sound of organized applause, the two monks in charge of the Golden Urn, which had been kept under the statue of Shakyamuni, brought it to the centre of the stage and placed it on a table. An assistant opened it up and took out three ivory tablets;

on them he glued pieces of paper on which the names of the three candidates were written, in Tibetan and Chinese.

Then Gyaltsen Norbu asked that the ivory tablets be checked. They were shown to the representatives of the State Council, who had come from Beijing specially for this purpose, to the leaders of the Autonomous Region, to high dignitaries and the most prominent *tulku*, and to the parents of the three children selected. Then each ivory tablet was put in a golden silk bag, which was sealed by a Chinese official.

At this point, Lama Tsering, who was in charge of the Democratic Management Committee of the monastery of Tashilhunpo, moved to the table. First he prostrated himself devoutly before the statue of Shakyamuni, then before the Golden Urn. He lifted it, shook it several times and put on the lid. Then Gyaltsen Norbu announced: 'Now place the Golden Urn in front of the statue of Shakyamuni and let us pray for the successful completion of the ceremony.'

The two monks in charge of the urn now carried it respectfully to its original position. The sound of chanting resonated around the room, yet a heavy atmosphere prevailed and fear was visible on the faces of the monks who had been forced to take part in the ceremony. With the exception of those who were pro-Chinese, none of them recognized the legitimacy of this occasion when a 'puppet' would be appointed as the reincarnation of the Tenth Panchen Lama. To them, as to the rest of the Tibetan population, the child selected by the Fourteenth Dalai Lama was the only one that mattered.

However, Gyaltsen Norbu invited the chairman of the Tibetan branch of the Buddhist Association of China[6] to proceed with the lottery. The man walked to the urn, bowed before the statue of Shakyamuni, prayed silently for a few minutes, then took the lid off the urn, shuffled the silk bags and seized one. In fact, in documents from Lhasa it was said that it could clearly be seen that one of the ivory tablets was larger than the others. When the lama in charge of the lottery put his hand in the urn, it was therefore easy for him to pick the 'right' tablet.

He announced in a muted voice: 'Fate has decreed that it is Gyantsen Norbu from the county of Lhari ...' The ivory tablet bearing his name was then presented to the officials and to Sönam Trampa and Sangyi Drolma, the parents of young Norbu, who had been members of the Chinese Communist Party since 1977. Norbu was born on 13 February 1990 in the same village as Gendün Chökyi Nyima. The deceit was obvious. The Chinese communists had wanted to create confusion in the minds of both Tibetans and Westerners.

As the monks and representatives of the official delegations shouted: '*Lhagyalo! Lhagyalo!* ... The gods have won!', and threw barley seeds and flowers into the air as auspicious symbols of happiness, the fake reincarnation of the Tenth Panchen Lama was suddenly produced. The whole ceremony had, in fact, been a huge sham, for young Norbu had been standing behind a red curtain at the back of the stage the whole time, already dressed in ceremonial attire for the enthronement.

He was asked to approach the statue of Buddha, before which he bowed. He was then offered a *khata*, a white silk scarf. In turn, Lama Tsering received a *khata* from Gyantsen Norbu. The monk who was to become his teacher came up to the child and they too respectfully exchanged *khatas*. Then young Norbu was seated in front of the statue of Shakyamuni and the teacher proceeded with the head-shaving ceremony. He also gave the child his religious name: Jigten Lobsang Jampa Lhundrup Chökyi Gyelpo Palzangpo.

The masquerade ended in jubilation for the Chinese and fear for the Tibetans. It was a most serious moment: Tibet was in more danger than ever.

In Beijing, the Chinese authorities commented: 'Now it is our turn.'

18

The Child Elected by Tibet

As soon as the death of the Tenth Panchen Lama was announced, the Dalai Lama offered to send a delegation of ten lamas to Tibet to carry out religious ceremonies and initiations. On 30 January 1989, two days after the Panchen Lama's death, the head of the Democratic Management Committee of the monastery of Tashilhunpo, Chadrel Rinpoche, sent an official letter on behalf of the committee to the Dalai Lama, via the Chinese embassy in India; he simply asked him to pray for the speedy discovery of the late Panchen Lama's reincarnation. On the following day, the letter was published in *Tibet Daily*, the Chinese government's official newspaper in Tibet.

After he had been appointed head of the search committee, Chadrel Rinpoche met with representatives of the Tibetan government in exile in Beijing and gave them another letter for the Dalai Lama. In March 1991, Tenzin Gyatso once again let Beijing know that he wished to take part in the search by sending a delegation of monks to consult mystical signs on the two sacred lakes of Tibet, Lhamo Latso and Yongtsa Lutso, in the county of Ripung in the prefecture of Shigatse. The Chinese answer reached Dharamsala in June: 'There is no need for any interference.'

In July 1993, Chadrel Rinpoche sent a message 'via official channels' to the Dalai Lama saying that the signs observed on the lakes of Lhamo Latso and Yongtsa Lutso confirmed that the Panchen Lama had been reincarnated. The Tibetan ruler sent his answer, dated 5 August, to this very important letter via the Chinese embassy in Delhi. He invited the search committee to come to India for consultations, but his letter remained unanswered.

In January 1995, the Fourteenth Dalai Lama, Tenzin Gyatso, met a Chinese contact who was close to the communist authorities. He reminded him, as he had done so before in October 1994, that he was still awaiting an answer to his letter of 5 August 1993. He stressed in particular the importance of traditional religious procedures in the search for the reincarnation.

Two months later, Chadrel Rinpoche went to Beijing to attend the yearly meeting of the National People's Congress. In the course of the meeting, the lama insisted that he be officially put in touch with the Dalai Lama to consult him about the conclusions of the search committee. Before he announced the identity of the selected candidate, Chadrel Rinpoche wanted to receive the Dalai Lama's approval and blessing, so as to legitimize the child in the eyes of the Tibetan population. He emphasized the importance of the Tibetan spiritual leader's participation in the selection and the important role played by tradition.

The members of the United Front opposed him, citing the historical role of the emperors which had been adopted by the Chinese Communist Party; in effect they thought that the Golden Urn procedure was sufficient to give the child legitimacy. Chadrel Rinpoche tried in vain to make them understand the significance of the issue and that, to Tibetans, the nature of the Golden Urn lottery was unacceptable, irreverent even. In April, the Chinese government announced their new regulations governing the search, selection and approval of reincarnations of great lamas. In Tibet, various signs indicated that the communists were trying to replace Chadrel Rinpoche, increasingly considered a nuisance, with someone who would be more obedient and comply with their plans.

When the monk appeared before the State Council – at which it is reported both premier Li Peng and president Jiang Zemin were present – he was categorically refused permission to meet Tenzin Gyatso officially. Such a meeting was deemed not only 'impossible' but also 'unnecessary', because Beijing could get by very well without the Dalai Lama. 'His intentions,' said Beijing, using words which have been repeated over and over again, 'have nothing to do with religion. His purpose in trying to oppose the final say of the central government on the question of the reincarnation of the Tenth Panchen Lama, is to deny Chinese sovereignty over Tibet and to create chaos there ... to change the historical tradition of the Panchen Lama's love for the motherland and dedication to Buddhist faith. By doing so, he is trying to exert influence on Tibetan

Buddhist believers in a bid to realize his plot to push for the "independence of Tibet" and split the motherland. This is the Dalai Lama's real purpose, and one for which he would move heaven and earth. Naturally, the Tibetan population strongly oppose the interference of the Dalai Lama in the work of determining the reincarnation of the Panchen Lama.'[1] Beijing was once again taking a unilateral decision on what should be done. Chadrel Rinpoche stressed the need to consult with the other members of the search committee and then hurried back to Shigatse, as the State Council had instructed him to announce as soon as possible the name of Chökyi Gyaltsen's successor.

When the Fourteenth Dalai Lama, Tenzin Gyatso, officially announced on 14 May 1995 that the reincarnation of the Tenth Panchen Lama was Gendün Chökyi Nyima, all Tibetans celebrated the happy news which, especially for those living in Tibet, heralded the end of an uncomfortable period of emptiness and uncertainty created by the conflict between the secrecy of the search group and the statements of the Chinese government, who had so often announced that only its voice mattered in the selection of the candidate.

Beijing reacted to Tenzin Gyatso's announcement without delay. In the Autonomous Region of Tibet, the authorities launched an intense political campaign encouraging people to denounce the Dalai Lama's illegal action and 'ask' the Chinese government to carry out the 'correct' identification of the Panchen Lama's successor. Diverse measures of pressure and repression were then implemented in villages of the Autonomous Region. On 17 May, Chadrel Rinpoche and his secretary, Jampa Chung, were arrested in Chengdu, in Sichuan, and placed in custody. One week later, on 24 May, at the end of a special meeting, the Chinese People's Political Consultative Conference (CPPCC) denounced the Dalai Lama's declaration as 'illegal and invalid'. Simultaneously, people heard that the barely-six-year-old child recognized as the Eleventh Panchen Lama by the Dalai Lama had disappeared with his parents and brother. It was reported that he had been immediately taken to Beijing. According to reliable sources, the Chinese communists had abducted the child simply to prevent Tibetans from officially recognizing the legitimacy of the Panchen Lama by paying homage to him according to the tradition of Tibetan Buddhism.

In June, traders who knew Chadrel Rinpoche were also arrested and accused of complicity in the transmission of letters between the lama and the Tibetan ruler. A few days earlier, a work group composed of 50 cadres from the Board of Public Security, the Religious Affairs Bureau and the CPPCC was set up in the monastery of Tashilhunpo. By the middle of June, the group intensified its activities: the cadres, equipped with tape recorders, visited the monks individually in their cells, persuading them to talk by stating that other monks had accused them of 'supporting the Dalai Lama's choice'. Utter confusion reigned. The resulting demonstrations were immediately suppressed by the Chinese troops surrounding the monastery. For the monks, *thamzing* sessions, beatings and torture with electric shocks became their daily lot.

Beijing, of course, denounced the Dalai Lama's announcement as a political manoeuvre. To the communists, it was an obvious attempt by the former ruler in exile to sabotage the various procedures implemented by the central powers in their search for the reincarnated Panchen Lama: 'The Dalai Lama and his like cheated people and practised fraud ... All of their acts blasphemed the last wishes of the Panchen Lama.'[2]

Furthermore, the Chinese affirmed that the Dalai Lama had created his own 'search group' while he was out of the country and that the group had set off for Tibet immediately after its creation on 24 March 1994. Beijing stressed that the delegation had no legitimate power whatsoever as, according to them, no *tulku* from Tashilhunpo was among its members. Even in Tashilhunpo, the cadres reported that, following the orders of the Dalai Lama, an individual had called the monastery and stated: 'We must persist ... and should not accept the drawing of lots from the Golden Urn ... It will be a disaster if an inappropriate candidate is chosen by drawing lots.'[3]

It was also said that the Dalai Lama had asked one of his men in Tashilhunpo to introduce secretly the name of the child he had chosen into the list of candidates. When the search group of Tashilhunpo proceeded to a new selection in January 1995, the same 'individual' had been instructed to put Gendün Chökyi Nyima's name among those of the eight remaining candidates. Although the members of the search group opposed such a step, which, according to Beijing, was contrary to all ethics, the 'individual' had prevented all further investigation. It was for this reason that the communists accused the Dalai Lama of cheating.

The Chinese also said that the Dalai Lama had asked his agent to appoint Gendün Chökyi Nyima as the 'one and only candidate for the reincarnation' by carrying out a fake divination and drawing lots from a bowl containing three balls of *tsampa*, each one of which was supposed to bear the name of a candidate. Beijing was suspicious of the procedure: for one thing it had been carried out behind closed doors, and, in addition, nobody knew what the other balls contained. Therefore, in the eyes of the occupying authorities, the lottery was totally illegal.

This is how Beijing saw the Dalai Lama and his government in exile:

> The Dalai Lama's clique ruled Tibet before the peaceful liberation of Tibet in 1951. For a long time, Tibet was under the yoke of an inhuman and feudal serf system. The upper-strata lamas and aristocrats were dictators who cruelly exploited and enslaved their serfs, the Tibetan masses. As a ruler, the Dalai Lama was the upholder of the backward feudal system in Tibet. In 1959, he betrayed the motherland and fled abroad. Since then he has been engaged in activities aimed at splitting the motherland and has served as a willing tool of the international anti-China forces. What the Dalai Lama has done in the Tenth Panchen Lama incident has proved once again that he has neither given up his old dream of becoming the 'King of Tibet', nor changed his ethnic separatist stance in defiance of the central government. Hence the 1.2 billion Chinese people, including the masses of Tibetan compatriots, will by no means let the Dalai Lama get away with his scheme.[4]

Luckily, only the Chinese are convinced by this type of polemic. It is true that Tibet's traditional political system was feudal and it is true that it was often unfair, but it should be added that the Tibetans lost a lot in the 'liberation' which Beijing persists in describing as 'peaceful', in spite of the million deaths that resulted from it. Today the Tibetans have lost the fundamental freedoms of movement, thought, belief and even procreation. The United Nations in vain condemned the totalitarian policy of China in Tibet. To credit the Dalai Lama with the desire to become 'King of Tibet' is to imply he desires to return to a feudal system. Yet, as early as 1959, Tenzin Gyatso set up democratic structures for Tibetans in exile. Not only did he state clearly that these structures would be maintained when Tibet was no longer under the yoke of Beijing, but he also did not hesitate to announce the end of his political authority. He intends free Tibet to be a democracy respecting the rights of man, where he would be only an 'ordinary monk' among others. However, the Tibetans themselves do not support this last decision; the majority of them wish the Dalai Lama to retain political authority, but to exercise it within a democratic framework. Therefore there are no legitimate grounds for Beijing's assertions.

On 11 July 1995, the governor of the Autonomous Region of Tibet summoned together all the monks of Tashilhunpo to disavow Chadrel Rinpoche, thus leaving the way clear for the appointment of another leader of the Democratic Management Committee. The monks hailed the end of his speech with an emphatic 'Long Live Chadrel Rinpoche'. Simultaneously, cadres of the work group brought forth Chadrel Rinpoche's secretary, Jampa Chung, in handcuffs and with chains around his feet, and demanded that he denounce his master. He proudly refused. The next day many cadres refused to attend a public ceremony. Only 11 of the 70 monks turned up. With the cancellation of the ceremony, the Chinese authorities lost face. They sent away the numerous tourists present in Shigatse and closed the monastery and its surroundings to the public.

During the night of 12 July, the police entered Tashilhunpo: 32 monks and 12 lay people were arrested. Among the prisoners was the venerable Gyaltrul Rinpoche, an eminent lama and prominent member of the monastery's Democratic Management Committee. Abandoning all pretence of democracy, the authorities appointed Sengchen Lobsang Gyaltsen, a lay politician, to replace Chadrel Rinpoche at the head of the committee. Sengchen Lobsang, also called 'Lama Tsering', had played a large part in sending the Panchen Lama to jail in 1964 and, as an ambitious collaborator, had long coveted the leadership of the monastery. Assisting him was Jamyang, who had headed the Democratic Management Committee during the Cultural Revolution, before being replaced by Chadrel Rinpoche in 1979. Only two trustworthy lamas remained from the previous committee.

On 21 August, the Chinese government announced that Gendün Chökyi Nyima and his family were being 'looked after' by the authorities somewhere in Tibet, 'in the interest of their security'. Chadrel Rinpoche was not 'under arrest' but had been 'having treatment' in hospital since May.

Yet when school started again, the children of Shigatse were made to learn by heart the contents of a pamphlet describing in detail the crimes committed by the lama and setting out the methods accepted by the Chinese Communist Party for the search for reincarnations. Through the intermediary of different authorities, the Chinese government maintained that 'the search for the reincarnation of the Panchen Lama had not been completed, but was still well under way, in spite of the disturbances created by the Dalai Lama's illegal action'. The authorities also discussed how to organize enthronement ceremonies in the absence of a true Buddhist 'emperor'. Still in August, a rehearsal for the Manchu ceremony of the Golden Urn was performed in the temple of Jokhang, filmed by a television crew sent specially from Beijing.

In November, 300 monks were summoned to a conference in Beijing, under threat of punishment: 'Your presence will be proof of your nationalism and your political allegiance.' On the day after the conference, Beijing announced that 'the lamas of Tashilhunpo refused to recognize the child appointed by the Dalai Lama'. The other lamas present were not mentioned. Prominent in the official photograph of the conference were the leader of the Chinese Communist Party, Jiang Zemin; the most prestigious general of China, General Liu; two deputy prime ministers – the president of the Supreme Court and the director of propaganda. All of Chadrel Rinpoche's previous actions were described as a plot demonstrating hostile interests.

In one of Lhasa's daily newspapers, the official conference photograph was faked so that Jiang Zemin, General Liu and the four other Chinese officials were shown in the second row, behind a row of monks. Consequently the newspaper suspended its publication for a few days ... Someone was reported to have been seriously injured when a bomb exploded at Sengchen's house.

Then the ceremony for the enthronement of Norbu Rinpoche took place, as described earlier. However, in the film of the event, shown on television in Lhasa over the following six weeks, the main stars were two Chinese officials – Luo Gan, a representative of the State Council who was close to Li Peng, and Ye Xiaowen, of the Religious Affairs Bureau – and Gyaltsen Norbu, the governor of the Autonomous Region of Tibet. Manipulation of the media was in full swing.

Conclusion

O ver 1,000 years ago, Chinese armies fell beneath the pikes and
sabres of the troops sent by Tibetan emperors to attack the
wealthy oases in the heart of Asia. But history has surely taken its
revenge, for Tibetans have now been living under Chinese rule for
50 years.

How many deaths will it take before the great powers condescend
to feel real and active concern for the fate of an oppressed people?
How many names must be added to the already over-long list of
anonymous people who have been lost in concentration camps, put
under house arrest, or died in oblivion? How many Gendün Chökyi
Nyimas will have to disappear? Sadly there is no answer to such
questions.

How could people have any idea that the Panchen Lamas were
among the spiritual masters of the emperors of China, knowing that
the holder of the title today is the hostage of a totalitarian policy?
His crime is very simple: it is being alive. This ten-year-old child
perpetuates a tradition and a belief which the government of the
Chinese People's Republic is determined to suppress in Tibet.

Once the communist government of Beijing had put an end to
Tibet as a political entity in the 1950s, it attacked lay and religious
people alike. However, it did not reckon with their noble and

tenacious character: for half a century now they have been resisting the Chinese steamroller – a nun dares to shout 'Free Tibet', a peasant refuses to buy Chinese equipment, a man scribbles the names of relatives who have disappeared on a piece of paper and slips it into the pocket of a tourist.

In the face of this stubborn resistance, Beijing decided to strike harder and higher. High-ranking lamas, *tulkus*, became a prime target. The government aimed to legitimize the lamas, as had been tried before in the old empire, but there was one major problem: since the seventeenth century the Tibetans had believed that only the Dalai Lama had the right to do this.

In the early 1990s the communist authorities were bypassed when the Dalai Lama officially recognized the reincarnation of the new Karmapa, the spiritual leader of the Kagyupa, one of the major lineages in Tibetan Buddhism. His enthronement in 1992 gave China the opportunity to demonstrate its power and leniency. People in exile were allowed to come back to Tibet to celebrate the occasion and to see for themselves that criticisms of Chinese policy in Tibet were unfounded. At least, this is what Beijing hoped for, but the ceremony somehow got beyond the control of the soldiers who had come to supervise the crowds. In spite of the propaganda praising the wisdom and tolerance of the Beijing government, to all the Tibetans present it was the Dalai Lama who had been responsible for the blessing and recognition of the newly enthroned Karmapa. They felt that, even from his exile, he continued to protect his fellow countrymen. But to the Chinese, once again the Dalai Lama appeared as a spoilsport.

In 1995, following the recognition of Gendün Chökyi Nyima, Beijing seized the opportunity to find another candidate, who was presented as the only truly valid one. In doing this the Chinese had two aims. First of all they wanted to show that the Dalai Lama had been mistaken and that he, the so-called spiritual leader, was just a manipulator, abusing the people's credulity to interfere with China's policies in Tibet. They declared that the Dalai Lama was a 'backward-looking character who tried to slow down the development of a people who, thanks to communism, had left the dark age of feudalism'. But the Tibetans did not show too many signs of caring what the Chinese thought on this subject.

Their second aim was more insidious for it played for time, which Mao Tse-tung had said was the only thing that could triumph over the Tibetans.

Several attempts have already been made to give the Panchen Lama more power than the Dalai Lama. They haven't succeeded, but if we do not pay heed, this is what is likely to happen. The puppet Panchen Lama, young Gyantsen Norbu Rinpoche, has been invested with a huge *de facto* authority. If Beijing manages to educate him according to Chinese views, the government will have an agent who could bring about tragic developments in the Tibetan situation.

According to his status, he will play a key role in the recognition of the next Dalai Lama. Several possible candidates may appear. The Dalai Lama recognized by carefully indoctrinated Norbu Rinpoche will not necessarily be recognized by Tibetans in exile. This might create a fatal split in the Tibetan community. The Panchen Lama could also decide that the lineage of the Dalai Lamas has come to an end and take direct control of the country, under the benevolent gaze of Beijing, who would finally be rid of the undesirable intruder in their plans.

Therefore, the present situation is very serious, particularly in humanitarian terms. Beijing is playing chess with ten-year-old children. Gendün Chökyi Nyima has disappeared; nobody knows for sure where he is, but it is certain that he is no longer enjoying the freedoms and pleasures to which a child is entitled: the warmth of a home, playing and exploring, receiving an education. The lot of Norbu Rinpoche is no better because, in addition, he embodies the way in which Beijing has deceived the people. Both children are victims, like so many others in China.

Beijing's totalitarianism is well known. Human rights stand for nothing in the former empire. Gendün Chökyi Nyima and Norbu Rinpoche are hostages: one of them is silenced, the other is held in a position which does not belong to him. As they have both been deprived of the right to speak, we have to speak for them. According to the Dalai Lama, campaigns for Gendün Chökyi Nyima have already prevented him from disappearing altogether. His story summarizes the recent history of Tibet. It is full of the miseries and pain that were unknown in the country before the Chinese communists took over. It also illustrates the intransigence of Beijing wherever its authority is contested, be it in Tibet or elsewhere. Beijing dictates a pace which everybody must accept, very often under physical, moral or economic threat.

When Western powers pay court to the fabulous wealth of riches and potential clients which China represents, perhaps the motivations of both sides should be questioned. For the sake of lucrative contracts, Europe and the United States turn a blind eye to the worst atrocities, and the sons of Mao get away with them by playing on these countries' financial greed.

Yet one question remains: what would have happened over 50 years ago if nobody had heard the calls for help when the Nazis made their bid to control a large part of the Western world? The disappearance of the Panchen Lama reminds us that personal freedoms are still in danger, and once again we must answer the calls for help.

1999

Gendün Chökyi Nyima,[1] his parents, his elder brother, Chadrel Rinpoche, and his secretary, Jampa Chung, are still missing. United Nations' experts on the rights of children have been unsuccessful in their attempts to meet the child, who is still 'the youngest political prisoner in the world'.

The monks of Tashilhunpo, including Gyaltrul Rinpoche, are still imprisoned in Shigatse for having refused to co-operate with the selection masquerade staged by the authorities. In November 1995, eight monks were given jail sentences ranging from 6 to 30 months. In Gyantse, other monks have been arrested on the same grounds and given 5-month jail sentences.

A recent dispatch from the German agency DPA stated that Gendün Chökyi Nyima and his family were somewhere in eastern Tibet. Nobody is able to confirm or invalidate this news apart from the Chinese authorities. If this information is true, why does Beijing not allow experts to meet them, if only to make sure that they are in good health?

In Tashilhunpo the atmosphere remains tense, with zealous officials permanently in residence. Monks have to suffer *thamzing* sessions of public criticism. Those who remain faithful to the Dalai Lama and Panchen Rinpoche, the Eleventh Panchen Lama, are jailed or killed. The situation in Tashilhunpo has become unbearable for the followers of the two spiritual authorities of Tibet. Yet in spite of the tension, numerous monks still dare denigrate the Chinese Panchen, Norbu Rinpoche. It is said that the child is afraid of monks and asks to be allowed to live in town or in Beijing. Nobody comes to pay him homage when he stays in Tashilhunpo, except under the threat of arms.

It is reported that the child's humiliated parents now regret having taken part in official intrigues and, in a late and symbolic move, have asked that the child be allowed to resume a normal life.

Notes

Introduction

1 According to Chineses sources this was Gyaltsen Norbu.

2 The title of emperor (*tsanpo*) conferred on the rulers of Tibet from the seventh to the eleventh century equates to the title of *tianzi* conferred on Chinese rulers.

3 Born in Uddiyana in the north of India, he introduced Buddhism into Tibet in the seventh century. From Kashmir, he travelled the length of the Himalayas to Sikkim and Bhutan. Padmasambhava embodies the ideal apostle for the 'Roof of the World'.

4 Atisha, or Dipamkara Shri Jnana (982–1054), was the superior of the monastery of Vikramashila in India. He was descended from two great lineages of transmission of the Word of the Buddha (Manjushri/Nagarjuna and Maitreya/Asanga). He was invited to Tibet, where he spent the last 13 years of his life.

5 Tsongkhapa (1357–1419) was the founder of the Gelugpa lineage. His works represent a synthesis of *sutras* and *tantras*.

6 Amithaba was immensely popular in China, Japan and Tibet, as well as in the regions of the Himalayas. He belonged to the Lotus family, or *Padma*, the family of Buddhas to which human beings belong.

7 Chenrezig (in Tibetan) – Avalokiteshvara in Sanskrit – was also revered in China as Guanyin, and in Japan as Kannon. In both countries he was sometimes represented as a female figure.

8 Other names given by the Tibetans to the Dalai Lama include: Kyab Rinpoche or Gyalwa Rinpoche ('Precious Protector'), Kyabgön Buk ('Internal Protector'), Lama Pönpo ('Priest-Officer'), or simply Kundun ('Presence').

9 'The Wheel of Time', a spiritual system combining the *mandalas* and meditations of Tantric Buddhism. Considered one of the highest *tantras* of Vajrayana.

10 Monasteries come under the Department of Antiquities.

Chapter 1

1 In K Dhondup, *The Water Bird and Other Years*, Rangwang Publishers, New Delhi, 1986.

2 Construction of the central, 'white' section of the Potala was begun in 1645, under the rule of the Fifth Dalai Lama. It was built on a hill, on the site of a meditation pavilion built 1,300 years earlier by Songtsen Gampo, the thirty-second ruler of Tibet. The 'red' section was added in 1690 by regent Sangye Gyatso (1653–1705).

3 A famous treaty signed with China in 821/22 by Emperor Trisong Detsen, alias Ralpachen (815–38). For a long time, the agreement served as a basis for relations between the two countries. Its

text, in both Tibetan and Chinese, can be seen on a pillar in front of the Jokhang in Lhasa.

4 Roland Barraux, *Histoire des Dalaï-Lamas*, Albin Michel, Paris, 1993.

5 Gilles Van Grasdorff, *Paroles des Dalaï-Lamas*, Ramsay, Paris, 1996.

6 Ibid.

7 1653–1705. He concealed the death of the Fifth Dalai Lama for about 15 years. During his regency he ordered the construction of the 'red' section of the Potala. He resigned in 1703. Koshut Mongols invaded Tibet and put him to death in 1705.

8 Demo Tulku Ngawang Jampal Gelek Gyatso (1757–77) was the first Rinpoche to be appointed a regent (in Tibetan, *Gyeltsab*), during the minority of the Eighth Dalai Lama.

Chapter 2

1 Laurent Deshayes, *Histoire du Tibet*, Fayard, Paris, 1997.

2 Born on 27 May 1876, he was recognized as the reincarnation of the Twelfth Dalai Lama on 12 February 1878 and enthroned on 31 July 1879. He was given his name – meaning 'Ocean of the Doctrine of Shakyamuni' – by the Eighth Panchen Lama. In 1882 the latter also gave him the first ordination of *getsul* (preliminary vows); this was the Panchen Lama's last intervention in the life of Thubten Gyatso.

3 Another version of this story says that Demo Rinpoche offered the boots directly to the Thirteenth Dalai Lama.

4 In yet another version of the story, when Lama Sogya discovered the possibility of a conspiracy against the Dalai Lama, he informed the authorities. It is also reported that the Nechung oracle himself took the boots

apart and discovered the *yantra*. It was said that Sogya became a favourite of Thubten Gyatso and was given numerous valuables which had belonged to Demo Rinpoche.

5 In 1903/4 Demo Rinpoche's party discovered that the regent's reincarnation was a nephew of the Dalai Lama. This enabled the Demo lineage to be once again officially recognized.

6 The Sino-Japanese war ended with the Shomonoseki Treaty. The Manchu empire ceded Korea and Formosa.

7 The 1793 edict openly questioned the nature of relations between China and Tibet or, more exactly, between the emperor of the Manchu dynasty and the Buddhist school in charge of Tibet. The imperial text specified that the Dalai Lama and other high-ranking lamas were to be selected by a lottery administered by the *amban* in Lhasa. The candidates' names were to be written on pieces of paper, folded and inserted in a Golden Urn. In spite of this obligation, the ceremony was seldom respected.

8 1863–1942; born in India, he was trained at Sandhurst and spent his career in the plateaux of Persia and Manchuria.

9 Deshayes, op cit, pp 242–54.

10 Jacques Bacot, *Introduction à l'histoire du Tibet*, Société Asiatique, 1962.

11 'Political Representative of Sikkim to British India', 7 July 1906.

12 Melvyn Goldstein, *A Modern History of Tibet, 1913–1951*, University of California, Berkeley, 1989, p 47.

13 Charles Bell, *Portrait of a Dalai Lama*, Wisdom Publications, London, 1946, p 78.

14 Ya Hanzhang, *The Biographies of the Dalai Lamas*, Foreign Languages Press, Beijing, 1991.

15 The Convention resembled a form of protectorate. First of all it stipulated that Tibet pay an indemnity of 7.5 million rupees, in 75 annual instalments of 100,000 rupees, starting on 1 January 1906. As a guarantee, the British were to occupy the Chumbi valley. In addition, Lhasa agreed to raze all fortifications, withdraw all troops from the Tibeto-Indian border, and consult the occupying authorities concerning any changes in border taxes. Furthermore, no foreign powers were to be allowed diplomatic representation in Tibet.

16 Charles Bell, op cit, p 69.

Chapter 3

1 Gautama, the historical Buddha (sixth century BC).

2 One of the protectors of esoterical teachings.

3 A collection of the Words of Shakyamuni Buddha.

4 Deshayes, op cit, pp 256–7.

5 Bacot, op cit.

6 Tibetan Blue Book of 1910, in Goldstein, op cit, p 51.

7 Goldstein, op cit, pp 51–2.

8 The Yellow Church (or 'Yellow Hat') refers to the Gelugpa. The term 'Red Hat' refers to the Nyingmapa, the Kagyupa and the Sakyapa.

9 Imperial decree of 25 February 1910, communicated to the British in a note dated the same day; in Goldstein, op cit, pp 52–3.

10 Bell, op cit, p 110.

11 Ibid, p 135.

12 The magpie refers to the Panchen Lama – the black and white body is a symbol of his duplicity; the cuckoo refers to the Dalai Lama.

Chapter 4

1 This was fairly common. When a great family was in danger of dying out for lack of male heirs, its name, properties and status were conferred on the eldest daughter's husband. Jensey Namgang married the two daughters of the minister who had collaborated with the Chinese.

2 The British agent posted to the Chumbi valley; he later became a close friend of the Dalai Lama's during his exile in India.

3 In Dhondup, op cit, p 68.

4 Lungshar had accompanied the four young Tibetans sent to England in 1913. This marked the beginning of his ascent in Tibetan society.

5 The song implied that Tsarong (the root) should be eradicated rather than the young generals who were merely the branches.

6 Van Grasdorff, op cit.

7 One ke is approximately 6lb.

8 Tibetans greet each other by sticking out their tongues to show that no evil prayer has turned them black.

9 Goldstein, op cit, p 252.

10 It is reported that the Panchen Lama confided his intentions to Marshall Zhang Xueliang, a warlord in the Beijing-Tianjin area, who reported them to W H Donald (a member of the British diplomatic service).

11 In Goldstein, op cit, p 254.

12 In 1932 this title was conferred on him in Beijing by the warlords Wu Peifu and Zhang Hueliang.

13 In Goldstein, op cit, pp 255–6.

Chapter 5

1 Extract from his political testament.

2 In Tibetan, *Tchamdjom pawo Tchudun.*

3 Lama Gendün Chödar, Trimön Norbu Wangyel (also called Norbu Wangchen), and Langcunga.

4 In Tibetan, *Chazö Chenmo.*

Chapter 6
1 Jampa Tsultrim was an old *ganden thriba* with no estates. Since he was close to 80 years old, he refused the regency.

2 Reting Tulku Thubten Jampey Yeshe Gyaltsen.

3 Reting Tulku Ngawang Yeshe Tsultrim Gyaltsen.

4 Changlochen Gung Sonam Gyelpo, Kusung Rupon Chapase, Sherpang Gyalkar Nangpa, Shod-drung Drakthonpa Dorje Rigdzin, Shod-drung Manriwa, Kyitöpa, Tsedrong Yulha Tenpa Tsewang and Dodam Thubten Delek.

5 In Goldstein, op cit, p 230.

6 The wireless unit became an India consulate after 15 August 1947, the famous 'Night of Freedom' celebrating Indian independence. It was closed in 1962, during the Sino-Indian war.

Chapter 7
1 A unit of Tibetan currency. Tibet had been issuing its own banknotes and stamps since 1912. They were handprinted using woodblocks (xylographs) – one block for each banknote, 12 stamps to a block – on locally made paper, hence the variety of colours and differences in the quality of printing.

2 An area south-east of Lhasa, on the right bank of the Tsangpo river (the upper half of the Brahmaputra).

3 Extract of 27 March 1937, *Yung Pao.*

4 Minutes of 31 December 1934, India Office.

5 A proposal for an agreement between the Tibetan government and the Panchen Lama was incorporated in the draft of the Sino-Tibetan settlement which was presented to the Kashag on 1 November 1934.

6 Deshayes, op cit, p 37.

7 Tenzin Gyatso, *My Land and My People*, McGraw Hill, New York, 1962, pp 22–3.

8 Ibid., pp 23–4.

Chapter 8
1 Ngawang Lobsang Gyatso, Fifth Dalai Lama, in Van Grasdorff, op. cit.

2 Gyatso, op cit, p 28.

3 In Tibetan, *Sitri Ngasöl.*

4 A religious monument often containing relics; the equivalent of the Sanskrit *stupa.*

5 Gyatso, op cit, p 43.

6 Tenzin means 'Holder of the Teachings'.

7 For further information on this period, see Deshayes, op cit, p 302 onwards.

8 The 'River of Bliss', the Brahmaputra.

9 Tibetan term for doctor.

Chapter 9
1 According to Chinese sources these were Lungri Gyatso, Pashöbon Lama, Chökyong Tashi, Tsepa Dorje, Ngagdo Gyashen and Lobsang Tseten.

2 Deshayes, op cit, pp 261–85.

3 This anecdote was related to the author by an elderly nun from Dolmaling nunnery. Kelsang Dolma, who came from the area, is now a refugee in Dharamsala.

4 Dated 3 July 1942. The letter was given to the Dalai Lama by two

American agents who had been sent to Tibet.

5 In Goldstein, op cit, p 392.

Chapter 10

1 Area of Lhasa; sadly, now best known for its NI prison, from which few Tibetans emerge alive.

2 Van Grasdorff, op cit.

3 Special knots made in strings which were worn to protect against external and internal obstacles.

4 Gyatso, op cit, p 57.

5 A reference to the discovery of the Fourth Dalai Lama, Yönten Gyatso, in a princely family of the Tümed Mongols. From then on the Tümeds became protectors of the Gelugpa.

6 The treasure stayed in this hiding place for nine long years.

7 The document is dated 23 November 1949.

Chapter 11

1 A book of grammar attributed to Tönmi Sambotha, a minister of Emperor Songtsen Gampo (seventh century), the father of Tibetan writing.

2 In Van Grasdorff, op cit.

3 Gyatso, op cit, pp 113–14.

4 The Buddha; his teaching (*Dharma*); and the spiritual community (*Sangha*).

5 Gyalwa Gendün Gyatso, Second Dalai Lama, in Van Grasdorff, op cit.

6 Tenzin Gyatso, *Freedom in Exile*, Abacus, London, 1998, pp 97–8.

Chapter 12

1 The people of the large eastern province of Kham, which was split into two in the eighteenth century. The western part of Kham remained under the rule of Lhasa; the eastern part

became part of the Chinese province of Sichuan. Both regions were affected by the Khamba uprising.

2 Such debates, on topics relating to the holy scriptures, were a specific tradition of the Gelugpa.

3 Jetsun Pema, *Tibet: My Story*, Element Books, Shaftesbury, 1997, pp 54–6.

4 Gyatso, *Freedom in Exile*, p 137.

5 Ibid, pp 150–1.

6 One of the names given by Tibetans to the Dalai Lama.

7 The equivalent of a prefecture bureau.

Chapter 13

1 The announcement was made on 20 June 1959. Although Nehru refused to recognize officially the Dalai Lama's government in exile, the Indian prime minister told him: 'You are in a free country, do as you please.'

2 A commune near Lhasa, nicknamed 'Red Flag' by the Tibetans.

Chapter 14

1 In Paris, Geneva, Canberra, Moscow, New York, Budapest and New Delhi – and, more recently, in South Africa and Taiwan.

Chapter 15

1 In western Tibet; a site of pilgrimage for both Hindus and Buddhists, as well as for followers of the Bön religion.

Chapter 16

1 Gyatso, *Freedom in Exile*, pp 260–1.

2 This figure was put forward by Harry Wu, a Chinese dissident who spent 19 years in *laogai*. A refugee in the United States since 1985, he now lives in California.

3 An estimate; there are no official statistics.

4 Phrase addressed by Lin Biao to Mao Tse-tung in a speech on 18 September 1966.

5 A reference to the 'trap' of the Hundred Flowers.

6 One of the historical leaders of the Red Army (1899–1974). In 1959 he denounced the disastrous effects of the Great Leap Forward and was subsequently eliminated from political life by Mao Tse-tung. One of the first victims of the Cultural Revolution, he was imprisoned in 1965. He died in 1974 as a result of the harsh treatment he endured.

7 Wei Jingsheng, 'An Autobiographical Essay', in *The Courage to Stand Alone*, Penguin, London, 1997, pp 247–8. The author was released in November 1997 and now lives in the United States.

8 Van Grasdorff, op cit.

9 Jetsun Pema, op cit, p 151.

10 Another name for the Jokhang temple.

Chapter 17
1 One yuan is worth approximately 7 new pence (UK), 12 cents (US).

2 The monastery of Kumbum in Amdo (Chinese Qinghai).

3 The letter, dated 17 June 1996, was written in French.

4 Deshayes, op cit, pp 123–6, 186–8.

5 Then vice-chairman of the National Committee of the Chinese People's Political Consultative Conference.

6 According to Chinese sources, Pomi Jampa Lodrup.

Chapter 18
1 *The Reincarnation of the Panchen Lama*, compiled by Shan Zhou, China Intercontinental Press, Beijing, p 68.

2 Ibid, p 75.

3 Ibid, p 71.

4 Ibid, p 75.

Conclusion
1 It is reported that the marks resulting from torture and beatings endured by the Tenth Panchen Lama can be seen on the body of the Eleventh Panchen Lama.

APPENDIX

The Fourteen Dalai Lamas

First Dalai Lama	Gendün Drub	(1391–1475)
Second Dalai Lama	Gyalwa Gendün Gyatso	(1475–1542/3)
Third Dalai Lama *(first holder of the title)*	Gyalwa Sönam Gyatso	(1543–1588)
Fourth Dalai Lama	Yönten Gyatso	(1589–1617)
Fifth Dalai Lama	Ngawang Lobsang Gyatso	(1617–1682)
Sixth Dalai Lama	Rigdzin Tsangyang Gyatso	(1683–1706)
Seventh Dalai Lama	Kelsang Gyatso	(1708–1757)
Eighth Dalai Lama	Jampel Gyatso	(1758–1804)
Ninth Dalai Lama	Lungtok Gyatso	(1806–1815)
Tenth Dalai Lama	Tsultrim Gyatso	(1816–1837)
Eleventh Dalai Lama	Khedrup Gyatso	(1838–1856)
Twelfth Dalai Lama	Trinle Gyatso	(1856–1875)
Thirteenth Dalai Lama	Thubten Gyatso	(1876–1933)
Fourteenth Dalai Lama	Tenzin Gyatso	(6 July 1935–)

The Lineage of the Panchen Lamas

FIRST PANCHEN LAMA
Khedrup Gelek Pelsang (1385–1438)
The First Panchen Lama studied in the monastery of Sakya. At the age of 23 he met Tsongkhapa and became one of his main disciples and his biographer. He was a great scholar and wrote nine volumes on the *sutras* and *tantras*; at the request of the local prince, in 1418 he founded Palkhor Chöde, the monastery of Gyantse, in Tsang. At 49 he was appointed head of the monastery of Ganden. He died at the age of 53.

SECOND PANCHEN LAMA
Sönam Choklang (1439–1504)
He studied under such masters as Lodren Bepa, and became an eminent scholar. He spent some time in the monastery of Sangphu before going on to found the nunnery of Chökhör Uding in Wensa. He died at the age of 65.

THIRD PANCHEN LAMA
Wensa Lobsang Döndrub (1505–64)
As the main disciple of Mahasiddha Chö Dorje, he received from him the *Miraculously Created Book of the Kadampa (Kadam Trulpai Legbam)*. Founder of the monastery of Chökyi Phodrang at Wensa. At the age of 33 he went for the first time to the monastery of Drepung, where he was ordained by the Second Dalai Lama, Gendün Gyatso (1475–1542/3). His great spiritual qualities enabled him to achieve the highest mystical powers. He died at the age of 61.

FOURTH PANCHEN LAMA
Lobsang Chökyi Gyaltsen (1570–1662)
He was recognized as the reincarnation of Wensa Lobsang Döndrub by Khedrup Sangye Yeshe, an immediate disciple of Lobsang Döndrub, and was ordained a novice when he was 13. At the age of 17 he went to study sacred texts in Tashilhunpo, in the province of Tsang. He received his full ordination from Panchen Damchö Yarphel at the age of 22 and became the abbot of Tashilhunpo nine years later.

In 1604, Lobsang Chökyi Gyaltsen went to Drepung to give the Fourth Dalai Lama, Yönten Gyatso (1589–1617), numerous teachings on the *sutras* and *tantras*. He also ordained him. When the Fourth Dalai Lama passed away, Lobsang Chökyi Gyaltsen initiated the search for the reincarnated child. In 1620, he acted as a mediator during the war between the ruler of Tsang and the Mongols.

Two years later, he announced that the Fifth Dalai Lama had been born in Chonggye, in the valley which was the birthplace of the Tibetan empire, in 1617. He presided over the head-shaving ceremony of Yönten Gyatso's successor and gave him the name of Ngawang Lobsang Gyatso (1617–82). He officiated at the initiation of the young Dalai Lama as a novice (1625), and his full ordination (1638), and taught him many *sutras* and *tantras*.

To show his gratitude, the Fifth Dalai Lama, who was the first Gelugpa to impose his role as the spiritual and temporal leader of Tibet, put Lobsang Chökyi Gyaltsen, his master and teacher, in charge of the monastery of Tashilhunpo. He conferred on him the title of Panchen, a half-Tibetan, half-Sanskrit word meaning 'great scholar'. His three previous incarnations were retrospectively given the title of Panchen. From then on the lineage of the Panchen Lamas developed in Shigatse, in the monastery of Tashilhunpo, which was designated their seat.

Panchen Lobsang Chökyi Gyaltsen was also the abbot of the monastery of Shalu, some 15 miles from Shigatse, for 20 years. Highly respected by all lineages of Tibetan Buddhism, he was considered as Tsongkhapa himself by the Gelugpa. He wrote five volumes on the *tantras* and *sutras* and died at the age of 82.

FIFTH PANCHEN LAMA
Lobsang Yeshe (1663–1737)

Recognized by the Fifth Dalai Lama as the reincarnation of Panchen Lobsang Chökyi Gyaltsen, Lobsang Yeshe was ordained as a novice by and received his first teachings from the Great Fifth at the age of 8. He ordained the Sixth Dalai Lama as a novice and gave him the name of Lobsang Rigdzin Tsangyang Gyatso (1683–1706).

Lobsang Yeshe received the title of Panchen Erdeni with a golden seal from the Manchu Emperor Kangxi (1663–1722) in 1713. Seven years later he went to Lhasa where the Seventh Dalai Lama, Kelsang Gyatso (1708–57) had just arrived in the Potala. The Panchen Lama officiated at the Dalai Lama's *upaseka**** ordination and gave him the name of Lobsang – hence his name Lobsang Kelsang Gyatso – and he also taught him about the *sutras* and *tantras*, and presided over his full ordination. The Seventh

Dalai Lama felt deep respect for his teacher, who put into practice many sacred texts.

When the Manchu Emperor Kangxi invited the Fifth Panchen Lama to China, the latter refused on the pretext that he might catch smallpox during the journey. He also felt he was too old to embark on such a trip. Lobsang Yeshe was the head of the monastery of Tashilhunpo for 67 years, and wrote four books on the *sutras* and the *tantras*.

SIXTH PANCHEN LAMA
Palden Yeshe (1738–80)

Born in Tashitse, in the district of Shang (province of Tsang), Palden Yeshe was recognized by the Seventh Dalai Lama, Kelsang Gyatso, as the reincarnation of Panchen Lobsang Yeshe. Kelsang Gyatso ordained him as a novice and gave him numerous religious teachings.

In the monastery of Tashilhunpo, Palden Yeshe announced the reincarnation of the Eighth Dalai Lama in 1761. He officiated at his *upaseka* ordination and gave him his religious name, Jetsun Lobsang Tenpe Wangchug Jampel Gyatso (1758–1804).

The Panchen Lama also presided over the Dalai Lama's two other ordinations in Lhasa in 1765 and 1777. Jampel Gyatso received some teachings on the *sutras* and *tantras* from him. During his rule in Tashilhunpo, he received an emissary from the East India Company, with whom he initiated discussions on the opening up of trade between Tibet and India.

In answer to an invitation from the Manchu emperor Qianlong, who made Tibetan Buddhism one of the official religions of the empire, the Sixth Panchen Lama went to China in 1779 and delivered numerous teachings to him. The latter appointed him his spiritual master and showed him much respect.

Palden Yeshe caught smallpox and died in Beijing at the age of 42. Following his death, very serious events took place. Greedy for the riches offered to the Panchen Lama, his two brothers – one of them his secretary and treasurer, the other the Tenth *Shamarpa*, a high-ranking *Karma-Kagyupa* lama – fought ruthlessly. When the Gurkhas of Nepal invaded the country in 1788 and 1791, the Manchu emperor intervened and took Tibet under his protection (1791–93).

SEVENTH PANCHEN LAMA
Tenpe Nyima (1782–1854)

Tenpe Nyima was born in Panam (Tsang) in the family of the Eighth

Dalai Lama, who recognized him as the reincarnation of Panchen Palden Yeshe. The Eighth Dalai Lama ordained him as a novice in 1789 and officiated at his full ordination in 1801; he also gave him his name, Lobsang Palden Tenpe Nyima, and numerous teachings.

In 1808, the Panchen Lama performed the head-shaving ceremony of the Ninth Dalai Lama, on whom he conferred the name of Lobsang Tenpe Jungne Lungtok Gyatso (1806–15). He also gave him numerous teachings on the practice of *sutras* and *tantras*.

Because the Dalai Lama died young (as did the next three), the Panchen Lama also discovered his successor, Lungtok Gyatso (1816–37), and presided over his head-shaving ceremony in 1822 and his full ordination in 1833. He also gave him his name, Ngawang Lobsang Jampel Tenzin Tsultrim Gyatso. The second premature death – of the Tenth Dalai Lama – gave the Panchen Lama important responsibilities. First of all he presided over the head-shaving ceremony of the Eleventh Dalai Lama, to whom he gave the name Ngawang Kelsang Tenpe Drönme Khedrup Gyatso (1838–56). The political situation was extremely tense and regent Tshomöling was forced to resign. Although Panchen Lamas do not usually exert any political power, at the request of the Chinese emperor's representative in Lhasa, the Panchen Lama agreed to act as regent (*sikyong*) for a few months (1844–45).

Panchen Tenpe Nyima wrote three books on the *sutras* and *tantras*. He always deeply revered his spiritual master, the Eighth Dalai Lama. The Seventh Panchen Lama died in the monastery of Tashilhunpo at the age of 73.

EIGHTH PANCHEN LAMA
Tenpe Wangchug (1855–1882)
Born in Thobgyal, in Tsang, he was sent to Kükyob Ling in 1857. He was ordained as a novice by regent Reting Ngawang Yeshe at the age of five and received his full ordination from Vinaya holder Jampa Tashi Damchö at the age of 23. He ruled over the monastery of Tashilhunpo from 1860 till 1882 and wrote three books on the *tantras* and the *sutras*. He died in his birthplace at Thobgyal at the age of 27.

NINTH PANCHEN LAMA
Chökyi Nyima (1883–1937)
He was born in the region of Dagpo, in south-eastern Tibet, and received both his novice (1888) and full ordination (1902) from the Thirteenth Dalai Lama, Thubten Gyatso (1876–1933). Thubten Gyatso went to India in

1906, at the official invitation of the Anglo-Indian government in Calcutta. Not long after he was back in Tibet he was forced to flee again when Chinese troops invaded in 1910. The Panchen Lama retained an ambiguous attitude until the departure of the Chinese in 1912, and refused to support the resistance movement set up by Thubten Gyatso's men. In 1914 he ordered the construction of a huge Maitreya* Buddha in Tashilhunpo.

Following conflict with the Tibetan government in Lhasa, Chökyi Nyima left for China in 1923. He spent many years travelling from place to place, in an attempt to return to Tibet with Chinese support. However, he did not neglect his religious duties and gave nine *Kalachakra* initiations and many other spiritual teachings.

In Jyekundo, he received Kewtsang Rinpoche, who was in charge of one of the search groups for the reincarnated child of the Thirteenth Dalai Lama. He gave the selected child his three names, including that of Tenzin Gyatso.

At a time when negotiations for his return to Tibet seemed to be progressing favourably, the Ninth Panchen Lama died at the age of 54 in the monastery of Kyegu Döndrub Ling (Jyekundo) in 1937.

TENTH PANCHEN LAMA
Chökyi Gyaltsen (1938–89)

The Panchen Lama was recognized by Lhasa through the Seventeen-Point 'Agreement' (1951), which the new Chinese communist power forced the Tibetans to sign. One year later he went to the Tibetan capital to meet the spiritual and temporal leader of Tibet. Both religious hierarchs attended the National People's Congress in China in 1954. Chökyi Gyaltsen was appointed a member of the Work Committee of the Congress and a high-ranking member of the Chinese People's Political Consultative Conference. In 1956, he was made vice-chairman of the Preparatory Committee for the Autonomous Region of Tibet (PCART). The Fourteenth Dalai Lama was appointed chairman. That year the Panchen Lama travelled to India with the Dalai Lama for the 2,500th anniversary of the birth of the Buddha.

After the Dalai Lama's departure into exile, Chökyi Gyaltsen became chairman of PCART (1959). While maintaining good relations with communist China, he managed to undertake some initiatives to promote the well-being of the Tibetan people. Once he realized that the actions of the Beijing authorities were contrary to their so-called 'fundamental' policy, based on 'lack of racial discrimination' and 'freedom of religion', and that their sole aim was to annihilate Tibetan culture, he began openly to oppose the communists.

He wrote a report containing 70,000 characters and submitted it to the authorities of the People's Republic of China. The communists immediately accused him of anti-Chinese and counter-revolutionary activities. In 1964, after having stated his support for the Dalai Lama at a public meeting in Lhasa, Chökyi Nyima was dismissed from all his duties. Humiliated, he was subjected to numerous *thamzing* sessions of public criticism, particularly in 1966 at the National Institute of Minorities in Beijing. He was then put under house arrest and spent nine years and eight months in jail. Only in 1975 was he released.

In 1979 he was appointed vice-chairman of the Chinese People's Political Consultative Conference and vice-chairman of the National People's Congress. He travelled extensively, particularly in Amdo and Kham, and constantly advised the Tibetans to maintain good relations with the Chinese while cultivating their Tibetan identity.

Chökyi Gyaltsen ordered the construction of a memorial *stupa* commemorating the silver mausoleums of the Panchen Lamas in Tashilhunpo which had been destroyed during the Cultural Revolution of 1966–76. He consecrated the monument and presided over the inauguration ceremonies, but died shortly afterwards, on 28 January 1989. Some sources report that the Tenth Panchen Lama might have been poisoned.

Eleventh Panchen Lama

Gendün Chökyi Nyima (25 April 1989–   )

On 14 May 1995 His Holiness the Fourteenth Dalai Lama officially recognized Gendün Chökyi Nyima as the reincarnation of the Tenth Panchen Lama. A few days later, the new Panchen Lama, his parents and his brother were arrested.

The child was born on 25 April 1989, in Lhari, in the district of Nagchu. At the urging of experts from the United Nations Committee for Children's Rights, the Chinese ambassador declared that his government had taken over guardianship of the child at his parents' request. The experts demanded to meet him, but to no avail.

The two personalities most involved in the discovery of the child Panchen, Chadrel Rinpoche and Jampa Chung, were given long jail sentences. In Tashilhunpo, the atmosphere remains extremely tense and communist officials are much in evidence around the monastery.

In the spring of 1999, Gendün Chökyi Nyima and his family were still missing. Now ten years old, he is still the youngest political prisoner in the world.

Boundaries of Tibet, India and China

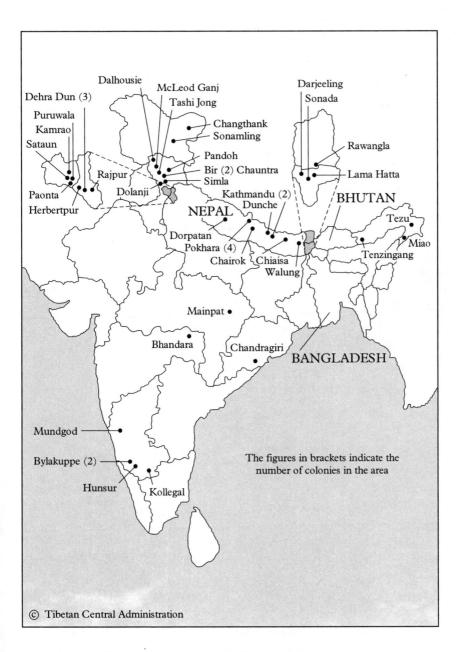

Colonies of Tibetan refugees in India and Nepal

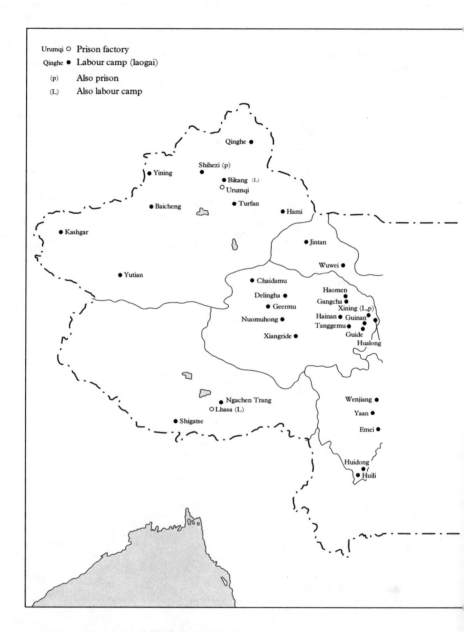

Legend:
- Urumqi ○ Prison factory
- Qinghe ● Labour camp (laogai)
- (p) Also prison
- (L) Also labour camp

Qinghe ●
Shihezi (p) ●
● Yining
● Bikang (L)
○ Urumqi
● Baicheng
● Turfan
● Hami
● Kashgar
● Jintan
● Yutian
Wuwei ●
● Chaidamu
Delingha ●
Haomen ●
Gangcha ●
● Geermu
Xining (L,p) ●
Nuomuhong ●
Hainan ● Guinan ●
Tanggemu ●
Guide ●
● Xiangride
Hualong
● Ngachen Trang
Wenjiang ●
○ Lhasa (L)
Yaan ●
● Shigatse
Emei ●
Huidong
● Huili

The Main Prison and Labour Camps

234

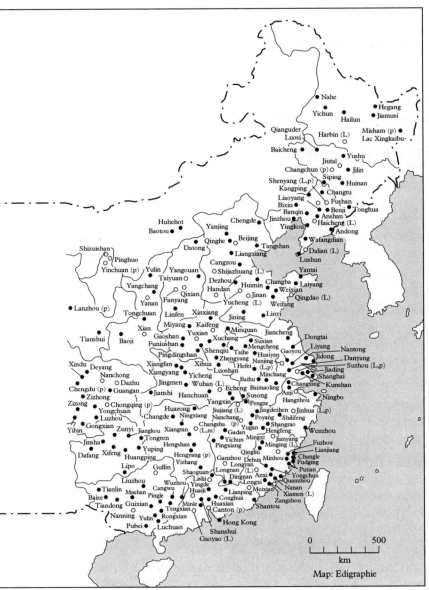

Nahe
Yichun
Hailun
Hegang
Jiamusi
Qianguder
Luosi
Harbin (L)
Misham (p)
Lac Xingkaibu
Baicheng
Yushu
Jiutal
Changchun (p)
Siping
Jilin
Shenyang (L,p)
Huinan
Kangping
Changtu
Liaoyang
Fushan
Bixin
Benji
Banqin
Anshan
Tonghua
Huhehot
Chengde
Jinzhou
Haicheng (L)
Baotou
Yanjing
Yingkou
Andong
Qinghe
Beijing
Wafangdian
Shizuishan
Datong
Tangshan
Dalian (L)
Pinghuo
Liangxiang
Lushun
Yinchuan (p)
Yulin
Yangouan
Cangzou
Yantai
Yangchang
Taiyuan
Shijazhuang (L)
Changba
Laiyang
Yanan
Qixian
Dezhou
Huimin
Weixian
Lanzhou (p)
Fanyang
Handan
Jinan
Qingdao (L)
Tongchuan
Linfen
Xinxiang
Yucheng (L)
Weifang
Xian
Miyang
Kaifeng
Jining
Linyi
Tianshui
Baoji
Gaoshan
Yuxian
Minquan
Jiancheng
Funiushan
Xuchang
Suxian
Dongtai
Xindu
Deyang
Pingdingshan
Shenqiu
Taihe
Mengcheng
Liyang
Nantong
Nanchong
Xiangfan
Xihua
Zhengyang
Huaiyan
Gaoyou
Jidong
Danyang
Suzhou (L,p)
Chengdu (p)
Dazhu
Jingmen
Yicheng
Luoshan
Hefei
(L,p)
Jiading
Zizhong
Guangan
Jianshi
Wuhan (L)
Baihu
Minchang
Shanghai
Zizong
Chongqing (p)
Hanchuan
Echeng
Baimaoling
Changxing
Kunshan
Yongchuan
Huarong
Yangxin
Susong
Anji
Ningbo
Luzhou
Changde
Ningxiang
Nanchang
Jiujiang (L)
Pengze
Hangzhou
Yibin
Gongxian
Zunyi
Jiangkou
Xiangtan
Jingdezhen
Jinhua (L,p)
Jinsha
Tongren
Changsha (p)
Poyang
Shilifeng
Dafang
Xifeng
Yuping
(L,m)
Yugan
Shangrao
Wenzhou
Huangping
Hengshan
Gadan
Mingxi
Hengfeng
Lipo
Yizhang
Yichun
Jianyang
Fuzhou
Gullin
Hengyang (p)
Pingxiang
Minging (L)
Lianjiang
Liuzhou
Shaoguan
Qingliu
Minhou
Changle
Tianlin
Wuzhou
Lishi
Ganzhou
Dehua
Fudging
Baise
Mashan
Cangwu
Yingde
Longyan
(L)
Dingnan
Anxi
Putian
Yongchun
Tiandong
Guixian
Pingle
Huaiji
Longxi
Nanan
Quanzhou
Nanning
Tengxian
Minle
Lianping
Meixian
Xiamen (L)
Yulin
Rongxian
Huaxian
Conghua
Zangzhou
Pubei
Luchuan
Canton (p)
Shantou
Hong Kong
Shanshui
Gaoyao (L)

0   500
km

Map: Edigraphie

(Map taken from : J-L Domenach, *Chine: L' Archipel oublié*, Fayard, 1992)

235

Major Dates in the History of Tibet

558 BC Birth of Shakyamuni Siddharta in the north of India.

127 BC Nyatri Tsenpo proclaimed king of Tibet; he was one of the first kings of the Yarlung dynasty (named after the valley where they settled) which ruled over the country for some eight centuries. His rule marks the beginning of Tibet's recorded history.

617–49 *Reign of Songtsen Gampo, thirty-second king of Tibet*
Under his rule, Tibetan writing and grammar are adopted and codified.

Beginning of the Tibetan empire
641 Songtsen Gampo marries a Nepalese princess and a Chinese princess; he also has three Tibetan wives. The emperor becomes a Buddhist. He launches a massive building campaign: the temples of Ramoche and Jokhang are erected to house holy statues of the Buddha.

705–55 *Reign of Tride Tsugtsen*

755–97 *Reign of Trisong Detsen*
763 Tibetan armies invade the Chinese capital.

779 Buddhism becomes the official Court religion; Padmasambhava and his disciples begin to build the monastery of Samye.

792–4 Buddhist Council in Lhasa and Samye. Imperial edict establishes religious links with India.

799(?)–815 *Reign of Tride Songtsen*
The emperor confirms the propagation of Buddhism.

815–36 *Reign of Trisong Detsen, alias Ralpatchen*
Dissemination of Buddhism and repression of the bön religion.

821–3 Peace treaty with China.

838–42 Reign of Langdarma
The emperor initiates fierce persecutions against the Buddhists, who are also persecuted in China around 842–6.

842 The emperor is murdered by a monk, Pelgyi Dorje. His death marks the end of the Yarlung dynasty, and Tibet is split into many principalities.

The time of religious seigneuries:
1042–54 Atisha (982–1054) arrives on the Tibetan plateau and remains there until his death. He is considered the second reformer of Tibetan Buddhism.

1073 Construction of the monastery of Sakya, seat of the Sakyapa.

End of 11th–end of 12th century: beginning of Kagyupa lineage.

1249 Beginning of the Sakyapa rule over Tibet.

1271–1368 Reign of Kublai Khan, Emperor of China, Yuan dynasty

1357–1419 Birth of Tsongkhapa, one of the great reformers of Buddhism and founder of the Gelugpa order, to which the Dalai Lamas and Panchen Lamas belong. His death marks the onset of serious rivalry between Buddhist orders in Tibet. There follows over a century of struggle for power between princely families of the provinces of U and Tsang.

1368–1644 Downfall of the Yuan; Chinese Ming dynasty

1409–19 Construction of the three monasteries that became major centres for the Gelugpa lineage: 1409 Ganden; 1416 Drepung; 1419 Sera.

1391–1475 First Dalai Lama, Gendün Drub
1447 He lays the foundation stone of the monastery of Tashilhunpo, completed 15 years later. Requests artists to decorate the building and to make a statue of Maitreya – 560lb of gold and 150 tons of bronze were used to create this 78ft-high Buddha of the future. Aware that his oral teaching is not enough, Gendün Drub orders the construction of a printing house in Tashilhunpo.

1475–1542/3 Second Dalai Lama, Gyalwa Gendün Gyatso
Tibet undergoes a period of troubles. The country is divided: clans, families

and monasteries struggle. The Gelugpa order founded by Tsongkhapa is subjected to strong pressures. The Ming dynasty (1368–1644) ruling over China takes advantage of the situation to take over Tibetan border areas. Gyalwa Gendün Gyatso acts as unifier. He orders the construction of the temple of Ganden P'hodrang in the monastery of Drepung.

1543–88 *Third Dalai Lama, Gyalwa Sönam Gyatso*
Even before the completion of his studies, he visits the different monasteries throughout the country. His charisma is recognized by all Tibetans and his reputation spreads beyond the borders.

1576 In answer to an invitation from the ageing prince Altan Khan, Gyalwa Sönam Gyatso travels to the Mongolian capital of Tso-Kha, near lake Kokonor. They meet two years later.

1578 In the course of their conversations, the lama gives such a subtle and convincing explanation of the concept of reincarnation that the old prince realizes that he is himself the reincarnation of the great Kublai Khan. His great faith in the wisdom of the lama leads Altan Khan to initiate the conversion of the Mongolian nations to Buddhism. In his wish to raise the lama above common people, he confers on him the title of Dalai, meaning 'ocean' in Mongolian. Its Tibetan equivalent is Gyatso. The reincarnations of Gyalwa Sönam Gyatso are now given the title of Dalai Lama, meaning 'Ocean of Wisdom'. The title is also granted retrospectively to Gendün Drub and Gyalwa Gendün Gyatso in recognition of their work.

1589–1617 *Fourth Dalai Lama, Yönten Gyatso*
1589 Birth of Yönten Gyatso in Mongolian territory. The child is Altan Khan's great-grandchild.

1602 The young Dalai Lama leaves Mongolia for the monastery of Drepung in Tibet and immediately becomes involved in rivalries between the different Buddhist orders. According to his biographer, he liked to take himself off to little-used hermitages so he could dedicate himself to long meditation sessions. To preserve Buddhism in his country, shortly before his departure, the young Dalai Lama appoints a young Mongol as his representative during his absence. The child is the same age as Yönten Gyatso and occupies the position until 1635. Mongolian Buddhists continue to hold this position, under the name of *dari-Hutuktu,* for several centuries.

1617–82 *Fifth Dalai Lama, Ngawang Lobsang Gyatso*

1644–1911 Manchu dynasty of Qing (China)

1642 The Mongol Gushri Khan deposes the king of Tsang and gives the Dalai Lama temporal power over Tibet.

1643 The Dalai Lama begins to write a history of Tibet.

1645 He decides to establish the government in Lhasa and orders the construction of the Potala.

1650 The Dalai Lama creates the lineage of the Panchen Lamas, the second spiritual authority of the country, with the elder authority the teacher of the junior. The superior of the monastery of Tashilhunpo, Lobsang Chökyi Gyaltsen, who had assisted the Dalai Lama in his work as well as in his rise to power, is recognized as the reincarnation of an immediate disciple of Tsongkhapa. Khedrup Gelek Pelsang is thus the first Panchen Lama to be recognized. As he had three previous incarnations, he becomes the fourth Panchen Lama. Tashilhunpo becomes the seat of the Panchen Lamas. By the end of the rule of the Fifth Dalai Lama, Tibet has been unified and politically structured. Eventually feudal families submit to a centralized power. Tibet becomes a prosperous country and exists once again as a nation.

1682 Death of the Fifth Dalai Lama. For some 15 years his death is concealed to preserve the country's unity and independence from the Mongols and the Chinese. Power is secretly exercised by regent Sangye Gyatso.

1693 The construction of the Potala is at last completed.

1683–1706 *Sixth Dalai Lama, Rigdzin Tsangyang Gyatso.*

1685 The young Dalai Lama and his mother are taken to the monastery of Tsöna, north of Tawang, where he stays for 12 years.

1697 The Fifth Panchen Lama, Lobsang Yeshe, presides over the young Dalai Lama's first stage of ordination and gives him his name, Rigdzin Tsangyang Gyatso, meaning 'Ocean of Melody'. The Sixth Dalai Lama settles in the Potala. As one of the most famous writers of love poetry in the history of Tibet, he gives precedence to artistic pursuits.

1705 The leader of the Koshut Mongols, Labsang Khan, invades Tibet.

1706 On 27 June, Labsang Khan deposes the Sixth Dalai Lama. The people of Lhasa and the monks of Drepung, who try to stop the departure of their spiritual and temporal leader for China, are subjected to reprisals. According to his biographers, he died around 14 November.

1708–57 *Seventh Dalai Lama, Kelsang Gyatso*
1720 Enthronement of Kelsang Gyatso. Theocracy resumes precedence in Tibetan institutions, even though the Seventh Dalai Lama takes little part in the political life of the country. His numerous works testify to his spirituality and knowledge.

1758–1804 *Eighth Dalai Lama, Jampel Gyatso*
The history of Tibet during the rule of the Eighth Dalai Lama may be described as a time of military, political and religious troubles. He was possibly the weakest Dalai Lama in the lineage. The Manchus become increasingly involved in Tibetan affairs.

1790–91 War with the Gurkhas of Nepal.

1806–15 *Ninth Dalai Lama, Lungtok Gyatso*
He is born at a time of intrigues and foreign interference. Rumours of foul play surround his early death just after he had attended the Mönlam ceremonies.

1816–37 *Tenth Dalai Lama, Tsultrim Gyatso*
1834 He takes his vows and dies three years later. There were again questions as to whether this was a natural death. The Panchen Lama suspects the regent of having a hand in it. Many historians have since corroborated his suspicion.

1838–56 *Eleventh Dalai Lama, Khedrup Gyatso*
1854 Death of the Panchen Lama, Tenpe Nyima, at the age of 84. He had known four Dalai Lamas and lived through two wars and a troubled period of Tibetan history.

1855 With the enthronement of the Eleventh Dalai Lama, the regent relinquishes power. The young Dalai Lama faces a new attack from the Gurkhas of Nepal.

1856 Mysterious death of the Dalai Lama.

1856–75 *Twelfth Dalai Lama, Trinle Gyatso*
The young Dalai Lama exercises power for only two years. He dies while on a pilgrimage after a brief illness. To some people, it is yet another suspicious death.

1876–1933 *Thirteenth Dalai Lama, Thubten Gyatso*
1895 The Thirteenth Dalai Lama assumes temporal power over Tibet.

1904 The British occupy Lhasa. The Dalai Lama takes refuge in Mongolia and China. He comes back five years later, in 1909.

1910 Chinese troops occupy Lhasa. The Dalai Lama goes into exile in India.

1911 The Tibetans rebel against Chinese occupying forces.

1913 Return of the Dalai Lama, who declares the independence of Tibet. Creation of the Kuomintang in China.

1914 Convention between Great Britain, China and Tibet in Simla, which China then refused to recognize.

1921 Creation of the Chinese Communist Party.

1923 On his own initiative, the Ninth Panchen Lama, who refuses to be the cause of civil war in Tibet, goes into exile.

1933 Death of the Thirteenth Dalai Lama.

6 July 1935 *Fourteenth Dalai Lama, Tenzin Gyatso*
1937 Death of the Ninth Panchen Lama.

1940 Enthronement of the Fourteenth Dalai Lama in Lhasa.

1949 Creation of the People's Republic of China. Invasion of Tibet by Chinese communist troops. The Dalai Lama takes refuge in Sikkim. Returns to Lhasa while the United Nations examine the Tibetan issue for the first time.

1951 On 23 May the Seventeen-Point 'Agreement' was signed. This was reputedly falsified by the Chinese authorities but it is now held up as a reference point by Beijing.

1954 The Dalai Lama travels to Beijing, where he meets the Tenth Panchen Lama.

1959 The Dalai Lama flees from Lhasa into exile.

1960 Creation of the Tibetan government in exile. Government structures are set up in Dharamsala, India.

1965 The United Nations examine the Tibetan issue again.

1967 The Dalai Lama goes abroad for the first time, visiting Thailand and Japan.

1979–82 Three Tibetan delegations from India visit China and Tibet.

1985 The Dalai Lama presents his five-point peace plan in Washington.

1989 The Fourteenth Dalai Lama receives the Nobel Peace Prize. Death of the Tenth Panchen Lama.

1995 14 May: the Dalai Lama recognizes the Eleventh Panchen Lama (six-year-old Gendün Chökyi Nyima, born on 25 April 1989). Some time later the child is abducted by the Chinese communists.

1999 The Eleventh Panchen Lama is still missing. Now ten, he is still the youngest political prisoner in the world.

Glossary

Amala: honorary term for mother.

Amban: Chinese representative of the Manchu emperors, a position created in 1728.

Avalokitesvara: the Bodhisattva of perfect compassion. Called Chenrezig in Tibet, he is the protector of the country and its people. The same deity is highly revered in China as Guanyin, and venerated as the feminine deity Kannon in Japan.

Bodhisattva: a being who has perfected altruism and compassionate action and who renounces their own final liberation so as to deliver all living creatures into enlightenment. The Bodhisattva remains in this world of suffering, acting out of pure compassion, without any form of attachment.

Bön: the original Tibetan religion.

Chöyön: a term combing two words: *chöney* (that which is worthy of veneration, for instance a lama or deity) and *yöndag* ('he who gives offerings' – a patron).

Dalai Lama: *Dalai* is a Mongolian word meaning 'ocean'; *lama* is the Tibetan equivalent of the Indian word 'guru', meaning spiritual teacher. Put together these words are often loosely translated as 'Ocean of Wisdom'. But the Dalai Lama is first of all the spiritual leader and most eminent religious personage in the Buddhist world, as well as the temporal leader of Tibet and its head of government. The Dalai Lama is an incarnation of Chenrezig, the Bodhisattva of compassion. The title was first conferred on Sönam Gyatso (1543–88) by the Mongol leader Altan Khan in 1578.

Dharma: this Sanskrit word encompasses numerous meanings: Buddhist teaching, the order of things, the cosmic system, and absolute Truth. In plural form, written without a capital letter, *dharmas* are the phenomena ordered by this law. *Buddha Dharma* is the explanation of this Reality given by the Buddha. *Buddha Dharma*, abbreviated to *Dharma*, is the name given by Buddhists to Buddhism.

Ganden thriba: title given to the head of the Gelugpa lineage. *Ganden* is the name of the monastery, *thri* is throne in Tibetan, and *ba* is the article, thus, literally, 'the one who sits on the throne'.

Geshe: doctor in Buddhist philosophy in the *Gelugpa* school.

Jokhang: the most important temple in Lhasa, the Tibetan capital. Founded in the seventh century, it is the temple most venerated by Tibetan Buddhists.

Kalön: minister of the Tibetan government.

Karma: according to the meaning of *karma*, all life is a process of learning. Each event shapes a being so that, placed in a more or less similar situation, that being will instinctively react. Therefore our behaviour is not free, for our will and desires result from our deeds. In this way, *karma* is a conditioning and not a fate. Buddhism aims to free beings from this conditioning through awareness.

Kashag: council of ministers composed of three lay people (*kalön*s) and a religious man (*kalön lama*).

Khata: white silk scarf used as an offering by Tibetans, instead of flowers.

Khenpo (council of): administrative council of the monastery of Tashilhunpo, headed by the Panchen Lama. It is also called Panchen Khenpo.

Lama: Tibetan Buddhist teacher.

Laogai: Chinese abbreviation of 'reform through labour', the Chinese equivalent of the Russian Gulag.

Lönchen: foremost minister in the government. The position was created in 1907.

Losar: celebrations of the Tibetan New Year, beginning on the twenty-ninth day of the twelfth month, the day of Gyetor, when all the negativity of the previous year is exorcised. Numerous ceremonies are performed.

Maitreya Buddha: The Buddha of the Future, who embodies universal love.

Mala: rosary used to count *mantras* and to promote constant attentiveness.

Mandala: symbolic representation of the world, the cosmos, the celestial palace of a deity or a paradise. *Mandalas*, which can be painted, made of coloured sands or even three-dimensional, form a medium for meditation.

Manjushri: *Bodhisattva* of knowledge and wisdom.

Mantra: 1) ritual and initiatory formula used in both Hinduism and Buddhism as a form of meditation and prayer; 2) a syllable which, when uttered repetitively or concentrated on, helps a person to gain access to the innermost mind and to influence it. The most famous mantra is *Om mani padme hum*, the *mantra* of Chenrezig, the *Bodhisattva* of Compassion.

Repeating these words and imagining oneself in the form of this *Bodhisattva*, helps to gradually release innate universal compassion.

Mönlam: collective rituals of greeting performed on the occasion of *Losar*, the Tibetan New Year.

Mönlam Chenmo: literally 'the Great Prayer', instituted by Tsongkhapa in 1409. Up to 50,000 people gather in Lhasa for this religious festival which is celebrated during the two weeks following the New Year.

Nechung oracle: in Tibetan tradition, the word *oracle* means the spirit entering a person to enable him to act as a medium between natural and spiritual realms. Tibetans call the person *kutenla*, literally meaning 'physical medium': the article *la* is attached to the end of a first name or a family name to mark respect. It is said that the spirit of Nechung entered a human body for the first time in 1544. In this way, Drag Trang-gowa Lobsang Palden became the first Nechung *Kuten*.

Norbu Lingka: the Dalai Lama's summer palace.

Panchen Erdeni: this partly Mongol title was given to the Fifth Panchen Lama by the Chinese Emperor Kangxi in 1713.

Potala: the Dalai Lama's winter palace.

Puja: acts of worship.

Rinpoche: literally, 'Precious One', an honorary title for lamas with high spiritual realizations. Tibetans also call the Dalai Lama, Gyalwa Rinpoche – the Precious Protector.

Shape: literally 'lotus feet', honorary title for a high-ranking Tibetan civil servant since the nineteenth century.

Sutras: texts reporting the Buddha's original teachings. They often take the form of a dialogue between the Buddha and his disciples on a specific topic.

Stupa: religious monument, often containing relics.

Tantras: scriptures and teachings which form the fundamentals of *Vajrayana* Buddhism, a major Buddhist trend in Tibet – also called esoteric Buddhism in China and Japan. Tantric teachings are based on the idea of transforming an impure vision into a pure vision through work on body, energy and mind. Tantric texts usually describe *mandalas* and meditation practices associated with a particular state of enlightenment, or deity. The *mandalas* usually depict the sacred dwelling of a Buddha, or a *Bodhisattva*, whom the disciple visualizes during a tantric practice. The relation between master and disciple is a key element of *tantra*.

Tashilhunpo: the first Dalai Lama, Gendün Drub, a disciple of Tsongkhapa, founded this monastery near Shigatse in 1447. He became its first abbot under the name of Gyalwa Rinpoche ('Precious Protector'). He set up a printing house there to produce Tibetan translations of the Sanskrit *Kangyur* (a collection of the words of Shakyamuni Buddha) and *Tengyur* (a compilation of comments written by Indian masters). The Fifth Dalai Lama, Ngawang Lobsang Gyatso, made Tashilhunpo the seat of the Panchen Lama, an emanation of Amithaba, the Buddha of Infinite Light, and the second hierarch in the Tibetan Gelugpa lineage.

Thamzing: public self-criticism sessions implemented by Chinese communists; the accused stands for hours before relatives, children and friends, who are forced to take part.

Thanka: a Tibetan icon painted on silk or fabric, which can be rolled. It is based on the Indian religious art of the Pala dynasty. Deeply interested in Indian religious teachings, Tibetans scrupulously followed the teachings of Indian, and later Nepalese, artists. *Thanka* painting was developed in Tibet in the seventh century, during the reign of Songtsen Gampo. Around the same time, silkworms, stone mills, paper and ink were introduced into Tibet and Tibetan writing and grammar became codified.

Tsampa: roasted barley flour.

Tsipön: Secretary of State for Finance. There are four *tsipön*.

Tulku: the concept of reincarnation is part of the Buddhist philosophical framework. It was not part of the Buddha's teachings, but it is considered by all Asians, of whatever religion, to be a natural phenomenon. The Buddha taught that the 'ego' or 'soul' does not transmigrate; rather, one life follows on from another by means of the most subtle form of mind, a 'kinetic energy'. An individual who has reached a high level of spiritual development is said to be able to direct this energy in a special way at the time of death, so that it results in the birth of a *tulku* – a reincarnated lama. The *tulku* is not the same person as the lama who has just died, but represents the active continuation of his positive qualities, wisdom and blessings. This phenomenon had always existed in Buddhism, but no particular attention was given to it. It was not until the eleventh century that a Tibetan lama, Karmapa, talked about his *tulku*. The *tulku* was given the same name as his predecessor, thus initiating the first lineage of reincarnation. As the system proved to be useful at both a spiritual and material level, it developed over the course of the centuries, giving birth, in the fifteenth century, to the lineage of the Dalai Lama and, in the seventeenth century, to that of the Panchen Lama.

Upaseka: First degree ordination which can also be given to lay people. Those who receive it accept the Three Refuges (Buddha, Dharma, Sangha) and agree to respect the five *shila* (ethical rules).

Bibliography

Avedon, John F, *In Exile from the Land of Snows*, Alfred Knopf, New York, 1984

Bacot, Jacques, *Introduction à l'histoire du Tibet*, Société Asiatique, 1962

Barraux, Roland, *Histoire des Dalaï-Lamas*, Albin Michel, Paris, 1993

Bell, Charles, *The Land of the Lamas*, Seeley Service, London, 1929

— *The Religion of Tibet*, Oxford University Press, Oxford, 1968

— *Portrait of a Dalai Lama*, Wisdom Publications, London, 1987

— *Tibet Past and Present*, Motilal Banarsidass, Delhi, 1992

Commission internationale de juristes, 'La question du Tibet et la primauté du droit', Geneva, 1960

Comité juridique d'enquête sur la question du Tibet, 'Le Tibet et la République Populaire de Chine', Commission internationale de juristes, Geneva, 1960

Das, Sarat Chandra, 'The Hierarchy of the Dalai Lamas', *Journal of the Asiatic Society of Bengal*, 1904

— *Tibetan Studies*, K P Bagghi & Co, Calcutta, 1984

Deshayes, Laurent, *Histoire du Tibet*, Fayard, Paris, 1997

Dhondup, K, *The Water Bird and Other Years*, Rangwang Publishers, New Delhi, 1986

Djamyang Norbou, *Un cavalier dans la neige*, Maisonneuve, Paris, 1981

Donnet, PA, *Tibet mort ou vif*, Gallimard, Paris, 1990

Eco-Tibet France, Tibet, *Environnement et dévelopement*, Editions Prajna, Savoie, 1993

Fromaget, A, *Océan de pure mélodie: Vie et chants du sixième Dalaï-Lama*, Dervy, Paris, 1995

Goldstein, Melvyn C, *History of Modern Tibet, 1913–1951*, University of California Press, Berkeley, CA, 1986

Grasdorff, Gilles Van, *Cent mille Éclairs dans la nuit* (with Gilbert Collard), Presses de la Renaissance, Paris, 1999

— *Gendün, l'enfant Oublié du Tibet*, Presses de la Renaissance, Paris, 1999

— *Paroles des Dalaï-Lamas*, Editions Ramsay, Paris, 1996

Harrer, Heinrich, *Seven Years in Tibet*, Flamingo, London, 1994

His Holiness the Fourteenth Dalai Lama (Tenzin Gyatso), *My Land and My People*, McGraw Hill, New York, 1962

— *Universal Responsibility and the Good Heart*, Library of Tibetan Works and Archives, 1980

— *Four Essential Buddhist Commentaries*, Library of Tibetan Works and Archives, 1980

— *Kindness, Clarity and Insight*, Snow Lion Publications, New York, 1984

— *Opening the Mind and Generating a Good Heart*, Library of Tibetan Works and Archives, 1985

— *Freedom in Exile*, Hodder and Stoughton, London, 1990

— *Cultivating a Daily Meditation*, Library of Tibetan Works and Archives, 1991

— *Cent éléphants sur un brin d'herbe*, Le Seuil, Paris, 1991; Abacus, London, 1998

— *A Flash of Lightning in the Dark of the Night*, Shambala, Boston and London, 1994

— *Terre des dieux, malheur des hommes* (interview with Gilles Van Grasdorff), J C Lattès, Paris, 1994

— *Essential Teachings*, Souvenir Press, 1995

— *Dialogues on Universal Responsibility and Education*, Library of Tibetan Works and Archives, 1995

— *The Power of Compassion*, Harper Collins, India, 1995

Lillico S, 'The Panchen Lama', *The China Journal*, vol 21, Shanghai, 1934

Malik, Inder L, *Dalai Lamas of Tibet*, Uppal Publishing House, New Delhi, 1984

Maraini, Fosco, *Tibet Secret*, Arthaud, Paris, 1990

Mehra, *Tibetan Policy (1904–1937): Conflict between the 13th Dalai Lama and the 9th Panchen*, J Brill, Leiden, 1976

Mullin, Glenn H, *Selected Works of the Dalai Lama III: Essence of Refined Gold*, Snow Lion, Ithaca, 1982

— *Selected Works of the Dalai Lama VII*, Snow Lion, Ithaca, 1985

— *Selected Works of the Dalai Lama II: Tantric Yogas of Sister Niguma*, Snow Lion, Ithaca, 1985

— *Path of the Bodhisattva Warrior: The Life and Teachings of the Thirteenth Dalai Lama*, Snow Lion, Ithaca, 1988

— *Mystical Verses of a Mad Dalai Lama*, First Quest Edition, Wheaton, 1994

Ngabo Ngawang Jigme, *Tibet*, PML Editions, 1989

Patt, D, *A Strange Liberation: Tibetan Lives in Chinese Hands*, Snow Lion, Ithaca, 1992

Pema, Jetsun, *Tibet My Story*, (with Gilles Van Grasdorff), Element Books, Shaftesbury, 1997

Richardson, H E, *Tibet and its History*, Oxford University Press, Oxford, 1962

— *A Short History of Tibet*, Dutton & Co, New York, 1962

— 'The Dalai Lamas', Occasional Paper of the Institute of Tibetan Studies, London, no 1, Pandect Press/Shambala, 1971

Rinchen Dolma Taring, *Daughter of Tibet*, John Murray, London, 1970; Wisdom Publications, London, 1986

Rockhill, Woodwille W, *The Dalai Lamas of Lhasa and their Relationships with the Manchu Emperors of China, 1644–1908*, Brill, Leyden, 1910

Shakabpa, W D, *Tibet, a Political History*, Potala Publications, New York, 1984

Shan Zhou (comp), *The Reincarnation of the Panchen Lama*, China Intercontinental Press, Beijing

Snellgrove, D L and Richardson H., *A Cultural History of Tibet*, Weidenfeld & Nicolson, London, 1968

Sogyal Rinpoche, *The Tibetan Book of Living and Dying*, Rigpa Fellowship, 1992

Stein, R A, *La Civilisation tibétaine*, L'Asiathèque-Le Sycomore, Paris, 1981

Subba, T B, *Flight and Adaptation: Tibetan Refugees in the Darjeeling-Sikkim Himalaya*, LTWA, Dharamsala, 1990

Surkhang Wangchen Gelek, 'The Critical Years: The Thirteenth Dalai Lama', in *Tibet Journal*

Tendzin Tcheudrak, *Le Palais des arcs-en-ciel*, (with Gilles Van Grasdorff), Albin Michel, Paris, 1999

Tibetan Young Buddhist Association, *Tibet, the Facts*, TYBA, Dharamsala, 1990

Tokan Tada, *The Thirteenth Dalai Lama*, Tokyo, 1965

Van Walt Van Praag, Michael, *The Status of Tibet*, Colorado, 1987

various, *Tibet, des journalistes témoignent*, L'Harmattan, Paris, 1992

various, *Tibet, l'envers du décor*, Olizane, Geneva, 1993

various, *Tibet, la solution de l'indépendance*, Olizane, Geneva, 1995

Wang Furen and Suo Wenqing, *Highlights of Tibetan History*, New World Press, Beijing, 1984

Winnington, Alan, *Tibet*, London, 1957

Wu, Harry, *Laogai: The Chinese Gulag*, Westview, 1992

Ya Hanzhang, *The Biographies of the Dalai Lamas*, Foreign Languages Press, Beijing, 1991

Younghusband, Francis, *India and Tibet*, London, 1910

Books on Tibet by Gilles van Grasdorff

Terre des Dieux, malheur des hommes, entretien avec sa sainteté le Dalaï-Lama, J-C Latt, 1995; Grand Livre du mois, 1995, Livre de poche, 1996

Paroles des Dalaï-Lamas, Editions Ramsay, 1996; Marabout, 1997

Tibet: My Story, with Jetsun Pema, Element Books, Shaftesbury, 1997

Le Palais des arcs-en-ciel, Tendzin Tcheudrak, Albin Michel, Paris, 1998

Index

Afghanistan 21
Altan Khan xx, 33
Amdo (Qinghai) province xx, xxi, 10,
    20–1, 46, 50, 52, 70, 78, 79, 89,
    98, 100, 115, 117, 132, 133, 135,
    153, 156, 163, 164, 172, 176,
    188, 231
Amithaba xxii, xix, 130, 216n
Anglo-Russian convention (1907) 32
Arunachal Pradesh 37
Atisha xviii, 60, 216n
Avalokitesvara see Chenrezig

Bailey, Colonel 47, 48
Balfour, Lord 18
Bandung conference (1955) 133
Baoding 22
Batang 16, 134
Batang monastery 17, 148
Battye, Captain 71
Beijing 21, 22, 23–4, 47, 120, 124,
    129–31, 149, 156, 181, 195, 204,
    205, 209, 228
Beijing government xi, xvii, xxi,
    xxiii–iv, 4, 17, 18, 21, 26, 35, 40,
    116, 117, 133, 134, 137, 152,
    154, 170, 173, 177, 178, 179–80,
    181, 182, 187, 188, 191, 193,
    197, 199–200, 202, 203, 204,
    205, 206, 207, 211–12, 213,
    214, 215, 230
Bell, Sir Charles 28, 30, 31, 39, 41, 42
Bhutan 5, 16, 30, 92, 216n
Bhutan, Maharajah of 47
Bilung Rinpoche 86–9
Board for Public Security vx
Bön religion xvii
Brahmaputra valley xvii
Britain 12, 13, 14–16, 21, 26, 32, 37,
    39, 40, 44, 47–8, 49, 71, 73–4,
    92, 103, 116, 117; see also London
    government
British India 3, 4–5, 15, 18–19, 26, 27,
    30, 35, 39, 40, 42, 65, 66, 67, 71,
    103, 229–30

Buddhism xi, xiii, xvii–xix, xx, xxii,
    5–8, 15, 34, 37, 39, 63, 66, 86,
    93, 115, 128, 136, 148, 149, 159,
    162, 172, 173, 178, 198, 204–5,
    216n; see also Tibetan Buddhism
Buddhist Association of China 169,
    187, 188, 192, 201
Bukhara 13
Burma 4, 14

Cai Fangbo, ambassador 194
Calcutta 17, 18, 19, 26, 35
Calcutta government 18, 230
Campbell-Bannerman, Sir Henry 19
Chadrel Rinpoche xv, xvi, 191, 193,
    203–4, 205, 208, 209, 215, 231
Chamdo monastery 148
Chamdo region 50, 121, 134
Chang Jiang river 50, 77
Changchung region xvii
Chao Erh-feng 17, 26, 31, 40
Chapman, Spencer 74
Che college, Sera 60, 104–6, 109,
    110, 111
Che Jigme 180
Chen (intepreter) 160, 161, 162
Chen Yi, Marshall 134–5, 135–7, 166,
    167, 168
Chengdu xv, 31, 176, 205
Chenrezig (Avalokitesvara) xix, 129,
    130, 216n
Chiang Kai-shek 4, 46, 48, 49, 50, 89,
    103, 104, 108, 109, 115, 156, 157
Chinese Communist Party xxiii, 159,
    178, 202, 204, 209
Chinese People's Political Consultative
    Conference (CPPCC) xv, xvi,
    200, 205, 206, 230, 231
Ch'ing dynasty 33
Chödrub Tendar 105
Chökhör Uding nunnery 225
Chökhorgyal monastery 5, 13, 69
Chokse, lama 99
Chökyi Gyaltsen see Panchen Lama,
    Tenth

Chökyi Nyima *see* Panchen Lama, Ninth
Chökyi Phodrang monastery 225
Chökyong Tashi 99
Chömpel Thubten 105
Chonggye 226
Chou En-lai 124–5, 130, 133, 158, 162, 164, 171, 172, 179, 181
Chumbi valley 14, 32, 117, 218n
Ch'un, Prince regent 24
Chung Yin, General 26, 27
Cixi, Empress 23, 24
Commission (Assembly) of Tibetan People's Deputies 155
Communist Party xvi, 135, 147, 151, 156, 157, 158, 163, 165, 182; *see also* Chinese Communist Party
Council of Khenpo 5, 86, 100, 126, 127, 131, 135, 137, 142
Cultural Revolution xi, 147, 181, 182, 186, 187, 209, 221n, 231
Curzon, Lord 14, 16, 18, 19

Dagpo region 60, 229
Dalai Lama, First (Gendün Drub) xxi
Dalai Lama, Second (Gyalwa Gendün Gyatso) 5, 111, 184, 226
Dalai Lama, Third (Gyalwa Sönam Gyatso) xx, 125
Dalai Lama, Fourth (Yönten Gyatso) xxi, 220n, 227
Dalai Lama, Fifth (Ngawang Lobsang Gyatso, Great Fifth) xvi, xx–xxi, xxi, xxii, 9, 23, 43, 217n, 227
Dalai Lama, Sixth (Rigdzin Tsangyang Gyatso) 10, 122, 227
Dalai Lama, Seventh (Kelsang Gyatso) 9, 10, 44, 60, 227–8
Dalai Lama, Eighth (Jampel Gyatso) 10, 228, 229
Dalai Lama, Ninth (Lungtok Gyatso) 8, 10, 229
Dalai Lama, Tenth (Tsultrim Gyatso) 8, 229
Dalai Lama, Eleventh (Khedrup Gyatso) 8, 10, 59, 229
Dalai Lama, Twelfth (Trinle Gyatso) 8, 10, 59
Dalai Lama, Thirteenth (Thubten Gyatso) 3, 5, 6, 79, 97, 175, 217n, 218n, 229–30
takes leadership 10–11
life threatened 11–12
relationship with Panchen Lama 13–14, 19, 38, 44–5, 49, 51–2, 101
destroys Sikkim border stones 14
flees to Mongolia 15
contacts Russia 15, 19–20
relationship with *Jetsun dampa* 20
returns to Kumbum 20–2
visits Beijing 22, 23–4
returns to Lhasa 25
appeals for help against China 26–7
exile in India 27, 30–1
Chinese edict against 28–9
returns to Lhasa 31–3
proclaims independence and authority 33–5
modernization progamme 37–42
illness and death 53–5
tomb 69
Dalai Lama, Fourteenth (Tenzin Gyatso) 181–2, 230
on rebirth 6, 7–8
located 77–80
stays in Kumbum 89–90
travels to Lhasa 90–1
early life in Lhasa 104, 111, 113
assumes power 116–17
seeks refuge in Dunkhar monastery 117
returns to Lhasa 120
relationshhip with Panchen Lama 125–7
spiritual training 127–8
initiates reforms 128–9
visits Beijing 129–31
meets Chen Yi 135–6
visits India 138–40
returns to Tibet 140–1
flees Tibet 141
exile in India xvii, 143, 155
recognizes new Karmapa 212
involvement in search for Eleventh Panchen Lama 203–8
recognizes Eleventh Panchen Lama xi–xii, xv, 193, 197, 205, 231
Darjeeling 30, 42
de Broissia, Louis 194
Demo Chamnag 57
Demo Kundeling, regent 9
Demo Rinpoche (Trinle Rabgye), regent 8, 11, 12, 217n
Demo Tulku Ngawang Jampal Gelek Gyatso, regent 97, 217n

Derge 134
Derge monastery 148
Deyang college, Drepung 76
Dharamsala 155, 180, 182, 185
Dogra people 12
Doi 134
Donald, W H 218–19n
Dorje Tsegyal Lungshar see Lungshar
Dorjieff 14, 19
Dragyab 146
Drepung monastery 8, 9, 20, 27, 36, 41, 56, 62–3, 75, 76, 77, 93, 104, 126, 137, 226
Dromtömpa 60
Dunkhar monastery 117
Düwa college, Drepung 76
Dzasa Trumba 43, 45
Dzasa Tsethong 181
Dzungarian Mongols 199

East India Company 4, 228
El Salvador 117

Fan Ming, General 129
Feng Tsuen 16
Foreign Affairs Office 103
Formosa 217n
France xiii–xiv, 24, 27

Ganden monastery 8, 9, 20, 27, 55, 62–3, 75, 76, 93, 126, 137, 226
Gandhi, Mahatma 107
Gang of Four 182
Gansu 156, 163, 172, 188, 192
Gaozong, Emperor 118
Gartok 15, 137
Gautama Buddha 218n
Gelugpa lineage xviii, xix, xx, xxi, xxii, 15, 27, 36, 53, 216n, 218n, 220n, 227
Gendün Chökyi Nyima see Panchen Lama, Eleventh
Gendün Drub see Dalai Lama, First
Gengis Khan 33
George V 17, 19, 47
Golden Urn ceremony xvi, xii, 113–14, 188, 193, 195–6, 199, 200–2, 204, 206, 209, 217n
Gomang college, Drepung 76, 77
Gongya Rinpoche 99
Gould, Sir Basil 73, 74, 104
Great Leap Forward 152, 155, 166, 184, 221n

Guangxu, Emperor 23, 24, 197
Gurkhas 39, 199, 228
Gyaltrul Rinpoche 208, 215
Gyaltsen Norbu 200, 201, 210, 216n
Gyalwa Gendün Gyatso see Dalai Lama, Second
Gyalwa Sönam Gyatso see Dalai Lama, Third
Gyanpal Rinpoche 153
Gyantse district 15, 18, 19, 27, 32, 40, 42, 44, 45, 47, 71, 137, 215
Gyantse monastery 225
Gyantsen Norbu (Norbu Rinpoche, false Eleventh Panchen Lama), xvi, 202–1, 210, 213, 215
Gyatsa 60
Gyelo Thondup 91
Gyenag Rinpoche 112–13, 137
Gyepa college, Drepung 76
Gyume 53

He Long, Marshall, 168
Hinayana Buddhism xviii, xix
Ho Chi Minh 116
Hong Kong 115, 148
Hor 94
Hu Bing 141–2
Huang Mu-sung, General 65, 66, 67, 70
Huriet, Claude 194

India xviii, 116, 117, 133, 134, 138–40, 143, 155, 216n, 219n, 228, 230; see also British India
Indonesia 116

Jagsam ferry 38
Jakarta 116
Jampa Chödrak 54
Jampa Chung xvi, 205, 208, 215, 231
Jampa Gyaltsen 72
Jampa Khenrab Tenzin 108
Jampa Tashi Damchö 229
Jampa Tendar 30, 39, 40
Jampa Tharchin 97–8, 107
Jampa Tsultrim 219n
Jampa Yeshe 57
Jampel Gyatso see Dalai Lama, Eighth
Jamyang 209
Japan 12, 20, 80, 104, 216n
Jensey Namgang see Tsarong Dabzang Dradul
Jetsun Pema 139, 185

Jiang Zemin 204, 209
Jokhang temple xvi, 29, 34, 66, 72, 93, 114, 129, 195, 200, 209, 217n
Jyekundo region 50, 77, 80

Kabshöba Chögye Nyima 61, 62, 63, 64, 108
Kachen Ang Nyima 137
Kachen Pasang 100
Kagyupa lineage xviii, xix, xx, 212, 218n
Kailas, Mount 168
Kalachakra xxi
Kalimpong 27, 72
Kangxi, Emperor 226, 227
Kangyur 23
Kantse monastery 80, 81
Kantse region 108, 134, 146, 164
Karang Bidho monastery 101
Karma-Kagyupa group xix
Karmapa 212
Karmapa Rölpai Dorje monastery 79
Kashag (government authority) 5, 8, 12, 20, 21, 25, 40, 54, 56, 57, 58, 62, 63, 66–7, 72, 73, 74, 85, 86, 93, 106, 110, 114, 115, 117, 129, 135, 141
Kelsang Dolma 220n
Kelsang Gyatso *see* Dalai Lama, Seventh
Kewtsang Rinpoche 77–8, 79, 80, 89–90, 230
Kham province 11, 26, 34, 39, 40, 50, 52, 77, 81, 108, 120, 132, 134, 135, 143, 165, 231, 220n; *see also* Sichuan
Khamba Dzong 18
Khamba people 80, 133, 134, 165
Khardo Rinpoche 72, 93
Khedrup Gelek Pelsang *see* Panchen Lama, First
Khedrup Gyatso *see* Dalai Lama, Eleventh
Khedrup Sangye Yeshe 226
Khenrab Wangchug 105–6
Khiva 13
Khokand 13
Khön Könchog Gyelpo xix
Khyi-chu river 95, 129
Khyungram 94
Kim Il Sung 116
Kokonor region xxi, 81, 86
Kongpo Tseten 100

Korea 116, 121, 133, 217n
Koshut Mongols 217n
Kumar, Maharajah 138
Kumbela (Thubten Kumbela) 46–7, 50–1, 54, 56, 57
Kumbum monastery xxii, 21, 79, 89, 98, 112, 115, 117, 122, 126, 196
Kumbum valley 25
Kundeling Chökyi Gyaltsen, regent 8
Kundeling monastery 107
Kunsangtse 41
Kuomintang (Chinese National Party) 46, 48, 65, 67, 70, 80, 85, 90, 101, 108, 113, 114, 115, 196
Kyarsib 81
Kyego Döndrub Ling monastery 229
Kyicho Küntün movement 61–2, 63, 64
Kyikhang Khenpo 150–1

Ladakh 12
Lama temple 195
Lama Tsering *see* Sengchen Lobsang Gyaltsen
Langdarma, Emperor xviii
Langdün Kunga Wangchug, prime mnister 56, 57, 63, 65, 67, 71, 72
League of Nations 117
Lenin 116
Lhabsang Khan 10
Lhalu Tsewang Dorje 107, 108
Lhamo Latso lake 5, 86–8, 192, 203
Lhari xv, 193, 201, 231
Lhasa xvi, xvii, 4, 12, 14, 34, 35, 36, 37–38, 47, 48, 70, 103, 104, 106, 116, 125, 149, 167, 210
established as capital xx
Anglo-Indian army enters 15
Chinese activity in 17
Thirteenth Dalai Lama arrives 25
Chinese troops sent to 26, 27, 31
Chinese edict posted 28
Ninth Panchen Lama visits 29–30
Thirteenth Dalai Lama returns 32
opposition to militarization 39, 41
British school built 42
Trongdra created 50–1
Ninth Panchen Lama sends delegates 52
mourns death of Thirteenth Dalai Lama 55
Reting Rinpoche arrives 60–1
Lungshar affair 63, 64

Chinese mission visits 66–7
British delegation visits 73–4
mourns death of Ninth Panchen
    Lama 85
Fourteenth Dalai Lama arrives 91,
    92–3
Reting Rinpoche encourages
    festivities 94–5
Reting Rinpoche's arrest and death
    108, 109, 111
Chinese representatives expelled 115
Chinese troops enter 121
Tenth Panchen Lama visits 127
PCART inaugarated 134–5
Fourteenth Dalai Lama flees 141
under Chinese occupation 144, 147,
    175, 176, 185
Lhasa Convention (1904) 15, 16, 17,
    18, 21, 218n
Lhasa government 13, 14, 17, 19, 21,
    25, 29, 40, 45, 61, 65, 71, 77,
    105–6, 120, 135, 142, 218n
Lhoka 144
Lhundrup Dzong 105
Li Peng xvi, 188, 191, 204
Li Weihan 156, 158, 159, 160, 162,
    163, 171
Li Xinnian 182
Li Zhongren 196
Liberation Committee of Chamdo 131
Lien-yu 25, 27, 29, 30
Lin Biao 148, 221n
Litang monastery 134
Liu, General 209
Liu Man-ch'ing 49
Liu Shaoqi 158, 184
Liu Wen-hui 46, 50, 80, 81
Lobsang Chökyi Gyaltsen see Panchen
    Lama, Fourth
Lobsang Damchö 81
Lobsang Gyaltsen, regent 15, 18, 21,
    45, 52, 65, 98
Lobsang Samten 91
Lobsang Tashi 116
Lobsang Tseten see Panchen Lama,
    Tenth
Lobsang Tsewang 78
Lobsang Wangchug 65
Lobsang Yeshi see Panchen Lama,
    Fifth
Lodren Bepa 225
London government 14, 16, 17,
    18–19, 21, 65

Loseling college, Drepung 76, 77
Lu Singchi 35
Ludlow, Frank 42
Lukhangwa 116
Lungri Gyatso 99
Lungshar (Dorje Tsegyal Lungshar)
    41, 45, 47, 50–1, 55, 56–7, 61–2,
    63, 64–5, 72, 218n
Lungtok Gyatso see Dalai Lama, Ninth
Luo Gan vxi, 210

Ma Pu-fang 46, 50, 89, 90,
    117–18, 153
Macao 183
Macdonald, J 15
Mahasiddha Chö Dorje 226
Mahayana Buddhism xviii, xix, 137
Manchu empire 10, 12–13, 16, 17, 21,
    23, 31
Manjushri 130
Mao Tse-tung 116, 117, 119, 120,
    121, 125, 130, 131, 135, 136,
    148, 149, 151, 154, 158, 161,
    162, 163, 164, 166, 171, 174,
    179, 182, 183–4, 213, 221n
Merv 13
Ming dynasty 33, 194, 195
Minto, Lord 18, 19
Miwang Pholanay 43–4
Mongol peoples xiv, xx, 10, 33, 106,
    168, 198, 199
Mongolia 15, 20, 45, 199
Mönlam 129, 140, 182
Mönlam Chenmo 41, 53, 106
Morley, Lord 16, 19
Mustang 143

Nagchu province xv, 25, 193, 231
Namkhai Naldjor 112
Namling 71
Nangartse 71
Nangchen region 50
Nanjing 46, 48, 70, 108
Nanjing government 50, 65, 66, 67,
    71, 89, 157
National Assembly (tshongdu) 41, 43,
    52, 56, 57, 58, 59, 62, 64, 70, 72,
    73, 74, 94, 106
National People's Congress 200, 204,
    230, 231
Nechung oracle (Kutenla) 11, 54, 57,
    89, 110, 133, 141, 217n
NEFA (North-East Frontier Agency) 37

Nehru, Pandit 107, 133, 134, 140, 143, 220n
Nepal 12, 42, 44, 93, 143, 199, 227
New Delhi 107
New Delhi government 71
Ngaba 164
Ngabo Ngawang Jigme 120, 121, 131, 168–9, 180, 182, 200
Ngagchen Rinpoche 52
Ngagpa college, Drepung 76
Ngagpa college, Sera 105–6
Ngari 94
Ngari Korsum 34
Ngawang Lobsang Gyatso see Dalai Lama, Fifth
Ngulchu Rinpoche 98, 127, 137, 166, 169–71, 181
Nicholas II, Tsar 14, 19, 20
Norbu Döndub 66
Norbu Lingka palace 29, 41, 56, 91, 127, 135, 141
Norbu Rinpoche see Gyantsen Norbu
Norbu Tsering 11, 12
Nuri Pönpo 153
Nyagtrü 11, 12
Nyarong 11, 12
Nyingmapa lineage xviii–xix, 218n
Nyungne Lama 72, 93

O'Connor, Frederick 18, 19

Padmasambhava (Guru Rinpoche) xvii, xix, 216n
Pakistan 134
Palden Lhamo 87
Palden Yeshe see Panchen Lama, Sixth
Pamir 13
Pan-Asiatic conference 107
Panam 227
Panchen Damchö Yarphel 226
Panchen Lama, First (Khedrup Gelek Pelsang) 226
Panchen Lama, Second (Sönam Choklang) 226
Panchen Lama, Third (Wensa Lobsang Dondrub) 226
Panchen Lama, Fourth (Lobsang Chökyi Gyaltsen) xxi–xix, 227–8
Panchen Lama, Fifth (Lobshang Yeshe) 186, 227–8
Panchen Lama, Sixth (Palden Yeshe) 4, 118, 186, 199, 228
Panchen Lama, Seventh (Tenpe Nyima) 186, 228–9
Panchen Lama, Eighth (Tenpe Wangchug) 5, 186, 217n, 229
Panchen Lama, Ninth (Chökyi Nyima) 6, 186, 218n, 229–30
  enthronement 5
  relationship with Dalai Lama 13–14, 19, 38, 44–5, 49, 51–2
  visits British India 17–18, 19
  asserts faithfulness to Chinese emperor 25
  fraternizes with Chinese 29–30
  returns to Shigatse 31
  requests meeting with Dalai Lama 32
  flees to China 45–6
  possibility of return to Tibet 47–8, 62, 65, 67, 70–1, 73, 74
  honoured by Chinese 50
  locates Fourteenth Dalai Lama 77
  death 80, 85–6
  enshrinement 98
Panchen Lama, Tenth (Lobsang Tseten, Chökyi Gyaltsen) xvii, 135, 156, 159, 221n, 230–1
  birth 101–3
  search for 86–9, 98–101
  early life at Kumbum 112–13, 117–18, 122–4
  confirmed as reincarnation 114–15
  captured by Chinese 115–16
  exchanges letters with Mao Tse-tung 118–19
  visits Beijing (1951) 124–5
  relation with Dalai Lama 125–7
  visits Lhasa 127
  visits Beijing (1954) 129–32
  life at Tashilhunpo 137–8
  appears to support China 138
  visits India 138–40
  concern for Dalai Lama 141–2
  summoned to Beijing (1962) 149
  hears of Chinese atrocities 149–51
  increasing concern over Tibet 153
  criticizes China 151, 162–7, 168–74, 177–8, 180, 186–7
  arrest and trial 180–1
  imprisonment vx, 181–2, 182–3
  rehabilitation 184–5
  returns to Tibet 185–7
  death xi, 187–8
Panchen Lama, Eleventh (Gendün Chökyi Nyima) 221n, 231

search for xi, 187–8, 191–8, 203–7
recognized by Dalai Lama xi–xii, xv,
  193, 197, 205, 231
abduction xii, xvi, xviii–xxiv, 200,
  205, 209, 211, 213
current situation xii–xiv, 215
Pelgyi Dorje xviii
Penam 71
Peng Dehuai 184
People's Liberation Army 119, 120,
  136, 138, 140, 141, 142, 143, 153
People's National Congress 184,
  186, 187
Persia 21
Phagpala Gelek Namgyal 181, 192
Phembo 38
Phembo Sengge Lama 94
Phütso Wangye 130
Pokotiloff, Ambassador 15
Potala palace xvii, xx, 4, 25, 30, 38,
  41, 55, 61, 63, 69, 71, 74, 80,
  109, 126, 136, 185, 216n, 217n
Preparatory Committee for the
  Autonomous Region of Tibet
  (PCART) 131–2, 135, 137, 140,
  149, 168, 181, 230
Puyi (Xuantong), Emperor 24, 31

Qianlong, Emperor 13, 97, 113, 195,
  197, 198–9, 228
Qincheng jail 181, 182
Qing dynasty 12, 194, 195, 197, 199
Qinghai province *see* Amdo province
Quetta 40, 43

Raidi xvi
Ralung 32
Ramoche temple 34
Rampa, lama 108
Rawling, Captain 18
Religious Affairs Bureau xv, xvi
Republican Revolution, China 31, 155
Reting monastery 59, 60, 72, 110
Reting Ngawang Yeshe Tsultrim
  Gyaltsen, regent 12, 229
Reting Rinpoche (Jampey Yeshe
  Tenpe Gyaltsen), regent 58, 60–1,
  63, 64, 65, 66, 67–8, 69–70,
  71–5, 89, 93–6, 104–5, 106, 107,
  108, 109–11
Reting Trichen Ngawang Chogden 60
Rigdzin Tsangyang Gyatso *see* Dalai
  Lama, Sixth

Rinchen Dolma Taring 42
Ripung county 203
Riwoche 40
Rockhill W W 4, 24
Rongbatse 40
Roosevelt, Franklin D 104
Russia, Russian Empire 3, 12, 13, 14,
  16, 19–20, 21, 40

Sakya monastery 225
Sakyapa lineage xviii, xix, xx,
  198, 218n
Samarkand 13
Sambo Tsewang Rigdzin 105–6
Samye monastery xvii, 14, 34, 74, 94
Sangphu monastery 226
Sangye Gyatso, regent 9, 216n
Sangyi Drolma 202
Sengchen Lobsang Gyaltsen (Lama
  Tsering) xv, 193–4, 201, 202,
  208–9, 210
Sera monastery 8, 9, 20, 27, 39, 55,
  60, 62–3, 75, 76, 93, 104–6,
  126, 137
Che college 60, 104–6, 109, 110
Seventeen-Point 'Agreement' 120, 124,
  130, 133, 135, 141, 142, 143,
  156, 200, 230
Seventy-Thousand Characters
  (report) 151, 163, 166, 168–74,
  179–80, 231
Shagaw college, Drepung 76
Shakabpa 69
Shakyamuni Buddha 23, 196, 200,
  201, 218n
Shalu monastery 226
Shamser, Maharajah 42
Sharcenchog 57
Shazur 41
Shen Tsung-lien 104
Sherab Gyatso 156–62, 168, 169
Shigatse xvii, xxi, 13, 31, 32, 44, 46,
  48, 71, 129, 135, 137, 138, 144,
  181, 186, 203, 208, 209, 215
Shillong 40, 43
Shinje Tsheda 11
Shunzhi, Emperor xxi
Siberia 15
Sichuan (eastern Kham) province xv,
  16, 17, 31, 33, 46, 52, 103, 156,
  163, 164, 172, 188, 192
Sikkim 4, 5, 14, 15, 16, 30, 39, 48,
  52, 93, 117, 138, 216n

Sikkim, Maharajah of 47, 138
Simla convention (1914) 37, 40, 50
Singapore 183
Sino-British Convention (1906) 21
Sino-Tibetan settlement (1934) 219n
Sogya 11–12, 217n
Sönam Choklang see Panchen Lama,
   Second
Sönam Chöphel, regent 9
Sönam Drölma 100
Sönam Trampa 202
Songsten Gampo, Emperor
   216n, 220n
St Petersburg government 14, 21
Surkhang, Commander 42
Surkhang, kälon 108

Tachai 145
Tachienlu 70
Tachkent 13
Taduk monastery 34
Taiwan 115, 152, 157
Taktra Rinpoche, regent 93, 94, 95–6,
   97–8, 103, 104, 105, 106–7,
   107–8, 110, 111, 116, 126
Taktse 145
Taktser 78, 79
Talung Drag monastery 107
Tangut tribe xx
Tashilhunpo monastery xv, xvi, xvii, 5,
   17, 18, 19, 25, 29, 44, 45, 46, 52,
   80, 85, 86, 89, 98, 127, 137, 138,
   142, 143, 149–51, 181, 186, 191,
   194, 196, 203, 206, 208, 215,
   226, 227, 228, 229, 231
Tashitse 227
Tengyeling, regent 8
Tengyeling monastery 36, 38
Tenpe Gyaltsen, regent 27
Tenpe Nyima see Panchen Lama,
   Seventh
Tenpe Wangchug see Panchen Lama,
   Eighth
Tenzin Chödrak 182, 185
Tenzin Gyatso see Dalai Lama,
   Fourteenth
Thirty Songs 122
Thobgyal 228
Thubten Gyatso see Dalai Lama,
   Thirteenth
Thubten Kumbela see Kumbela
Tibetan Buddhism xi, xix, 64, 187,
   191, 194, 195, 197, 200, 205, 228

Times, The 48
Tongzhi, Emperor 13
Tönmi Sambotha 220n
Trantsa Tamdrin Gyelpo 181
Trimön 30, 56, 62–3, 69
Trinle Gyatso see Dalai Lama, Twelfth
Trisong Detsen (Ralpachen), Emperor
   xvii, 216n
Trongdra regiment 50, 56
Truman, President 133
Tsa Serkhang 47
Tsang province xvii, xxi, 44, 52, 138,
   142, 226, 228, 229
Tsangpo river 95
Tsarong Dabzang Dradul (Jensey
   Namgang) 36, 38–9, 40, 41–2, 43,
   55, 218n
Tsethang xvii
Tshomöling, regent 9, 229
Tsigang (Finance Office) 8, 41, 47,
   61, 111
Tsogo 41
Tsongkhapa xix, xxii, 53, 99,
   216n, 226
Tsultrim Gyatso see Dalai Lama,
   Tenth
Tümed Mongols xx, 220n
Turkestan 15
Turkmenistan 13

U region 52
United Nations 104, 134, 174,
   179, 208
   Committee for Children's Rights
      xvi, 231
   General Assembly 117
   Security Council xii
United States 104, 133, 157, 184, 214
Urga 15

Vajrayana Buddhism xviii, xix
Vietnam 116
Vikramashila monastery 216n

Wei Jingsheng 182, 183–4, 221n
Weir, J L R 48
Wendu 98, 100, 101–3, 153
Wensa Lobsang Dondrub see Panchen
   Lama, Third
Williamson W F 47, 52, 71, 73
Wu, Harry 221n
Wu Peifu 218n
Wu Zhunqing 199

Wutai Shan sanctuary 22

Xiangride 118
Xikang province 80
Xining 70, 196
Xinjiang 163
Xunhua 103, 153

Yarlung valley xvii
Yatung 14, 15, 27, 32, 42, 117, 137
Ye Xiaowen xvi, 210
Yellow Temple, Beijing 23, 24
Yeshe Tsultrim 181
Yigtsang (monastic council) 8
Yongtsa Lutso lake 203

Yönten Gyatso *see* Dalai Lama, Fourth
You Tai 15, 17, 20
Younghusband, Francis 15, 16, 18, 19
Yuan dynasty 194, 198
Yuan Shikai, General 31, 32, 35
Yunnan (principality of Djang) 33, 52, 156, 163, 172, 188, 192

Zhang Dingyi 141
Zhang Hueliang 50, 218n
Zhang Xueliang, Marshall 218n
Zhang Yin Tang 21, 25
Zhao Puchu 192
Zhu De 119, 130

If you would like to help the Tibetan community, you can:

Make a donation
Please send to:
Tibetan Center for Human Rights and Dignity
Narthang Building
Gangchen Kyishong
Dharamsala HP 176215
India

Sponsor a child in a Tibetan Children's Village (TCV)
You are requested to pay a minimum amount of US$ 30 or £20 per month, either by cheque or bank transfer.

Contribute to the funding of various TCV projects
You may choose the amount you want to pay, either by cheque or bank transfer.

Give donations in kind
Warm clothes (for children and adults), valid medicines – particularly vaccines against tuberculosis – and toys are always wanted. They will be sent to the various TCV homes.

For further information, write to:
Head Office
Tibetan Children's Village
Dharamsala Cantt-176216
Distt Kangra, HP
India

If you choose to pay by cheque, please make it out to TCV and send it to the above address. If you prefer to make a bank transfer (the best method), please transfer the funds to account no C-310 300 792 (American Express Bank) in New Delhi, India.